End-time Events
Journey to the End of the Age

by
Charles Capps

Harrison House
Tulsa, Oklahoma

End-time Events—
Journey to the End of the Age
ISBN 1-57794-325-2
Copyright © 1997 by Charles Capps
P. O. Box 69
England, Arkansas 72046

Reprinted 1999

Published by Harrison House, Inc.
P. O. Box 35035
Tulsa, Oklahoma 74153

Contents

PREFACE

Many different views have been taught through the years on the subject of Bible prophecy. Some of them have had many good points, while others did not seem to fit with the overall prophetic revelation found in the Bible.

God revealed His thread of truth concerning end-time events from the beginning of Genesis to the Book of Revelation. The Old Testament foreshadowed the actual events. The New Testament also reveals end-time events through parables.

We know that Jesus taught mostly in parables. A parable is a parallel, a simple story illustrating scriptural truth and insight. Parables are like windows which allow you to see truth that has been there all the time but was somehow hidden or out of sight.

This book will challenge you to take a fresh look at some of these parables and scriptural composites found in God's Word. I invite you to allow the Holy Spirit to give illumination as we investigate the prophetic Word of God.

—*Charles Capps*

INTRODUCTION

You are about to take a scriptural journey to the end of the age and learn how God reveals the sequence and time frame of end-time events. I challenge you to allow the Holy Spirit to bear witness with your spirit concerning this end-time revelation. I believe you will be enlightened as God's Word comes alive to you concerning the events that will transpire in God's timing to fulfill His Word. My purpose is not to set specific dates, but rather to bring to light what God's Word has already established concerning the timing of certain prophetic events.

We will discover that all Scripture is truly given by inspiration of God. (2 Timothy 3:16.) There is a special reason for every Scripture recorded in the Bible. Many Scriptures have a double reference, revealing prophetic insight and details in progressive revelations.

We will take a fresh look into the Old and New Testament Scriptures in a way that will bring you new insight. They will be referred to at times as scriptural composites, for they are word pictures revealing some events which have already been fulfilled and others that are about to be fulfilled.

God's Word to Daniel was: **"shut up the words, and seal the book, even to the time of the end..."** (Daniel 12:4).

We are the generation to which end-time revelation has come.

Since God reveals these revelations in numerical order, we will be dealing with biblical numerics. This simply means that God uses numbers as well as words to confirm revelation. Please don't get this confused with numerology, for there is a great difference.

We will find that God has stretched numerical truths through the Scriptures, from Genesis to Revelation, in a consistent pattern revealing the general time frame of all end-time events.

It seems that God has now lifted the curtain on end-time revelation. What former generations sought desperately to know, God is revealing to this last generation.

This book will take you through biblical prophecies and scriptural composites revealing events yet to come. It will give you a glimpse of God's infinite and unfailing love and determination to deliver those who believe in His Son and trust His prophetic Word. It will reveal details of God's way of escape for those who will dare to believe His Word and prepare for the transition that will end this age.

In His own words Jesus revealed that there was a way of escape:

"Watch ye therefore, and pray always, that ye may be accounted worthy to escape all these things that shall come to pass, and to stand before the Son of man" (Luke 21:36).

Then in the parable of the nobleman (Luke 19:12-27) the message is clear that we are to *occupy till He comes.*

This book is really a wake-up call for those who have not made preparations to DO SO NOW and for those who have drifted away from God to repent and be restored to fellowship.

The admonition to the Church is twofold:

Proclaim, "The King is coming!"

and

"Occupy until He comes!"

There's a Storm on the Horizon

This generation is blessed beyond any that has lived on planet Earth since the beginning of creation. We are living in a marvelous time of prophetic fulfillment, which is good news *if* you believe in the blessed hope, the glorious appearing of the great God and our Savior, Jesus Christ.

Yet, as one surveys the prophetic Scriptures and calculates the effect of their fulfillment on the modern world, the accumulated results are staggering. We live in a time when weapons of mass destruction are within reach of almost any nation in the world.

...We are being thrust—by time itself—into the time of prophetic fulfillment which will end the age.

What is yet even harder to comprehend is the magnitude of destruction that will come upon this planet from the gathering moral decay that is sure to bring God's wrath upon a wicked world. It is evident that our great society and our government-sponsored programs are hopelessly out of control, as we are being thrust—by time itself—into the time of prophetic fulfillment which will end the age.

There are times when I feel somewhat like a meteorologist issuing a warning of an approaching storm. You can imagine how he feels as he tracks a killer tornado on Doppler radar as it approaches a densely populated city. He knows he cannot stop the storm or divert its path. The only hope of saving lives is by warning those in its path in the quickest way possible so that they might escape before the storm strikes or make a desperate attempt to withstand its devastation.

This scenario is a perfect parallel of this generation, for so many today are unaware of the approaching storm. Some have heard the warning but are unprepared and without hope, believing there is no way of escape. To them, the only ray of hope seems to lie in a desperate attempt to withstand the storm of events that will usher in the seven years of tribulation destined for planet Earth.

There is a real storm brewing, as planet Earth spirals towards a cataclysmic transition into the last Millennium before eternity. The signs of the times are clear: Planet Earth is winding down, while fulfillment of prophetic events is escalating profoundly. Our society is now racing down the information superhighway at breakneck speed without even asking the question, *Where are we headed?*

However, people from every nation, race, and creed are now beginning to ask questions. Environmentalists are sounding alarms about the earth and its atmosphere. New diseases, as well as old ones, that are resistant to modern medicine seem to appear weekly. Economists juggle multitrillion-dollar debts, without any clear solutions to the problem. Major governments disarm and almost immediately lose control of their nuclear warheads. Wars and rumors of wars are heard around the world on a daily basis.

Yet for some, the quality of life has never been better. While for others, the cost of living has increased to the point that they are working around the clock to just barely meet their bills. Many are living only by increasing credit-card debt.

TWO IMPORTANT QUESTIONS

It is obvious why economic collapse is one of the most frequent warnings heard worldwide. The very complexity of these problems today cause us all to consider two questions: *Is there any hope for planet Earth?* And, *where will it all end?*

The answer to the first question is, yes, there is hope for planet Earth. But this hope is not based on the ability of man to solve the complex problems facing the inhabitants of the earth in the twenty-first century. This hope is in the Person of Jesus Christ—the Son of God, the anointed Messiah—and His promised appearance to catch away those who have placed their faith in Him and in His resurrection power.

This hope also includes Christ's Second Advent, which will occur immediately after the Great Tribulation has ended, to destroy the Antichrist and begin 1000 years of peace and righteous rule on Earth. During that time, the righteous will be the heads of His government and will rule and reign with Him. The earth will be free from Satan's influence for 1000 years. For Satan will be bound and confined to the bottomless pit as Jesus Christ rules and reigns in His Kingdom here on planet Earth.

THE END IS IN SIGHT

As we journey through the prophetic pages of God's Holy Word, we will find a clear answer to both of our important questions: *Is there any hope?* And, *where and when will it all end?* We are all well aware that time will eventually answer these questions, but by then it would be too late to escape the tribulation destined for those who remain on the earth.

Some have sensed the coming events but have many unanswered questions concerning the future. They are seeking for the answers in the wrong places. Millions seek answers from their horoscopes. Some call "psychic hot lines," not realizing they are seeking answers from demonic sources. Some put their hope in religious traditions, which so much of the time fail to give the right answers to these questions. Others have given up because they believe God doesn't want us to know.

But the truth is, God wants us to know what is about to happen so we can be prepared and *escape* the coming storm and stand before the Son of Man. (Luke 21:36.)

THE LIGHT IS NOW ILLUMINATING THE DARKNESS

I am sure you have at times walked into a room where the louvered blinds were tilted at a certain angle. The sun was shining, but until a certain time of day, the sun didn't shine into the room. So it is concerning the truth of many prophetic Scriptures which have been hidden from us in days past. We are now living in a time when the Holy Spirit's illumination on the prophetic Scriptures is dispelling the darkness.

We are now living in a time when the Holy Spirit's illumination on the prophetic Scriptures is dispelling the darkness.

What a glorious time to be alive! That is, if you are prepared to escape what lies ahead for those who are left on planet Earth during the seven years of tribulation that is destined for planet Earth.

SIGNS OF THE TIMES

One of the discourses given by Jesus predicting end-time events which will profoundly affect life on planet Earth is found in Matthew's gospel:

Matthew 24:3 **And as he sat upon the mount of Olives, the disciples came unto him privately, saying, Tell us, when shall these things be? and what shall be the sign of thy coming, and of the end of the world?**
4 And Jesus answered and said unto them, Take heed that no man deceive you.
5 For many shall come in my name, saying, I am Christ; and shall deceive many.

6 And ye shall hear of wars and rumours of wars: see that ye be not troubled: for all these things must come to pass, but the end is not yet.
7 For nation shall rise against nation, and kingdom against kingdom: and there shall be famines, and pestilences, and earthquakes, in divers places.

Jesus mentioned four things that would occur in one generation to signal that the end was drawing near: wars, famine, pestilence, and earthquakes. These signs are being fulfilled almost daily, making everyone consider how close we must be to the prophesied end.

"EARTHQUAKES IN DIVERS PLACES"

Jesus made it clear that the occurrence of many earthquakes in different places would be one of the signs of the end-time.

Some may say, "We have always had earthquakes." But earthquake information obtained from the u.s. Geological Survey National Earthquake Information Center in Denver, Colorado, shows an astounding increase in earthquakes over the past twenty-six years.

A recent U.S.G.S. report shows there were 4,139 earthquakes in 1970—and 19,996 in 1996.* This is an amazing difference showing an increase of 15,857 more earthquakes that occurred in 1996 than in 1970.

These facts simply prove once again the accuracy of the Bible's prophetic revelation. As we head toward the Seventh Millennium, earthquakes are definitely on the increase.

---

*United States Geological Survey, National Earthquake Information Center, P.O. Box 25046, DFC, MS 967, Denver, CO, *Data Global Search Statistics,* compiled February 19, 1997.

In the summer of 1995 USA *Today* reported that Yellowstone National Park experienced 2,300 mini-earthquakes in a five-day period.

"FAMINE AND PESTILENCE"

In the 1960s some medical schools discouraged students from entering the field of infectious diseases because they believed that the advances in vaccines and antibiotics would soon wipe out infectious diseases. However, thirty years ago, no one had heard of AIDS, and the Ebola virus hadn't left behind a wake of dead and dying.

The medical profession hadn't realized that bacteria could mutate and become resistant to antibiotics. The World Health Organization never dreamed that it would fear another outbreak of yellow fever or tuberculosis in the 1990s. But somehow, in spite of miraculous medical advances and worldwide social programs, the problems of pestilence and famine continue to grow, revealing the nearness of the end of this age.

"NATION WILL RISE AGAINST NATION"

Some have labeled the twentieth century as the "Century of War." This century has seen more wars than any other time in the history of mankind. Yes, there have always been wars, but there are a few things that distinguish the twentieth century from all others. First, it has the distinction of hosting the only "World Wars" in history; and second, at no other time in history has man had the weapons capable of destroying all life on planet Earth—until now.

Most nuclear, biological, and chemical warfare wasn't even thought of at the turn of the century. The potential for destruction by modern weapons paints a vivid mental picture, especially when considering the prophecy of Jesus.

Matthew 24:21 NKJV **For then there will be great tribulation, such as has not been since the beginning of the world until this time, no, nor ever shall be.**
22 And unless those days were shortened, no flesh would be saved; but for the elect's* sake those days will be shortened.†

It is rumored that the United States developed a weapon so deadly that they decided it was too terrible to use. It is called the neutron bomb. The neutron bomb emits neutrons that will incinerate flesh and all life in a given area. Yet, within a few minutes the radiation is gone and nonliving things, such as tanks and artillery, are again safe to use.

God has a plan to deliver His people from the judgment to come.

It is possible that other nations have the neutron bomb in their defense arsenals. The effect of this weapon's destruction corresponds with Zechariah's prophecy in chapter 14 about a war still to come in Israel:

Zechariah 14:12 NKJV **12 And this shall be the plague with which the Lord will strike all the people who fought against Jerusalem: Their flesh shall dissolve while they stand on their feet, their eyes shall dissolve in their sockets, and their tongues shall dissolve in their mouths.**

These weapons are terrible beyond comprehension. But, *God has a plan to deliver His people from the judgment to come.*

Wars. Famine. Pestilence. Earthquakes. These are just a few of the signs that show this age is drawing to an end. But God has

---

* This refers to the elect of Israel. Lockyer, Herbety, Sr. *Illustrated Bible Dictionary.* (Nashville: Thomas Nelson, 1986).

† The days of intense tribulation will be cut short, not the seven-year period.

always had a plan to deliver His people from the destruction that is soon to come upon the inhabitants of planet Earth. The plan was written by forty different authors on different continents, in three different languages, over a period of 1500 years.

The whole plan is revealed in His Holy Word, the Bible.

It has withstood the test of time.

It has withstood the test of history.

It has withstood the test of archaeology.

It has withstood the test of prophetic fulfillment.

Not one prophecy recorded in the Bible has ever failed. Most were spoken hundreds of years before the birth of Christ. Historical evidence has proven that every prophecy regarding Tyre, Nineveh, Gaza, and Babylon has come to pass.

For hundreds of years, Bible critics thought they had finally found the one prophecy that was false. None of them believed that Israel could ever become a nation again. They thought for sure the Bible was wrong concerning Israel.

But in 1948, in one divine act, God did what man had labeled impossible: He began gathering the Jewish people back to that tiny strip of real estate in the Middle East, restoring their nation. It was from that moment in 1948 that prophetic events began to accelerate towards complete fulfillment concerning Israel.

THE TIME IS SHORT

People of all nations of the world are now searching for answers concerning the future. We are being thrust by time itself into the twenty-first century, which will usher humanity into the greatest change in the history of this planet. Many have placed their hope in the United Nations for peace on earth. But until Jesus the Messiah returns to rule the earth in His righteous kingdom, there will be no lasting peace for planet Earth.

Every detail of God's plan to rescue mankind from certain destruction rests on the promised return of Christ. God has woven into the fabric of His Word His master plan to rescue the Church of true believers from His wrath that will be poured out on the wicked during the Tribulation Period. He has also given us scriptural profiles which reveal the sequence and general time frame of the Rapture, the Great Tribulation, the last Millennium, and eternity to follow. We will look at some of them in the following chapters.

The Triangle of the End

Several years ago while teaching a series of satellite meetings, the spirit of prophecy came upon me. The prophecy pertained to the *triangle of the end*. I saw in the Spirit a large acute triangle, and these words came forth: "As you approach the triangle of the end, time shall grow faster and closer, faster and closer...until the wicked shall be cut off."

As those words came forth, I saw in my spirit, as it were, a large acute triangle. It was standing on end, looking somewhat like an inverted pyramid, with a line drawn down the center from the wide top to the narrow point at the bottom. Being wide at the top and very narrow at the bottom, it resembled a funnel. Inside this triangle was light, but outside was darkness.

LINE UPON LINE, PRECEPT UPON PRECEPT

The prophetic word continued: "There was a time when you could be off from the center line of the triangle and still be inside the triangle of light. But as you approach the end of the triangle, you must move to the center line, for line must be upon line, precept upon precept."

I could see that if you were off from the center line, at the bottom end of the triangle you would be outside of the triangle of light and in darkness. I understood that was the way the wicked would be cut off. Even though they were to one side of the center line of God's Word at the top of the triangle of time, they were still in the light. But at the narrow end, which represented the end of the age, everyone who was not on the center line (precept of God's Word) at the end of the age would be in darkness.

We are spiraling faster and faster through the narrow end of the triangle of time....

As we approach the Seventh Millennium, time seems to have accelerated and prophetic events are being compressed together. We have entered the triangle of the end, in which both the time allotted and prophetic events are being compressed to maximum density to fulfill all the prophetic Scriptures and end this age in God's own time frame.

Time is reacting much the same as liquid flowing through a funnel, being drawn into the narrow end and released into a container of larger dimensions. It seems that there is not enough time to go around, and time controls us. We all, in one way or another, sense that we are being drawn by the vortex created by time itself. We are spiraling faster and faster through the narrow end of the triangle of time for the purpose of being released into a new Millennium that will forever change planet Earth.

What an exciting time it is to see prophecy being fulfilled almost daily, right before our own eyes. God has allotted a specific time for prophetic end-time events, and they must transpire in His timing to fulfill all prophetic Scriptures concerning the mature and glorious Church referred to by Paul in Ephesians 4:13 as a perfect man ministering in the fullness of Christ! This will be a short work of righteousness and will culminate with the Rapture of the Church.

Then the fulfillment of the Seventieth Week of Daniel will begin, which is seven years of tribulation. This will transition planet Earth into its last Millennium. Christ will return from Heaven with His saints at the end of that seven-year period; and there will be 1000 years of peace.

The end of that 1000 years of peace will bring about the appointed end of the wicked and rebellious of all ages. They will receive their just recompense of reward, with Satan and all of his emissaries being cast into the lake of fire.

Then the righteous of all ages will be enveloped into eternity with a new Heaven and a new earth, as the Holy City, the New Jerusalem, descends out of Heaven from God.

WHAT A GLORIOUS ETERNITY WE FACE.

THE LEASE IS ABOUT TO EXPIRE

Regardless of who you approach on the streets today, whether sinner or saint, they are conscious of the fact that time is about to run out for planet Earth. They know that some events of major proportion are about to take place. But without the light of God's Word, they really don't have a clue as to what they are or when they will take place.

Yet from the beginning, God has revealed the events of the end-time. This has been done two ways: through His prophetic Word and by past events recorded in the Scriptures that reveal the future in a very unique way.

There is a sequence of events that must transpire in God's timing to fulfill the prophetic Scriptures of all ages and usher in the seventh and last Millennium before eternity. The Scripture states that Jesus opened His mouth in parables and spoke things that had been **"kept secret from the foundation of the world"** (Matthew 13:35). I believe we are the last generation and should not be caught by surprise or be confused as to God's timing concerning these earth-shaking events. Jesus warned us that men's hearts would fail them **"...for fear, and for looking after those things which are coming on the earth..."** (Luke 21:26).

There are chaotic times ahead for the inhabitants of planet Earth who refuse to heed God's prophetic warning and continue to walk in their own darkness, defying God Who created them and taking the "right to life" from children yet unborn and putting that authority into the hands of mortals who terminate that life at their own will.

The prophet Malachi gives us a glimpse of their judgment:

Malachi 4:1 For, behold, the day cometh, that shall burn as an oven; and all the proud, yea, and all that do wickedly, shall be stubble: and the day that cometh shall burn them up, saith the Lord of hosts, that it shall leave them neither root nor branch.

The prophet Jeremiah in chapter 13 also sounds a warning for such a wicked generation:

16 Give glory to the Lord your God, before he cause darkness, and before your feet stumble upon the dark mountains, and, while ye look for light, he turn it into the shadow of death, and make it gross darkness.

Yet there is also good news, even in the same time frame. Solomon really puts it into biblical perspective with these words in Proverbs, chapter 4:

There is great darkness and deception ahead for those who find themselves outside the triangle.

**18 But the path of the just is as the shining light, that shineth more and more unto the perfect day.
19 The way of the wicked is as darkness: they know not at what they stumble.**

It is evident from many prophetic Scriptures that greater darkness is coming upon the wicked who dwell on planet Earth. They have been caught in the vortex of this triangle of the end and are about to be thrust into gross darkness, because they will not honor their Creator, and refuse to follow the guidelines set forth in the Creator's Handbook, which we call the Bible.

There is great darkness and deception ahead for those who find themselves outside the triangle. However, there will be brilliant light and revelation for those who are willing to repent and respond to God's warning.

The prophet Isaiah gives us a glimpse into this matter when referring to the time of Israel's restoration, at which time their blindness departs and they recognize Jesus as their Messiah.

> Isaiah 60:1 **Arise, shine; for thy light is come, and the glory of the Lord is risen upon thee.**
> **2 For, behold, the darkness shall cover the earth, and gross darkness the people: but the Lord shall arise upon thee, and his glory shall be seen upon thee.**

It is evident from these verses that during the same time frame in which gross darkness covers the wicked of the earth, great light will come by the revelation of the Holy Spirit to those who will follow God's precepts and worship Him.

Let's look once again at Solomon's statements from Proverbs 4: **But the path of the just is as the shining light, that shineth more and more unto the perfect day** (v. 18). **The way of the wicked is as darkness: they know not at what they stumble** (v. 19).

I believe that perfect day for the Church begins when the earth lease expires and God takes back control of the earth. The Scriptures seem to indicate that there will be a window of time for the end-time harvest of souls into His Kingdom. Then Christ will appear to catch away those who are looking for Him. He will at that time resurrect the bodies of the righteous dead of all ages and catch them up to Heaven, along with the righteous who are alive at His appearing. (1 Thessalonians 4:16-17; 1 Corinthians 15:51-52.)

This event will leave the wicked of the earth groping in their own darkness for the seven years of the Tribulation, which immediately follows this event that we call "the Rapture." There will then be wars, pestilence, troubles, and chaotic conditions in a measure which man has never experienced, even from the beginning of time.

But God has provided better things for us who are the children of light, as stated by the apostle Paul in 1 Thessalonians, chapter 5:

4 But ye, brethren, are not in darkness, that that day should overtake you as a thief.
5 Ye are all the children of light, and the children of the day: we are not of the night, nor of darkness.

Yet many today are asking the same question as Daniel did when he saw and heard the prophetic vision in his day.

Daniel 12:8 **And I heard, but I understood not: then said I, O my Lord, what shall be the end of these things? 9 And he said, Go thy way, Daniel: for the words are closed up and sealed till the time of the end.**

God's message to Daniel set a time for these things to be revealed. That revelation is being released to the Body of Christ in this generation as never before.

When God spoke through His prophets of old, His prophetic words established these events and the sequence in which they would transpire. God caused those prophetic utterances to be fused together with time so that they could not be separated from the segment of time to which they were assigned for complete fulfillment.

Some of these events could not be totally understood until the generation had arrived on the scene to which this assignment was made. *Time itself is prophetic and has released that revelation to this generation.*

God has established His timetable for prophetic events. Yet it has been partially veiled in a time capsule, so to speak, until we have arrived at the segment of time allotted for their fulfillment. Then that revelation immediately precedes the actual event itself. This could be described as time-released revelation. Time has veiled the Word for the simple reason that much of the prophetic Word could not be completely understood until knowledge and technology had increased.

Knowledge of God's Word has increased with technology to the point that in an instant of time, we have access to every Scripture in the Bible. This has made it easy to compare the prophetic Scriptures throughout the whole Bible. Technology is now in place that will allow all the nations of the world to see Christ as He descends from Heaven with the saints on the Mount of Olives at the end of the Tribulation Period.

Many of the answers to our questions have been partially veiled so that we could only see them as through a glass darkly. But God has revealed them in His own way.

It seems that God releases revelation to the generation which will be most affected by the events that are to follow. We detect this attitude in the prayer of Jesus in Matthew, chapter 6, as He taught His disciples to pray: **"Give us this day our daily bread"** (v. 11). To us today, this would mean, "Give us in our day (in this generation) the revelation needed for the time in which we live."

Some of the most profound revelation has been reserved for the end-time, for God does not want us to be frightened or confused concerning the sequence and timing of these end-time events. To repeat the words of Jesus: **"Unto you** [those who have ears to hear] **it is given to know the mystery of the kingdom of God..."** (Mark 4:11). Unto those who don't have ears to hear, it is not given, for they have no desire to know the truth. But anyone who truly seeks God and wants to know the truth will find it.

THE LAST MILLENNIUM

The earth and its inhabitants are caught in a vortex of time and are being hurled toward the Seventh and last Millennium.

There have only been five times in the history of the world that any generation has faced a new Millennium, much less the last one. The transition into that Millennium will bring joy and happiness to those who are prepared for the Rapture. But those who are unprepared will be hopelessly confused, fearful, and perplexed by the traumatic changes that will take place after the Church is taken out of the earth.

The earth and its inhabitants are caught in a vortex of time and are being hurled toward the Seventh and last Millennium.

Jesus, when referring to this time, said: **"Men's hearts failing them for fear, and for looking after those things which are coming on the earth: for the powers of heaven shall be shaken"** (Luke 21:26). But because of God's unfailing love, He has made a marvelous way of escape for those who are truly born again and have a personal relationship with our Lord and Savior, Jesus Christ. There are some who still scoff and blaspheme the Word of God. They ridicule those who preach the Good News of the blessed hope. But regardless of what the critics say, the true Church, which Paul refers to as the Body of Christ, will soon depart this earth for a period of seven years to be taught how to rule and reign with Him. (John 14:1-3.)

As we approach the last Millennium, the words that God gave Daniel are becoming much more meaningful and clear.

Daniel 12:4 AMP **But you, O Daniel, shut up the words and seal the Book until the time of the end. [Then] many shall run to and fro and search anxiously [through the Book], and knowledge [of God's purposes** as revealed by His prophets] shall be increased and become great.

8 And I heard, but I did not understand. Then I said, O my Lord, what shall be the issue and final end of these things?

9 And he [the angel] said, Go your way, Daniel, for the words are shut up and sealed till the time of the end.

10 ...but the wicked shall do wickedly. And none of the wicked shall understand, but the teachers and those who are wise shall understand.

These verses are a witness of the day in which we live, partly because knowledge has increased through new technology. But mostly because it is an appointed time, and the Holy Spirit is bringing to light things that have been hidden in God's Word for centuries. He is now revealing God's prophetic timetable and the sequence of end-time events in a marvelous way.

This generation, above all others, needs to understand the events that are about to transpire. We need this information so we can sound the alarm to the multitudes who don't have a clue as to what is about to take place here on the earth.

When the pieces of the prophetic puzzle are placed in the right time slots, they reveal a vivid composite (pictorial) drawing of the end-time. These events will happen in God's timing and will bring about a complete fulfillment of Bible prophecy. Their total fulfillment will usher in **"new heavens and a new earth, wherein dwelleth righteousness"** (2 Peter 3:13).

But, first, allow me to lay a scriptural foundation that will help you understand how God has woven threads of parallel truth through His Word, even into everyday events, which gives us great revelation and insight into God's grand finale that will end this age.

Keys to End-time Insight

We have all heard people say, "I've been hearing for fifty years that we're living in the *last days,* so that couldn't be true." The truth is that the last days are at least 2000 years long. If we include the Seventh Millennium in the last days, they are 3000 years long. But, generally speaking, the last days refer to the Church Age, which, according to what I see in Scripture, is a period of 2000 years.

Hebrews, chapter 1, gives us a valuable clue concerning this matter.

**1 God, who at sundry times and in divers manners
spake in time past unto the fathers by the prophets,
2 Hath in these last days spoken unto us by his Son.**

We know that God has already been speaking to us through His Son for almost 2000 years. However, in Luke 13:31-32 it seems possible that, by double reference, Jesus alluded to the third day, which could be prophetic of the millennial reign of Christ in which the Body of Christ (the Church) would be perfected.

God does not want us to be confused about these events that will end the Church Age. He has recorded certain events in Scripture that serve as signposts to keep us on the right road on our journey to the end of this age.

If you started a trip of several hundred miles and after a few hours were unsure if you were on the right road, you would be concerned and possibly confused. As soon as you saw a road sign revealing that you were on the right road, you would immediately be relieved of all doubt and confusion. However, if the sign revealed that you were on the wrong road, you would immediately begin to search for a map to see where you had missed it and how to get back to the right road.

God in His infinite wisdom has placed signs in His Word along our journey to eternity, to let us know when we are on the right track. One way you can tell whether or not you are on the right track in the prophetic Word is to find it in the Old Testament types and to be able to follow it into the New Testament. Many end-time events are foreshadowed in the beginning of the Old Testament, and their confirmations are interwoven into the New Testament, even to their complete fulfillment in the Book of Revelation.

JOURNEY TO THE END OF THE AGE

We will begin our scriptural journey into end-time insight in the Book of Isaiah, where God is speaking to Israel. He challenges their idols of wood, gold, and silver.

Isaiah 41:21 **Produce your cause, saith the Lord; bring forth your strong reasons, saith the King of Jacob. 22 Let them bring them forth, and shew us what shall happen:** let them shew the FORMER THINGS, WHAT THEY BE, THAT WE MAY CONSIDER THEM, AND KNOW THE LATTER END OF THEM; OR DECLARE US THINGS FOR TO COME.

Allow me to paraphrase God's challenge to the idols: "If you are really gods, then take the things that are now, and through those things, show us what the end of the whole matter shall be. Show us the future through present events."

God issued this challenge because that is the way He reveals many future events. He foreshadows things that are to come by things that have already happened. Sometimes this is called the law of double reference, which means there were to be two stages of fulfillment. The prophetic Word, or past event, had a literal fulfillment but by double reference pointed to a later prophetic fulfillment. Therefore, the present natural event was only a seed of confirmation of a greater fulfillment to come.

Evidently, it is from this concept that someone coined the phrase "History has a way of repeating itself." Allow me to bring that statement into biblical perspective—God has a marvelous way of completely fulfilling every aspect of His prophetic Word.

THE FIRST KEY

In Isaiah, chapter 46, we find our first key to unlocking the revelation of many end-time events:

9 Remember the former things of old: for I am God, and there is none else; I am God, and there is none like me,
10 DECLARING THE END FROM THE BEGINNING, and from ancient times the things that are not yet done, saying, My counsel shall stand, and I will do all my pleasure.

This far-reaching statement in verse 10 gives us our first key: *God has declared the end from the beginning.*

THE GENESIS ACCOUNT

More than twenty years ago, I had some insight into the fact that the Genesis account revealed God's *whole* plan for mankind. But it really didn't come into focus until I made a commitment to study and teach end-time events.

> *God has a marvelous way of completely fulfilling every aspect of His prophetic Word.*

After spending some time in prayer and meditating on these Scriptures, it seems that God has given us a blueprint in the Genesis account which extends from the creation of Adam to the end of the Seventh Millennium. I see this as a prophetic profile of the 6000 years of God's dealing with mankind prior to a transition into the last Millennium before eternity.

I believe the Genesis account reveals a time in which the earth had a face-lift. Evidently, some catastrophic event took place which flooded and destroyed life on earth. Then there was a replenishing of the earth, which we call the beginning of mankind as we know him on earth today. We see strong evidence of this in Psalm 104:30-31:

> **30 Thou sendest forth thy spirit, they are created: and thou renewest the face of the earth.**
> **31 The glory of the Lord shall endure for ever: the Lord shall rejoice in his works.**

KEY NUMBER TWO

We find the second key in 2 Peter, chapter 3:

> **1 This second epistle, beloved, I now write unto you; in both which I stir up your pure minds by way of remembrance:**
> **2 That ye may be mindful of the words which were spoken before by the holy prophets, and of the commandment of us the apostles of the Lord and Saviour:**
> **3 Knowing this first, that there shall come in the last days scoffers, walking after their own lusts,**
> **4 And saying, Where is the promise of his coming? for since the fathers fell asleep, all things continue as they were from the beginning of the creation.**
> **5 For this they willingly are ignorant of, that by the word of God the heavens were of old, and the earth standing out of the water and in the water:**

6 Whereby the world that then was, being overflowed with water, perished:

7 But the heavens and the earth, which are now, by the same word are kept in store, reserved unto fire against the day of judgment and perdition of ungodly men.

8 BUT, BELOVED, BE NOT IGNORANT OF THIS ONE THING, THAT ONE DAY IS WITH THE LORD AS A THOUSAND YEARS, AND A THOUSAND YEARS AS ONE DAY.

Peter reveals the second major key to understanding certain end-time events: *One day is with the Lord as a thousand years, and a thousand years as a day.* This simply means that in certain places in Scripture (at least by double reference), a day represents a 1000-year period. Yet, it can only be interpreted that way when it is obvious that it fits prophetically.

For instance, in the Scriptures you will find the phrase *the Day of the Lord.* This at times refers to a 1000-year day, which begins when Christ comes to the earth at the end of the Tribulation Period to set up His kingdom.

Peter implies that we could be ignorant about some things, but he admonishes us not to be ignorant about THIS ONE THING, for it is an important key to understanding end-time events.

> *One day is with the Lord as a thousand years, and a thousand years as a day.*

The second key concerning end-time events: *One day is with the LORD as a thousand years, and a thousand years as one day.*

I encourage you to give special attention to the following Scriptures from the Book of Genesis, for they are foundational Scriptures revealing how God uses things that happen in one time period to reveal later prophetic events in their own time frame.

It seems that God has divided the time of man's dominion on planet Earth into three segments of time. That time frame in general terms is considered to be 2000 years from the creation of Adam to Abraham. Two thousand years from Abraham to Christ. If we use the concept of "ONE DAY IS WITH THE LORD AS A THOUSAND YEARS, AND A THOUSAND YEARS AS ONE DAY," we could say this: There were approximately two days from Adam to Abraham and two days from Abraham to Christ, which would be four days from the creation of man to Christ. Then the parable of the Good Samaritan seems to reveal that from Christ to the end of the Church Age is also two days, or 2000 years, making a total of 6000 years. We will cover more details of this parable in chapter 5.

THE EARTH LEASE

The Genesis account states that God labored six days, creating the earth and making man in His own image, then rested the seventh day. The Scriptures indicate that God gave Adam a lease on planet Earth for a period of 6000 years.

> Genesis 1:26 **And God said, Let us make man in our image, after our likeness: and LET THEM HAVE DOMINION over the fish of the sea, and over the fowl of the air, and over the cattle, and over all the earth, and over every creeping thing that creepeth upon the earth.**
> **27 So God created man in his own image, in the image of God created he him; male and female created he them.**
> **28 And God blessed them, and God said unto them, Be fruitful, and multiply, and replenish the earth, and subdue it: and have dominion over the fish of the sea, and over the fowl of the air, and over every living thing that moveth upon the earth.**

The earth lease, which gave man dominion on earth for a limited time is subtly revealed in the first chapter of Genesis. Just as Isaiah had prophesied, God spoke the end from the beginning. (Isaiah 46:9-10.) The six days, by double reference, represent 6000 years of human history. It is within that time frame that mankind will be allowed to exercise dominion on the earth, and then God will take back control of this planet. Psalm 24:1 says: **"The Earth is the Lord's and the fulness thereof: the world and they that dwell therein."** It is evident that each of the six twenty-four-hour days in the Genesis account represents 1000 years of God's dealing with mankind under the earth lease agreement before the day of rest.

Paul, in Hebrews 4:3-5, states:

3 For we which have believed do enter into rest, as he said, As I have sworn in my wrath, if they shall enter into my rest: although the works were finished from the foundation of the world.
4 For he spake in a certain place of the seventh day on this wise, And God did rest the seventh day from all his works.
5 And in this place again, If they shall enter into my rest.

It is clear that the seventh day in the Genesis account represents the Seventh Millennium, which is a day of rest for God and his people. (Hebrews 4:1-11.) During that time, Satan will be bound and confined to the bottomless pit as Christ and His saints rule in His kingdom here on the earth. (Revelation 20.)

GOD'S COVENANT WITH ABRAHAM

In Abraham's day, God made a blood covenant with Abraham, and through that covenant the promised child, Isaac, was born. God told Abraham that through him all of the nations of the earth would be blessed and that great nations would come out of him because he obeyed God's voice. (Genesis 22:17-18.)

But when Isaac was grown, God asked Abraham to offer his son as a sacrifice on a mountain in the land of Moriah.

And He said to Abraham, **"Take now thy son, thine only son Isaac, whom thou lovest, and get thee into the land of**

Moriah; and offer him there for a burnt offering upon one of the mountains which I will tell thee of" (Genesis 22:2).

This foreshadowed what God was going to do with His own Son to redeem mankind. Abraham took his son to the mountain, bound him and laid him on the altar and raised the knife to kill him; but the angel of the Lord stopped him. (vv. 9-12.)

The covenant God made with Abraham would stand forever.

God proved that Abraham would keep the covenant He had made with him. He proved Abraham's willingness to give his only son. God called Isaac Abraham's "only son" because he was the only son of promise. Because Abraham kept his covenant by obeying God's command, it was legal under the earth-lease agreement for God to send His Son to earth to redeem fallen man.*

When Abraham raised the knife to kill his son, the Supreme Court of the universe, (Heavenly Father, His Son, and the Holy Spirit), ruled on the matter, declaring that covenant to be valid throughout eternity. The covenant God made with Abraham would stand forever. (Genesis 15:18; 17:1-7.)

Abraham had validated the Blood Covenant in an act of obedience by offering his son, thereby making it legal for God to send His Son to planet Earth to redeem mankind. It is evident that Abraham understood this, for in John 8:56 Jesus said, **"Abraham rejoiced to see my day: and he saw it, and was glad."** There is no doubt that Abraham received a revelation that day of God offering His Son as the sacrificial Lamb to redeem fallen man.

DOUBLE REFERENCE OF THE SECOND DAY

The second day in the Genesis account revealed what was done in that twenty-four-hour period concerning the separation of the

---

*For a complete teaching on this subject, see the author's book *Authority in Three Worlds*.

waters of the earth. However, the second day also has a prophetic fulfillment by double reference, which revealed what was going to happen in the second thousandth year on planet Earth.

> **Genesis 1:6 And God said, Let there be a firmament in the midst of the waters, and let it divide the waters from the waters.**
> **7 And God made the firmament, and divided the waters which were under the firmament from the waters which were above the firmament: and it was so.**
> **8 And God called the firmament heaven. And the evening and the morning were the second day.**

God divided the waters below from the waters above. So, at least by double reference, we could conclude that *waters* symbolizes salvation on two levels, of which the new birth is on a higher level.* (Isaiah 12:3; John 3:5; 15:3; Ephesians 5:26.)

As we investigate the apostle Paul's statement found in Galatians, chapter 4, we will get a better understanding of this matter:

> **21 Tell me, ye that desire to be under the law, do ye not hear the law?**
> **22 For it is written, that Abraham had two sons, the one by a bondmaid, the other by a freewoman.**
> **23 But he who was of the bondwoman was born after the flesh; but he of the freewoman was by promise.**
> **24 Which things are an allegory: FOR THESE ARE THE TWO COVENANTS; the one from the mount Sinai, which gendereth to bondage, which is Agar.**
> **25 For this Agar is mount Sinai in Arabia, and answereth to Jerusalem which now is, and is in bondage with her children.**

---

* One of the rules of Bible interpretation is that when it mentions water and does not name a particular river, stream, or ocean, it applies, or at least has a double reference, to people.

26 But Jerusalem which is above is free, which is the mother of us all.

These Scriptures seem to confirm what we saw in the second-day account. God separated the waters below from the waters above, which was a preview of the two covenants; for *water* is also a type of the Word that brings salvation. This foreshadowed people who were in bondage to sin and were operating in the flesh.

God separated that which was below (fleshly nature) from that which was above, being indicative of deliverance from sin by the new birth. This seems to fit as a parallel in the second day of the Genesis account, which reveals the beginning stage of a New Covenant.

We could say it was the embryo stage of the New Covenant, which was to come through Christ. For the promise was made to Abraham and his seed, and that Seed was Christ. (Galatians 3:16.) Abraham operated under that Covenant until the Seed (Christ) came, to Whom the promise was made.

It was through that covenant, which God made with Abraham and confirmed with Isaac, that Jesus Christ was born on earth 2000 years later.

The prophetic implications become much stronger as we view them in the light of the statements made by the prophet Jeremiah.

Jeremiah 51:15 He hath made the earth by his power, he hath established the world by his wisdom, and hath stretched out the heaven by his understanding. 16 When he uttereth his voice, there is a multitude of waters in the heavens; and he causeth the vapours to ascend from the ends of the earth....

We know in a natural sense that water in lakes, streams, and oceans becomes polluted; but through the evaporation process, water vapor will rise and form clouds, leaving all its pollution below.

Using this analogy, we know that vapor is water in a pure form ascending above the earth. Is it possible that this is God's marvelous way of illustrating both the rebirth of the human spirit and the catching away of the Church to Heaven in another form? Could it be that this also represents the Body of Christ, who will come back to the earth with Christ and cause the earth to be productive once again?

The prophetic implications are even greater when we study the context of Jeremiah's statement concerning God's punishment of Babylon. Even though Babylon has experienced a partial fulfillment of Jeremiah's prophecy, the total fulfillment will come near the end of the Tribulation Period. (Revelation 17:18.)

The prophecies of Jeremiah are also magnified by Psalm 148:

1 Praise ye the Lord. Praise ye the Lord from the heavens: praise him in the heights.
2 Praise ye him, all his angels: praise ye him, all his hosts.
3 Praise ye him, sun and moon: praise him, all ye stars of light.
4 Praise him, ye heavens of heavens, and YE WATERS THAT BE ABOVE THE HEAVENS.

It is quite possible in verse 4 that these *waters* represent people who ascended to Heaven. This corresponds perfectly with the words of Jeremiah and the implications found in day two of the Genesis account.

Could it be that God has woven the revelation of the Rapture of the Church into the second day of the Genesis account as well? The parallel seems to fit.

THE FOURTH DAY

As we take a closer look at the fourth day of the Genesis account, keep in mind that there were approximately 2000 years from Adam to Abraham and another 2000 years from Abraham to the birth of Christ, making a total of 4000 years.

> Genesis 1:14 **And God said, Let there be lights in the firmament of the heaven to divide the day from the night; and let them be for signs, and for seasons, and for days, and years:**
> **15 And let them be for lights in the firmament of the heaven to give light upon the earth: and it was so.**
> **16 And God made two great lights; the greater light to rule the day, and the lesser light to rule the night.**

Notice it was on the fourth day that God allowed great light to shine upon the earth in a literal sense. The *great light* was obviously the sun, for it rules the day; the moon, which would be the lesser light, rules the night.

However, there are prophetic implications also in the fact that the sun is symbolic of Jesus' (the Light of the world) coming to earth at the end of the fourth day, which reveals His first coming to be the four thousandth year of human history.

It is interesting that Malachi 4:2, in reference to a time of period after the earth lease expires, states: **"the Sun of righteousness** shall **arise with healing in his wings."** You will notice that in this verse the word is spelled *S-u-n*. This serves as a clue that God allowed the natural light of the sun to shine on the earth on the fourth day to foreshadow His supernatural Son bringing great Light to the earth after 4000 years of human history.

We find an interesting comparison in Psalm 19:1-5 which also would relate to the fourth day of the Genesis account:

> **1 The heavens declare the glory of God; and the firmament sheweth his handiwork.**
> **2 Day unto day uttereth speech, and night unto night sheweth knowledge.**

3 There is no speech nor language, where their voice is not heard.
4 Their line is gone out through all the earth, and their words to the end of the world. In them hath he set a TABERNACLE for the sun,
5 Which is as a bridegroom coming out of his chamber, and rejoiceth as a strong man to run a race.

These verses are classic examples of God's subtle way of revealing future prophetic events through present and past events. It was the prophet Isaiah who gave us this understanding of God's method of revealing future events.

Isaiah 42:9 **Behold, the former things are come to pass, and new things do I declare: before they spring forth I tell you of them.**

Solomon gives us the third key, which also has prophetic implications concerning the end-time.

Ecclesiastes 1:9 **The thing that hath been, it is that which shall be; and that which is done is that which shall be done: and there is no new thing under the sun.**
10 Is there any thing whereof it may be said, See, this is new? it hath been already of old time, which was before us.

These prophetic verses, together with the Genesis account of the fourth day, seem to reveal that God established the appointed time of Jesus' birth in the first chapter of Genesis. Then the apostle Paul gives support to this by stating, **"...when the fulness of the time was come, God sent forth his Son..."** (Galatians 4:4).

What would constitute the fullness of time? It had to fit the prophetic pattern established in Genesis 1:14-18. Therefore, Jesus' birth must fulfill God's timely appointment in the four thousandth year (fourth day) of human history.

CHRISTIANS REFLECT CHRIST

It is quite evident that Christ, the Son of righteousness, also rules the day in which we live by reflecting His Light to the world through the Body of Christ. This seems to be referred to in Genesis 1:16 as **"the lesser light to rule the night."** The moon reflects the sun as a Christian reflects Christ, Who is **"the Sun of righteousness"** (Malachi 4:2). Christians have been made new creations in Christ to rule and restrain the darkness on earth by reflecting the light of Christ Himself.

This is one of the major reasons the Antichrist cannot put his ambitions into effect until the Church is taken out of the earth. The Body of Christ (the Church) is restraining and will continue to restrain (hold back) the Antichrist's spirit until the Church is caught up to meet the Lord in the air. (1 Thessalonians 4:16-17.)

In the parable of the faithful and unfaithful servants in Luke 19:13, the words of Jesus give us a clear message that WE ARE TO OCCUPY TILL HE COMES.

CHAPTER FOUR

Resurrection Insight

In the Holy Scriptures there are many revelations woven into ordinary events which have not been recognized in other generations. These revelations have been placed there for this generation. But time itself has had much the same effect as a louvered blind. The revelation could not be clearly seen until we arrived at the time appointed for that revelation to be released.

This generation has arrived at that point in God's timing, and these things are now being unveiled as never before.

The prophet Isaiah and Jesus both seem to confirm this fact:

Isaiah 42:9 **Behold, the former things are come to pass, and new things do I declare: before they spring forth I tell you of them.**

John 16:12 **I have yet many things to say unto you, but ye cannot bear them now.**
13 Howbeit when he, the Spirit of truth, is come, he will guide you into all truth: for he shall not speak of himself; but whatsoever he shall hear, that shall he speak: and he will shew you things to come.

These verses indicate that many things Jesus wanted to reveal concerning the prophetic Scriptures could not have been clearly understood in that day. The implications were that the Holy Spirit would reveal them at a time in human history to the generation that would be able to understand them clearly.

LAZARUS' DEATH AND RESURRECTION

God used ordinary events in the Scriptures to give us insight into future events before they happen.

We find one such event recorded in the gospel of John, which gives us an account of Lazarus' death and his resurrection.

John 11:3 **Therefore his sisters sent unto him, saying, Lord, behold, he whom thou lovest is sick.**
4 When Jesus heard that, he said, This sickness is not unto death, but for the glory of God, that the Son of God might be glorified thereby. *

Notice Jesus' reaction when He heard the news that Lazarus was sick.

6 When he had heard therefore that he was sick, he abode two days still in the same place where he was.

The story of Lazarus was a type, or a parallel, of mankind who was spiritually dead when Jesus came to earth. When the runner left Bethany with the message, Lazarus was only sick; but by the time he arrived, Lazarus was dead, and Jesus knew it. After Jesus heard that Lazarus was sick, He stayed two days still in the same place where He was, before going to raise Lazarus from death.

> *God used ordinary events in the Scriptures to give us insight into future events before they happen.*

God's Word reveals in a marvelous way the past, the present, and the future. This fits perfectly with the profile we found in Genesis 1:14-18, which, by double reference, revealed that Christ's first coming to earth would be on the fourth day.

---

*It wasn't the sickness or death of Lazarus that brought glory to God, but rather his resurrection.

Follow this thought pattern very carefully, for this event seems to confirm the prophetic revelation woven into the fourth day of the Genesis account. I believe the fourth day reveals what was to happen in the four thousandth year on earth. Great light was to come to the earth in two ways: by the sun on the fourth natural day, and by the birth of Jesus in the four thousandth year by prophetic reference.

✳ We know Jesus was in Heaven at the time Abraham validated the Covenant by raising the knife on his son Isaac. It was that Covenant which made it legal for God to send His Son to the earth to pay the price for man's sin and redeem mankind from spiritual death. But He stayed two days (2000 years) still in the same place *where He was.* I believe He waited those two days to fulfill a scriptural profile in the Genesis account which revealed His first coming to be on the fourth day, representing 4000 years.

As Jesus was on His way to Bethany, He met Martha.

John 11:21 **Then said Martha unto Jesus, Lord, if thou hadst been here, my brother had not died.**
22 But I know, that even now, whatsoever thou wilt ask of God, God will give it thee.
23 Jesus saith unto her, Thy brother shall rise again.
24 Martha saith unto him, I know that he shall rise again IN THE RESURRECTION AT THE LAST DAY.

It is possible that the **"resurrection at the last day,"** to which Martha was referring, would be the one at the beginning of the millennial reign of Christ. For at that point in time, the revelation concerning the Rapture of the Church had not been revealed.

That revelation was given to us by Paul and Peter, who were both apostles to the Gentiles. It was spoken of by Paul in 1 Thessalonians 4:16-17 and 1 Corinthians 15:51-52; and it is the resurrection connected with the Rapture of the Church.

It seems Martha had no knowledge of the resurrection to which Jesus referred. Therefore, Jesus began to explain to her the resurrection of the righteous dead, which would take place at the time of the Rapture of the righteous who would be alive at His appearing. In response to Martha's statement, Jesus began to preach the Resurrection which will accompany the Rapture.

John 11:25 **Jesus said unto her, I am the resurrection, and the life: he that believeth in me, though he were dead, yet shall he live:**
26 And whosoever liveth and believeth in me shall never die. Believest thou this?

Notice the prophetic implications of His statement: **"...I am the resurrection, and the life...."** Jesus seems to be saying: "He that has believed in Me, though he has already died, when I appear (for the Church) he shall be resurrected and live. And whoever believes in Me and is alive at My appearing shall never die, but the mortal body will be changed and become immortal." The resurrection of the righteous dead of 6000 years will take place when Jesus appears. This statement fits prophetically with what the apostle Paul taught. Compare the following Scripture with what Jesus said to Martha.

1 Thessalonians 4:16-17 and 1 Corinthians 15:51-52.

16 For the Lord himself shall descend from heaven with a shout, with the voice of the archangel, and with the trump of God: and the dead in Christ shall rise first:
17 Then we which are alive and remain shall be caught up together with them in the clouds, to meet the Lord in the air: and so shall we ever be with the Lord.

1 Corinthians 15:51 **Behold, I shew you a mystery; We shall not all sleep, but we shall all be changed.**
52 In a moment, in the twinkling of an eye, at the last trump: for the trumpet shall sound, and the dead shall be raised incorruptible, and we shall be changed.

These verses leave no doubt that the statements made to Martha at least by prophetic implications, are in reference to the righteous who will be alive at the time of the Rapture, *revealing that they will never die.* I believe Jesus was actually preaching the Rapture to Martha, but she missed the intent of His message, as many Bible scholars have today. I challenge you to study these verses in depth. You will find that all three passages describe the very same event: the resurrection of the righteous dead and the Rapture of the Church.

THE STONE AND THE LAW

When Jesus arrived at the tomb of Lazarus, His first order was to remove the stone:

John 11:39 Jesus said, Take ye away the stone. Martha, the sister of him that was dead, saith unto him, Lord, by this time he stinketh: for he hath been dead four days.

After Jesus heard that Lazarus (mankind) was sick, He stayed two more days in the same place where He was so He would arrive on the scene to raise him up after four days.

This profiles the fact that when Jesus arrived on planet Earth, mankind had been spiritually dead for 4000 years:

Jesus was beyond Jordan, where John had first baptized, when He received the message that Lazarus was sick. It was approximately seventeen miles from Bethany where Lazarus was, and it took the messenger a day to travel that distance. After Jesus heard Lazarus was sick, He stayed two days still in the same place where He was, making a total of three days.

Then it took Jesus another day to get to Bethany, which made four days in all.

Some might suggest that mankind was not spiritually dead before the Law was given, concluding that mankind had not been spiritually dead for a 4000-year period.

God gave the Law to Moses approximately 2500 years after the creation of Adam. But mankind was spiritually dead from the time that Adam sinned. This is what Paul was referring to in Romans 5:13: **"For until the law sin was in the world: but sin is not imputed when there is no law."**

Man had actually been spiritually dead for 4000 years, but he did not recognize that fact until the Law came.

The very first thing Jesus did when He arrived on the scene was to remove the stone from the tomb. The stone represented the Law, for the Law had kept mankind entombed in spiritual death.

Let's compare the following Scriptures in Galatians with Jesus' statement in Matthew 5:17-18.

Galatians 3:22 **But the scripture hath concluded all under sin, that the promise by faith of Jesus Christ might be given to them that believe.**
23 But before faith came, we were kept under the law, shut up unto the faith which should afterwards be revealed.
24 Wherefore the law was our schoolmaster to bring us unto Christ, that we might be justified by faith.
25 But after that faith is come, we are no longer under a schoolmaster.

Matthew 5:17 **Think not that I am come to destroy the law, or the prophets: I am not come to destroy, but to fulfil.**
18 For verily I say unto you, Till heaven and earth pass, one jot or one tittle shall in no wise pass from the law, till all be fulfilled.

It was through the law of works that sin had flourished. The Law was to bring man to Christ by revealing that he couldn't be righteous within himself, and there was no power in the Law that would help him to keep it.

THE MINISTRATION OF DEATH

In 2 Corinthians, we find scriptural precedent that the stone represented the Law in this event:

2 Corinthians 3:6 **Who also hath made us able ministers of the new testament; not of the letter, but of the spirit: for the letter killeth, but the spirit giveth life.**
7 BUT IF THE MINISTRATION OF DEATH, WRITTEN AND ENGRAVEN IN STONES, was glorious, so that the children of Israel could not steadfastly behold the face of Moses for the glory of his countenance; which glory was to be done away:
8 How shall not the ministration of the spirit be rather glorious?

In these verses Paul called the Law **"the ministration of death, written and engraven in stones,"** because God had written the Law in stone. Today we keep the spirit of the Law but not the letter of the Law. (2 Corinthians 3:6.) We know that spiritually dead people can't keep the Law and those who are spiritually alive don't need the Law. We are not under the law of the Old Covenant but are under the law of the New Covenant, which is the law of faith, and faith works by love. (Galatians 5:6,13.)

LAW FULFILLED

Jesus did what no man had been able to do: He lived and walked perfectly and uprightly under the Old Covenant for thirty years. He fulfilled it to the letter, and it passed away, as stated by Paul in Romans 10:4: **"For Christ is the end of the law for righteousness to every one that believeth."**

Let's compare this verse from the *King James Version* with that found in *The Amplified Bible:*

Romans 10:4 AMP **For Christ is the end of the Law [the limit at which it ceases to be, for the Law leads up to**

Him Who is the fulfillment of its types, and in Him the purpose which it was designed to accomplish is fulfilled. That is, the purpose of the Law is fulfilled in Him] as the means of righteousness (right relationship to God) for everyone who trusts in and adheres to and relies on Him.

...eternal life is in the Person of Jesus Christ.

In Paul's day, the Jews were still trying to obtain righteousness by the Law, as many are today, but Christ made an end of the Law for righteousness. In this dispensation of grace, those who believe Jesus is the Messiah, the Son of God, and confess Him as Lord of their lives have eternal life. That eternal life is in the Person of Jesus Christ. If you are in Christ, you are a new creature and you have eternal life.

The apostle John brings the biblical perspective of eternal life into sharp focus in the following verses.

1 John 5:11 **And this is the record, that God hath given to us eternal life, and this life is in his Son.**
12 He that hath the Son hath life; and he that hath not the Son of God hath not life.

Yes, it's that simple. That's why it is called the simple plan of salvation.

RESURRECTION–LIFE–IMPARTED

When Jesus removed the stone from the tomb, there was a glorious resurrection.

John 11:43 **And when he thus had spoken, he cried with a loud voice, Lazarus, come forth.**
44 And he that was dead came forth, bound hand and foot with graveclothes: and his face was bound about with a napkin. Jesus saith unto them, Loose him, and let him go.

This was the way people were embalmed in those days: by being wrapped in strips of linen soaked in spices.

The grave clothes in which Lazarus was wrapped represented religious bondage. All kinds of man-made rules and regulations had been added to the Law. For instance, they couldn't eat with unwashed hands; they couldn't even walk through the fields and eat grains of wheat on the Sabbath day. Those regulations turned out to be religious bondage for the people. Jesus commanded them to loose Lazarus (mankind) and let him go from that which had him bound.

There are many today who are still bound in that same manner; but Jesus came that they might have life and have it more abundantly. (John 10:10.)

CHAPTER IN REVIEW

This synopsis will serve to bring the major points of this chapter into clear focus concerning the prophetic implications of the biblical record of Lazarus' sickness, death, and resurrection.

When Lazarus fell sick, his two sisters, Mary and Martha, sent a messenger to beckon Jesus for the purpose of healing their brother.

Jesus was beyond Jordan in the place where John first baptized. (John 10:40.) It was approximately seventeen miles to Bethany, where Lazarus lived.

When the messenger was sent to Jesus, Lazarus was only sick, but it took him a day to get the message to Jesus. When Jesus heard of Lazarus' situation, He declared that the end result of the whole matter would not be death, but that it would bring glory to God.

After Jesus had assessed the situation, knowing that Lazarus was dead, He stayed two days still in the same place. This made a total of three days from the time the messenger was sent to Him. We know it took Jesus a day to get to Bethany, where Lazarus had been buried. So, from the time the messenger was sent until Jesus arrived at Lazarus' tomb, four days had passed.

We know this was a natural event that happened as it is recorded. However, it has prophetic implications because of the exactness of the four days it took for Jesus to arrive on the scene to raise Lazarus from the dead. It parallels the prophetic profile we saw in the Genesis account of the second day and the fourth day.

The second day implies prophetic importance because in the second thousandth year from Adam, Abraham validated the Covenant. He proved that he would keep the Covenant, making it legal for God to send His Son to redeem mankind. However, God did not send His Son at that time. Jesus stayed two days, or 2000 more years, in Heaven before He was born on the earth.

The fact that Jesus arrived on the scene and raised Lazarus from the dead on the fourth day is prophetic of 4000 years of human history. Jesus' first act when He arrived on the scene was to roll away the stone, which prophetically represented the Law.

The record of this event in the Scriptures leaves no doubt that it was God's way of weaving into natural events the revelation of God's plan to remove the Old Covenant and to establish the New Covenant, which would impart eternal life to mankind.

This record of Lazarus' sickness, death, burial, and resurrection is an example of the way God, through His infinite wisdom, reveals things to come by actual events that happened before the time of their prophetic fulfillment.

CHAPTER FIVE

Secrets Revealed in the Parables

In former generations, much of the prophetic Word concerning the end time had been sealed or partially veiled because of the time in which that generation lived. They simply could not grasp a clear understanding of the many events that were prophesied; they did not know about inventions such as television, computers, modern weapons of mass destruction, and fast transportation. Therefore, they couldn't identify with certain prophecies for lack of this knowledge. So they were sort of seeing through a glass, darkly. But today, knowledge has increased dramatically and prophetic revelations are being unveiled by time itself to this end-time generation.

Matthew refers to such revelation being hidden in parables:

Matthew 13:34 **All these things spake Jesus unto the multitude in parables; and without a parable spake he not unto them:**
35 That it might be fulfilled which was spoken by the prophet, saying, I will open my mouth in parables; I will utter things which have been kept secret from the foundation of the world.

The things that have been kept secret from the foundation of the world will not be hidden from this generation. We have arrived at the point in God's timing where there are no longer any hindrances to block the revelation and insight concerning end-time events.

As we have taken a closer look at the second and fourth days of the Genesis account, we have found it just as Isaiah had stated: God spoke the end from the beginning, revealing an overall view of His working with mankind to be six 1000-year days.

The things that have been kept secret from the foundation of the world will not be hidden from this generation.

Scriptural implications indicate the Body of Christ (Church) will be caught up to Heaven, after 6000 years of human history and before the seven years of tribulation begin on planet Earth. This period is exactly seven years long. It seems to be a parenthetical week of years which God has set aside to deal with Israel and the wicked of the world in order to bring them to a decision, either for or against God.

When those seven years have been fulfilled, Christ will come back to the earth with the saints who were raptured, Satan will be bound, and Christ will set up His earthly kingdom for 1000 years of righteous rule. At the end of that 1000 years of peace, Satan will be loosed for a little season. Then all wickedness will be totally destroyed from the earth in the last battle between the righteous and the wicked of the earth. (Revelation 20:7-15.)

The last two days of the six-day period (6000 years) are very significant, for this is the length of the Church Age.

THE GOOD SAMARITAN REVELATION

Luke 10:30 **And Jesus answering said, A certain man went down from Jerusalem to Jericho, and fell among thieves, which stripped him of his raiment, and wounded him, and departed, leaving him half dead.**

In this parable, the man seems to represent Adam as well as all of mankind; Jerusalem is a type of Heaven, for it is the city of the Great King; and Jericho represents the way of the wicked world. Jerusalem was higher in elevation, and the road down to Jericho was called "the bloody way." It was the most dangerous road in Palestine because of robbers infesting the country.[1] Yet, Jericho was a city of priests, for it was a religious city.

The man in this parable represented mankind, who was stripped of his right standing with God by Satan through sin and was left spiritually dead. This basically reveals what happened to Adam and all of mankind through the Fall.

> Luke 10:31 **And by chance there came down a certain priest that way: and when he saw him, he passed by on the other side.**
> **32 And likewise a Levite, when he was at the place, came and looked on him, and passed by on the other side.**

The priest, who was an official of the Law, was just as spiritually dead as the man was, so he couldn't help him. The Levites, who were in charge of the blood sacrifices, couldn't help him either, for the blood of bulls and goats could not take away the consciousness of sin.

> Luke 10:33 **But a certain Samaritan, as he journeyed, came where he was: and when he saw him, he had compassion on him.**

Take note of the fact that the Good Samaritan was on a journey; he had a mission to perform. There is no doubt that the Good Samaritan in this parable symbolically represents Jesus. Verse 33 states, "**...as he journeyed,** [he] **came where he was....**"

Jesus was born here; He came to the earth in a natural body, for He had a mission to perform. He came to where man was, to pay the debt of sin and to resurrect mankind from spiritual death.

He became sin for us that we might be made alive spiritually and become the righteousness of God in Him. (2 Corinthians 5:21.)

Notice this phrase in Luke 10:33: "**...and when he saw him, he had compassion on him.**" We see this phrase many times in the Scriptures concerning Jesus' attitude toward suffering humanity. (Matthew 9:36; 14:14; 18:27; Mark 1:41; 6:34.)

> Luke 10:33 **...and when he saw him, he had compassion on him,**
> **34 And went to him, and bound up his wounds, pouring in oil and wine, and set him on his own beast, and brought him to an inn, and took care of him.**

In Matthew 9:17, Jesus said that new wine is not put into old bottles. The bottles were actually wineskins made of leather and would crack with age. In order to renew them, oil would be rubbed into them, enabling them to hold the new wine, which is a type of the Holy Spirit. The oil mentioned in this parable is a type of the work of the Holy Spirit in the human spirit, as Paul states in his letter to Titus:

> Titus 3:5 **Not by works of righteousness which we have done, but according to his mercy he saved us, by the washing of regeneration, and renewing of the Holy Ghost.**

When Nicodemus came to Jesus at night, He explained to him that he must be born again to be able to see the kingdom of God. (John 3:1-7.)

In this parable, the oil and the wine symbolize the work of the Holy Spirit through the Word, to bring salvation by the washing and regeneration of the human spirit by the Holy Spirit. The Samaritan poured in the oil and the wine and set the man on his *own beast,* which represents *His property.* The Scriptures reveal that God has translated us out of the kingdom of darkness into the kingdom of His dear Son. (Colossians 1:13.) The Good Samaritan took the man to an inn to be cared for while he was gone. The inn in this parable seems to represent the Church, which was to care for those born again until Jesus returns.

> Luke 10:35 **And on the morrow when he departed, he took out two pence, and gave them to the host,* and said unto him, Take care of him; and whatsoever thou spendest more, when I come again, I will repay thee.**

There is great significance in the amount of money that was given to the host in this parable. A pence is the same as a penny referred to in Matthew 20:2. You will notice in that passage that a penny was the wage for a day's work. The Greek word translated "penny" in Matthew 20:2 is *denarion*.[2] It is the same word which is translated "pence" in Luke 10:35. Therefore, a pence, or a penny, in biblical times was a day's wage.

The Good Samaritan paid the host to take care of the man for two days, which seem to represent 2000 years, the time span allotted to the Church Age. (See Hosea 6:1-2.) History reveals there were 4000 years from the creation of Adam to Christ. That only leaves 2000 years (two days) for the Church Age. This would be consistent with what is revealed in the Genesis account concerning God having completed His work in six days.

The implication of the fact that the Good Samaritan gave the *host* two days' wages to take care of him seems to be prophetic, revealing his plan to return two days later. This would correspond perfectly with the 1000-years-as-a-day interpretation of the Genesis account.

In this parable, Jesus spoke things which had been kept secret from the foundation of the world. Yet the parable itself seems to

---

* The host in this parable would seem to represent the Holy Spirit.

have been veiled by time until the arrival of the generation which would be affected the most by this revelation.

Verse 35 leaves no doubt that Christ intends for the Body of Christ to be fully equipped for the end-time harvest at the end of the Sixth Millennium. This is obvious from the words that Jesus used in this parable: "**...and whatsoever thou spendest more, when I come again, I will repay thee.**" What an astounding statement, which will no doubt have a far-reaching effect concerning whatever is needed for the end-time harvest to be completed on time.

...there is no limit to what the Holy Ghost will do to bring the Body of Christ into complete maturity....

This statement gives the definite impression that nothing will be spared that is needed. *Money will be no object; neither will the anointing that is required for the Body of Christ to come to full maturity and be victorious at the close of the Church Age.* These words imply, "Spare no expense. See to it that they get whatever is needed, and put it on the Master's card, and He will take care of it when He comes again." This parable reveals that there is no limit to what the Holy Ghost will do to bring the Body of Christ into complete maturity in that time frame. (Ephesians 4:11-13.)

This parable also has a prophetic implication that the Good Samaritan (Jesus) expected to return after two days.

It seems that God dropped a subtle clue in Genesis, chapter 1, which in our day seems to confirm the time when the Church (Body of Christ) will come to full maturity.

Genesis 1:27 **So God created man in his own image, in the image of God created he him; male and female created he them.**
31 And God saw every thing that he had made, and, behold, it was very good. And the evening and the morning were the sixth day.

It was at the end of the sixth day that God saw everything He had made, and it was very good. So you can rest assured that at the *end of the sixth day* it will be very good for the Body of Christ (the Church). God saw it from the beginning, and I believe we will see it prophetically fulfilled after 6000 years of human history.

It seems evident that God has indeed spoken the end from the beginning. There are some who might accuse me of setting dates, but I am only reviewing what God has already revealed from the beginning. The Bible states that not even Jesus knew the day and the hour.

> Mark 13:32 **But of that day and that hour knoweth no man, no, not the angels which are in heaven, neither the Son, but the Father.**

God is the Master Timekeeper of the universe, and He alone knows our exact date in human history. Man's calendar is probably not accurate, so it is not wise to try to set specific dates. If we knew the day and the hour of His appearing to catch away the Church, we still wouldn't know the exact time, unless we knew which time zone He would pick for the moment of Christ's appearing.

You can be sure that the Body of Christ will be taken out after completing His work on the earth through the Church. But at the present time, God has reserved the exact timing of this great event to Himself alone. There are, however, Scriptures that would seem to indicate that He will reveal the exact day before the Rapture takes place. I will give more information about this in later chapters.

Concerning the Second Advent, although we don't know the time of this event when Jesus will return to earth from Heaven with the saints, we know both the time zone and location. Zechariah 14:1-5 plainly states that He will descend on the Mount of Olives just outside of Jerusalem—the very place where

He ascended to Heaven. If we knew the time of the Second Advent we would know the exact time of the Rapture, for it would be exactly seven years before that event.

As Christians, we are children of light, and you can rest assured we will not be left in the dark concerning the Rapture. The critics of the Rapture refer to it as "the great escape," "Rapture theory," or "the great snatch." But regardless of what the critics say, when the time comes, the Body of Christ will leave planet Earth for a period of seven years. Then we will return with Him at the end of the Tribulation as prophesied in Zechariah 14:1-5 and Revelation 19:11-21.

CHAPTER SIX

Redemption of the Body

God sent His only Son to the earth to redeem mankind from spiritual death. Jesus redeemed us from spiritual death and made the experience of the new birth available to all mankind. The new birth comes about by the *washing of regeneration* and renewing of the Holy Spirit in the human spirit. (Titus 3:5.)

But there is another redemption coming that will complete the work that the Holy Spirit began in us—a redemption so glorious that Paul called it "that blessed hope."

Titus 2:13. **Looking for that blessed hope, and the glorious appearance of the great God and our Saviour Jesus Christ;**

Colossians 1:18. **And he is the head of the body, the church: who is THE BEGINNING, THE FIRSTBORN FROM THE DEAD; that in all things he might have the preeminence.**

Paul reveals Jesus to be *the head, the beginning of the Church,* and the *firstborn from the dead.* In Revelation 1:5, He is called the first begotten of the dead.

RECONCILED TO GOD

We have been reconciled and presented holy, blameless and above reproach in His sight.

Colossians 1:21 **And you, that were sometime alien-ated and enemies in your mind by wicked works, yet now hath he reconciled**

22 In the body of his flesh through death, to present you holy and unblameable and unreproveable in his sight:

23 IF YE CONTINUE IN THE FAITH GROUNDED AND SET-TLED, AND BE NOT MOVED AWAY FROM THE HOPE OF THE GOSPEL....

Paul states that the mysteries hidden for ages are now being revealed.

Jesus did reconcile us to God through His death to present us holy, blameless, and above reproach in His sight. However, Paul reveals in verse 23 that this promise is conditional.

In Titus 2:13, Paul referred to the glorious appearing of Jesus Christ as *that blessed hope*. In fact, he spoke of it in one way or another in all of his epistles to the Church. Since faith is the substance of things hoped for, it is clear that faith has a connection with that blessed hope of the Rapture.

Yet, there are many today who once believed in that blessed hope and now scoff at it. They call it a theory or "escape mentality." They have been moved away from their faith and hope concerning this vital part of the Gospel.

HIDDEN MYSTERIES REVEALED

In Colossians 1, Paul states that the mysteries hidden for ages are now being revealed.

Colossians 1:25 **...I am made a minister, according to the dispensation of God which is given to me for you, to fulfil the word of God;**

26 Even the mystery which hath been hid from ages and from generations, but now is made manifest to his saints:

27 To whom God would make known what is the riches of the glory of this mystery among the Gentiles; which is Christ in you, the hope of glory.

In other words, Paul said: "Christ in you is your hope of being glorified." In Romans 8:10-11 Paul said:

10 ...if Christ be in you, the body is dead because of sin; but the Spirit is life because of righteousness.

11 But if the Spirit of him that raised up Jesus from the dead dwell in you, he that raised up Christ from the dead shall also quicken your mortal bodies by his Spirit that dwelleth in you.

I believe this Scripture has a double reference to the Holy Spirit making your spirit totally alive to God at His appearing.

DEAD AND BURIED BUT RAISED WITH CHRIST

When we were baptized into Christ, that act portrayed our death to sin, our burial, and our resurrection to new life. As far as God is concerned, we are already risen *with* Christ.

Colossians 3:2 Set your affection on things above, not on things on the earth.

3 For ye are dead, and your life is hid with Christ in God.

4 When Christ, who is our life, shall appear, then shall ye also appear with him in glory.

These verses give a perfect description of the dead in Christ and the righteous who will be alive at the time of the Rapture of the Church referred to in 1 Thessalonians 4:17.

CROWN OF REJOICING

In 1 Thessalonians 2 Paul says:

19 For what is our hope, or joy, or crown of rejoicing? Are not even ye in the presence of our Lord Jesus Christ at his coming?
20 For ye are our glory and joy.

Then in 1 Thessalonians Paul admonishes us to sorrow not as those who have no hope:

1 Thessalonians 4:13. **But I would not have you to be ignorant, brethren, concerning them which are asleep, that ye sorrow not, even as others which have no hope.**

The phrase *no hope* in this verse seems to refer to those who don't believe in the resurrection that is connected with the Rapture, which Paul referred to as *that blessed hope.*

Titus 2:11 **For the grace of God that bringeth salvation hath appeared to all men,**
12 Teaching us that, denying ungodliness and worldly lusts, we should live soberly, righteously, and godly, in this present world;
13 Looking for that blessed hope, and the glorious appearing of the great God and our Saviour Jesus Christ.

When Paul uses the words *glorious appearing,* there is no doubt about which appearance Paul is referring to in this Scripture. The Rapture is the only appearance that would fit this description, for the Day of the Lord will be a day of darkness and gloom for the wicked, as described by the prophet Zephaniah.

THE DAY OF THE LORD IS NEAR

Let's compare the prophecy of Zephaniah with Acts 2:20 and also 1 Thessalonians 5:2.

ZEPHANIAH

Zephaniah 1:14 **The great day of the Lord is near, it is near, and hasteth greatly, even the voice of the day of the Lord: the mighty man shall cry there bitterly.**
15 That day is a day of wrath, a day of trouble and distress, a day of wasteness and desolation, a day of darkness and gloominess, a day of clouds and thick darkness.

ACTS

Acts 2:20 **The sun shall be turned into darkness, and the moon into blood, before that great and notable day of the Lord come.**

FIRST THESSALONIANS

1 Thessalonians 5:2 **For yourselves know perfectly that the day of the Lord so cometh as a thief in the night.**

All of these Scriptures imply that Christ's Second Advent will be a day of darkness, which corresponds perfectly with Matthew 24:29-30.

29 Immediately after the tribulation of those days shall the sun be darkened, and the moon shall not give her light, and the stars shall fall from heaven, and the powers of the heavens shall be shaken:
30 And then shall appear the sign of the Son of man in heaven: and then shall all the tribes of the earth mourn, and they shall see the Son of man coming in the clouds of heaven with power and great glory.

These Scriptures refer to Christ's coming physically to the earth after the tribulation to set up His kingdom. This is not the Rapture but rather the Second Advent.

WE SHALL BE LIKE HIM

John gives us a unique glimpse at the event we call the blessed hope.

1 John 3:2 **Beloved, now are we the sons of God, and it doth not yet appear what we shall be: but we know that, when he shall appear, we shall be like him; for we shall see him as he is.**
3 And every man that hath this hope in him purifieth himself, even as he is pure.

Jesus bought us back from the slavery of sin. He paid the price to redeem us!

We are sons now, for Christ has redeemed us by His blood. He has bought us back from sin. In Paul's day, it was legal to buy slaves. They were bought for a certain number of years.

Jesus bought us back from the slavery of sin. He paid the price to redeem us! All the legal matters have been settled, and He has already made the earnest payment. The Holy Spirit is called the earnest of our inheritance. (2 Corinthians 1:22, Ephesians 1:14.)

When you buy a piece of property, you pay a certain amount of earnest money to hold the deal until the transaction is completed. It is a down payment that will legally hold the property for you. When you do that, all legal matters have been set in order to guarantee that no one else can interfere with the purchase, until the time of the total redemption of the purchased possession.

This is why Ephesians 2:6 reveals that He has "**...raised us up together, and made us sit together in heavenly places in Christ Jesus.**" In the mind of God, we are already seated "**in heavenly places in Christ Jesus.**"

In Ephesians Paul states that God has predestined us unto adoption:

Ephesians 1:3 **Blessed be the God and Father of our Lord Jesus Christ, who hath blessed us with all spiritual blessings in heavenly places in Christ:**

4 According as he hath chosen us in him before the foundation of the world, that we should be holy and without blame before him in love:

5 Having predestinated us unto the adoption of children by Jesus Christ to himself, according to the good pleasure of his will.

"Having predestinated us unto the adoption of children." That means Jesus paid the price, and everyone who receives Him as Savior and Lord is predestined to the adoption process. All the legal work has been signed and sealed. He gave the earnest of our inheritance when He sent the Holy Spirit on the Day of Pentecost. He plans to complete the transaction when He gathers all who are in Christ together unto Him at His appearing at the time of the Rapture.

Ephesians 1:9 **Having made known unto us the mystery of his will, according to his good pleasure which he hath purposed in himself:**

10 That in the dispensation of the fulness of times he might gather together in one all things in Christ, both which are in heaven, and which are on earth; even in him.

I believe beyond a doubt these verses are in direct reference to the Rapture of the Church. He will gather us together unto Him when the fullness of that appointed time comes. Paul continues in verses 11-14 revealing that we were sealed with the Holy Spirit until the redemption of the purchased possession.

SEALED WITH THE HOLY SPIRIT

Ephesians 1:11 **In whom also we have obtained an inheritance...**
13 In whom ye also trusted, after that ye heard the word of truth, the gospel of your salvation in whom also, after that ye believed, ye were sealed with that holy Spirit of promise,
14 Which is the earnest of our inheritance until the redemption of the purchased possession....

JESUS IS THE HEAD

Paul reveals in Ephesians 1:21 that Jesus is far above all dominion and power and is the Head of the Church.

Ephesians 1:21 **Far above all principality, and power, and might, and dominion, and every name that is named, not only in this world, but also in that which is to come:**
22 And hath put all things under his feet, and gave him to be the head over all things to the church,
23 Which is his body, the fulness of him that filleth all in all.

GOD'S PLAN FOR FULLNESS

Jesus is the Head, and the Church is the Body. It seems then that the Body joined together with the Head constitutes God's plan of fullness. In other words, God's plan for Christ's Body (the Church) is to be in Him, and He in us, that we may be made perfect in one. (John 17:20-24.)

The first stage of Jesus' coming in His kingdom will be to bring the Body together with the Head. Jesus, being the Head, will give direction to the Body. But the Body as sons of God, will carry out His plans on earth during His 1000-year reign.

Romans 8:14 **For as many as are led by the Spirit of God, they are the sons of God.**
15 For ye have not received the spirit of bondage again to fear; but ye have received the Spirit of adoption, whereby we cry, Abba, Father.

John said, **"Beloved, now are we the sons of God..."** (1 John 3:2). The documents have already been signed with Christ's own blood. So, as far as God is concerned, in the realm of the spirit, it is already accomplished. Yet, we are awaiting the redemption of our bodies. They have not yet been redeemed, but we know beyond a shadow of a doubt that we are already the legal sons of God. Paul gives us insight into this in Romans, chapter 8:

Romans 8:16 **The Spirit itself beareth witness with our spirit, that we are the children of God:**
17 And if children, then heirs; heirs of God, and joint-heirs with Christ; if so be that we suffer with him, that we may be also glorified together.
18 For I reckon that the sufferings of this present time are not worthy to be compared with the glory which shall be revealed in us.

This glory Paul referred to, no doubt alludes to the complete fulfillment of the adoption process, which is the redemption of the body, at the time of the Rapture.

THE MANIFESTATION OF SONS

Romans 8:19 **For the earnest expectation of the creature waiteth for the manifestation of the sons of God.**
20 For the creature was made subject to vanity, not willingly, but by reason of him who hath subjected the same in hope,
21 Because the creature itself also shall be delivered from the bondage of corruption into the glorious liberty of the children of God.

The "time of the manifestation of the sons of God" refers to the time when the literal adoption is complete just before we are taken to the Father's house.

This body which now holds us in bondage to the limitations of the flesh will be changed....

We will be *completely* liberated at that time from the elements of the flesh. This body which now holds us in bondage to the limitations of the flesh will be changed and made like His glorious body. Paul also reveals the reason for the change:

1 Corinthians 15:50 **Now this I say, brethren, that flesh and blood cannot inherit the kingdom of God; neither doth corruption inherit incorruption.**
51 Behold, I shew you a mystery; We shall not all sleep, but we shall all be changed,
52 In a moment, in the twinkling of an eye, at the last trump: for the trumpet shall sound, and the dead shall be raised incorruptible, and we shall be changed.
53 For this corruptible must put on incorruption, and this mortal must put on immortality.

Romans 8:22 **For we know that the whole creation groaneth and travaileth in pain together until now.**
23 And not only they, but ourselves also, which have the firstfruits of the Spirit, even we ourselves groan within ourselves, waiting for the adoption, to wit, the redemption of our body.

When you were born again, your body did not experience the same change as your spirit did. You noticed that the next day, when your body still wanted to continue some of the same old habits, you had to **"...mortify the deeds of the body..."** (Romans 8:13).

At the time of this writing, we are still waiting for the completion of the adoption process in which our bodies will be changed and made immortal. The redemption of the body, in simple terms means our physical bodies will be clothed with immortality.

Here is how the apostle Paul describes the final process of our bodily redemtpion:

> 1 Corinthians 15:54 **So when this corruptible shall have put on incorruption, and this mortal shall have put on immortality, then shall be brought to pass the saying that is written, Death is swallowed up in victory.**

What a victory that will be!

The Blessed Hope

Paul makes an interesting statement in Romans 8, which, at first glance, would seem to contradict his own writing in Ephesians.

Romans 8:24. FOR WE ARE SAVED BY HOPE: **but hope that is seen is not hope: for what a man seeth, why doth he yet hope for?**

This statement has posed a question in the minds of many for years. Why did Paul say, "We are saved by hope"? We know that in Ephesians 2:8 he said, **"For by grace ye are saved through faith...."**

I believe Paul's statement in Romans 8:24 was referring to the *blessed hope, which saves us from the wrath to come.* (See 1 Thessalonians 5:9.) Let's look at it in the context in which it was written.

Romans 8:22 **For we know that the whole creation groaneth and travaileth in pain together until now.**
23 And not only they, but ourselves also, which have the firstfruits of the Spirit, even we ourselves groan within ourselves, waiting for the adoption, to wit, THE REDEMPTION OF OUR BODY.
24 FOR WE ARE SAVED BY HOPE: **but hope that is seen is not hope: for what a man seeth, why doth he yet hope for?**
25 But if we hope for that we see not, then do we with patience wait for it.

It seems obvious that the hope being referred to here is the redemption of our physical bodies, which will happen at the time of the Rapture. The Scriptures plainly teach that the righteous will be saved from the wrath to come—through that blessed hope. If we hope for that which we have not yet seen (Rapture), then we should also have patience to wait for it.

In John 14, Jesus reveals that hope which will save us from the wrath to come.

2 In my Father's house are many mansions: if it were not so, I would have told you. I go to prepare a place for you.
3 And if I go and prepare a place for you, I will come again, and receive you unto myself: that where I am, there ye may be also.

He will, at the appointed time, come and receive us unto Himself that we may be with Him in Heaven.

This passage reveals that Jesus was going to the Father's house to prepare a place for us. It also implies that when our place is prepared, He will, at the appointed time, come and receive us unto Himself that we may be with Him in the Father's house.

JUDGING THE INTENT

When I taught a Sunday school class, I always tried to motivate people to do their own thinking. One day I made the statement, "There is not one Scripture in the Bible that says that you have a mansion in Heaven," and we almost had a riot in the church.

I didn't say they didn't have mansions in Heaven. I just said that there wasn't one place in the Scriptures which stated that they had mansions in Heaven. The Scripture they thought made that statement was John 14:2.

It *may be* a mansion that He is preparing, but the Scripture doesn't say the place being prepared is a mansion. Nevertheless, we can rest assured that a place will be prepared for us and that He will honor His Word by coming to receive us unto Himself so we will be with Him in His Father's house.

TO THE JEW FIRST, THEN TO THE GENTILES

The reason Jesus didn't do more direct teaching concerning the catching away of the Church was that His ministry was primarily to the Jews. In Romans, the apostle Paul also mentions the fact that the Gospel was to the Jews first. **"For I am not ashamed of the gospel of Christ: for it is the power of God unto salvation...to the Jew first, and also to the Greek"** (Romans 1:16).

Then, in Matthew 10, we see Jesus sending out the twelve disciples with an anointing to heal the sick, cleanse the lepers, raise the dead, and cast out devils. He also instructed them where to go with this message.

> **5 These twelve Jesus sent forth, and commanded them, saying, Go not into the way of the Gentiles, and into any city of the Samaritans enter ye not:**
> **6 But go rather to the lost sheep of the house of Israel.**

His disciples were sent to the lost sheep of the house of Israel and were forbidden, at that time, to go to the Gentiles. This reveals why, while He was on earth, Jesus did not give more direct reference to the Rapture of the Church—the reason being that His ministry was primarily to Israel, who, generally speaking, rejected Him.

Therefore, most of His discourse in Matthew 24 was in reference to the time of tribulation and His Second Advent, rather than the Rapture. He knew the Jews were not going in the Rapture if they didn't receive Him as the Messiah. Therefore, He only referred to the Rapture indirectly on a few occasions. (See John 11:25; 14:1-3; Luke 21:36.)

PETER AND PAUL—APOSTLES TO THE GENTILES

Peter and Paul were both apostles to the Gentiles. So it was through them that God revealed a major part of the revelation concerning the Rapture. Even though Paul wrote most of the epistles to the Church, God used both Peter and Paul to give us the revelation of the catching away of the Church.

The Gospel they preached brought great hope to the Body of Christ.

> 1 Thessalonians 4:13 **But I would not have you to be ignorant, brethren, concerning them which are asleep, that ye sorrow not, even as others which have no hope.**

The hope he referred to here is the Resurrection that takes place at the time of the Rapture. In Titus, chapter 2, Paul refers to it as *that blessed hope.*

> Titus 2:11 **For the grace of God that bringeth salvation hath appeared to all men,**
> **12 Teaching us that, denying ungodliness and worldly lusts, we should live soberly, righteously, and godly, in this present world;**
> **13 Looking for that blessed hope, and the glorious appearing of the great God and our Saviour Jesus Christ.**

Then in 1 Thessalonians, Paul began to lay out God's plan for the Body of Christ to escape the seven years of tribulation destined for planet Earth:

> 1 Thessalonians 4:14 **For if we believe that Jesus died and rose again, even so THEM ALSO WHICH SLEEP IN JESUS WILL GOD BRING WITH HIM.**

This verse is in reference to the spiritual bodies of those who have died in Christ. He will bring them with Him to be united with their physical bodies, which will be resurrected from the grave at the shout of Michael the archangel blended with the trump of God.

There are some who think this verse is in reference to Revelation 19:11-16 and Matthew 24:29-30, which are passages describing the Second Advent. But they don't fit in the context, for verses 15-17 clearly establish the fact that verses 13-17 are all direct references to the Rapture of the Church.

> 1 Thessalonians 4:15 **For this we say unto you by the word of the Lord, that we which are alive and remain unto the coming of the Lord shall not prevent** (precede) **them which are asleep.**
> **16 For the Lord himself shall descend from heaven with a shout, with the voice of the archangel, and with the trump of God: and the dead in Christ shall rise first.**

When Paul says, **"For this we say unto you by the word of the Lord..."** he means it came by a personal revelation from Jesus Christ Himself. Paul received many revelations directly from the Lord Jesus Christ. (Galatians 1:11-12.)

Many people are confused by verse 16. Take note of the fact that *the trump of God* in verse 16 is not the same as the "trumpet of the seventh angel" mentioned in Revelation 11:15, as many have supposed. If you believe that the "trump of God" and the "trumpet of the seventh angel" are the same, you will be hopelessly confused in trying to understand end-time events and the sequence in which they occur. Neither should we confuse the last trump, mentioned in 1 Corinthians 15:52, with the "trumpet of the seventh angel," for they are not the same.

Let's compare these two verses in 1 Thessalonians 4 with two verses in 1 Corinthians 15:

> 1 Thessalonians 4:16 **For the Lord himself shall descend from heaven with a shout, with the voice of the**

archangel, and with the trump of God: and the dead
in Christ shall rise first:
17 Then we which are alive and remain shall be caught
up together with them in the clouds, to meet the Lord
in the air: and so shall we ever be with the Lord.

1 Corinthians 15:51 **Behold, I shew you a mystery; We
shall not all sleep, but we shall all be changed,
52 In a moment, in the twinkling of an eye, at the last
trump: for the trumpet shall sound, and the dead
shall be raised incorruptible, and we shall be changed.**

These verses from 1 Thessalonians 4 correspond perfectly
with 1 Corinthians 15:51-52. There is no doubt that these two
Scriptures are describing the very same event. *The Bible must be
interpreted with the Bible,* and it is apparent in both of these passages that Paul is referring to the Rapture of the Church and not
the Second Advent. It is possible that the trump of God could
sound at the time of the last trumpet of the Feast of Trumpets.

THE DAY OF THE LORD

1 Thessalonians 5:1 **But of the times and the seasons,
brethren, ye have no need that I write unto you.
2 For yourselves know perfectly that the day of the
Lord so cometh as a thief in the night.**

The day of the Lord here also refers to the Second Advent, not
the Rapture. I don't believe the Rapture is ever referred to in
Scripture as *the day of the Lord* or Jesus' coming as *a thief in the
night,* as many have assumed.

Generally speaking, the Day of the Lord is 1000 years long.
It will begin when Jesus descends from Heaven with the saints to
the Mount of Olives and destroys the armies of the Antichrist.
(Revelation 19:11-21, Zechariah 14:1-5.) He will, at that time,
set up His kingdom, and the saints will rule and reign with Him

for 1000 years. That seems to be the event most often referred to as *the day of the Lord.*

A careful study of the scriptural context where the Bible refers to Jesus' coming **"as a thief in the night"** will always show the reference to be concerning His Second Advent. A thief usually comes in the darkness of night. Concerning 1 Thessalonians 5:1, Paul said he didn't need to write to the Church concerning the times or seasons, for they knew that the Day of the Lord (Second Advent) would come as a thief in the night—the reason being that the Church will have already been in Heaven for seven years at the time of His Second Advent, and we will be coming back with Christ. (Zechariah 14:1-5, Revelation 19:11-20.)

> *It is very possible that the phrase "peace and safety" in this Scripture refers to the peace accord....*

PEACE AND SAFETY

1 Thessalonians 5:3 **For when they shall say, Peace and safety; then sudden destruction cometh upon them, as travail upon a woman with child; and they shall not escape.**

It is very possible that the phrase "peace and safety" in this Scripture refers to the peace accord which government leaders are so desperately trying to put together between Israel and the PLO at the time of this writing.

However, that peace will be short-lived, and the prophesied sudden destruction that Paul mentions in verse 3 seems to be already in the making.

Today, we are seeing prophetic fulfillment taking place before our eyes as never before. This peace agreement may, or may not be the one the Antichrist will confirm for a seven-year period, but it is possible that it will at least lay the foundation for that peace covenant mentioned in Daniel 9:

27 And he shall confirm the covenant with many for one week: and in the midst of the week he shall cause the sacrifice and the oblation to cease, and for the overspreading of abominations he shall make it desolate, even until the consummation, and that determined shall be poured upon the desolate.

This Peace Accord could be the very thing that will cause Russia to begin the prophesied invasion of Israel. It is even possible that we will see this very peace agreement signed before the Rapture takes place.

It is significant that when addressing the brethren of the Church, Paul says, **"...Ye have no need that I write unto you"** (1 Thessalonians 5:1). However, in verse 3, he uses the word **they** which does not refer to the Church, but rather to the people on earth during the Tribulation Period.

THE HOPE OF DELIVERANCE

When the Body of Christ is taken out of the earth, multitudes will realize that the Word of God is true and that they have missed God's way of escaping all the things coming on the earth during the Tribulation.

Luke 21:36 **Watch ye therefore, and pray always, that ye may be accounted worthy to escape all these things that shall come to pass, and to stand before the Son of man.**

The Scriptures reveal that there will be 144,000 Jewish men born again immediately after the Rapture of the Church. God will seal them in their foreheads (Revelation 7:4), and they will have an assignment to evangelize the nation of Israel and the Gentiles. (Isaiah 49:6.) The Antichrist won't be able to harm them in any way. They will be divinely protected until they are caught up to Heaven sometime after Mid-Tribulation. They will preach the everlasting Gospel, and multitudes of Jews and Gentiles alike will be saved through their ministry. (Isaiah 60:3.)

Paul also reveals another reason that the Church has no need of certain information concerning the times and seasons:

> 1 Thessalonians 5:4 **But ye, brethren, are not in darkness, that that day should overtake you as a thief.**
> **5 Ye are all the children of light, and the children of the day: we are not of the night, nor of darkness.**
> **8 But let us, who are of the day, be sober, putting on the breastplate of faith and love; and for an helmet, the HOPE OF SALVATION.**
> **9 For God hath not appointed us to wrath, but to obtain salvation by our Lord Jesus Christ.**

Verse 8 in this passage is in reference to the hope of deliverance from the wrath of God that will be poured out upon the wicked during the Tribulation. This blessed hope which we call the Rapture will deliver the Body of Christ from the wrath of God which is destined to come on the wicked of the earth. (Revelation 3:10.) God has reserved His wrath for His enemies—not the Church.

> Nahum 1:2 **God is jealous, and the Lord revengeth; the Lord revengeth, and is furious; the Lord will take vengeance on his adversaries, and he reserveth wrath for his enemies.**

> Revelation 16:1 **And I heard a great voice out of the temple saying to the seven angels, Go your ways, and pour out the vials of the wrath of God upon the earth.**

THE SECOND ADVENT

Now let's examine some Scriptures concerning the Second Advent.

2 Thessalonians 1:6 **Seeing it is a righteous thing with God to recompense tribulation to them that trouble you;**
7 And to you who are troubled rest with us, when the Lord Jesus shall be revealed from heaven with his mighty angels,
8 In flaming fire taking vengeance on them that know not God, and that obey not the gospel of our Lord Jesus Christ:
9 Who shall be punished with everlasting destruction from the presence of the Lord, and from the glory of his power.

It is evident from these Scriptures that Paul is referring to the Second Advent described in Revelation 19:11-21 (and Zechariah 14:1-5). This is the same event he had referred to in 1 Thessalonians 5:2, when he said the Lord shall come **"...as a thief in the night."** He mentions the Second Advent first because after he had written the first epistle to the Thessalonians, it seems from the context that someone had written a letter (possibly forging Paul's name to it) saying that the Day of Christ (referring to the Second Advent) was upon them. So Paul dealt with this in chapter 2.

TWO SEPARATE EVENTS

2 Thessalonians 2:1 **Now we beseech you, brethren, by the coming of our Lord Jesus Christ, and by our gathering together unto him.**

At first glance, it would seem that **"the coming of our Lord Jesus Christ"** and our **"gathering together unto him"** are the same event. However, after studying the context closely, I believe the phrase **"the coming of our Lord Jesus Christ"** is referring to the Second Advent, which is also called the "Day of Christ" in the next verse.

I believe Paul mentioned the Second Advent first because some false teachers were saying that the Day of Christ was at hand. He was trying to assure them that it was not true. He also pointed out the difference between the coming of the Lord to the earth at His Second Advent and *our gathering together unto Him at the time of the Rapture.* This seems to be the reason he mentioned them both in the same verse. Yet, these are definitely separate events. They are different in purpose and separated in time by exactly seven years.

TWO MAJOR EVENTS BEFORE THE DAY OF CHRIST

2 Thessalonians 2:1 **Now we beseech you, brethren, by the coming of our Lord Jesus Christ, and by our gathering together unto him,**
2 That ye be not soon shaken in mind, or be troubled, neither by spirit, nor by word, nor by letter as from us, as that the day of Christ is at hand.
3 Let no man deceive you by any means: for that day shall not come, except there come a falling away first, and that man of sin be revealed, the son of perdition.

Paul assured them that he had not changed his doctrine. He said that there were two things which absolutely had to come to pass before the Day of Christ (Second Advent), which refers to Christ's coming to the earth to set up His kingdom.

First: There would come *a falling away.*

Second: *The Man of Sin (Antichrist)* would be *revealed.*

FALLING AWAY OR A DEPARTURE?

Let's investigate the Greek word *apostasia,* which is translated "falling away." It is only used in two places in the New Testament. Here, in 2 Thessalonians 2:3, it is translated "falling away," but in Acts 21:21 it is translated "forsake."

The Amplified Bible footnotes 2 Thessalonians 2:3, stating, "A possible rendering of the Greek *apostasia* is 'departure [of the Church].'"[1]

> *The Amplified Bible footnotes 2 Thessalonians 2:3, stating, "A possible rendering of the Greek apostasia is 'departure [of the Church].'"*

When you give time and thought to these verses, that seems to be the only possible meaning it could have in the context in which it was written.

I don't believe there will be wholesale backsliding in the Church before the return of Christ. There are some who have departed from the faith; there have always been backsliders. But Paul is not referring to a backsliding Church. In the context, I am convinced he is referring to the departure of the Body of Christ from the earth before the Man of Sin (Antichrist) is revealed.

As we continue in this passage, we find more support that the phrase *falling away* could be translated "departure."

MAN OF SIN REVEALED

Let's read verses 3 through 7 together for continuity of thought:

2 Thessalonians 2:3 **Let no man deceive you by any means: for that day shall not come, except there come a falling away first, and that man of sin be revealed, the son of perdition;**
4 Who opposeth and exalteth himself above all that is called God, or that is worshipped; so that he as God sitteth in the temple of God, shewing himself that he is God.
5 Remember ye not, that, when I was yet with you, I told you these things?
6 And now ye know what withholdeth that he might be revealed in his time.
7 For the mystery of iniquity doth already work: only he who now letteth will let, UNTIL HE BE TAKEN OUT OF THE WAY.

The Scriptures reveal that there is an appointed time for the Antichrist to be revealed, and he will not be revealed until that time. The time allotted to him is an exact period of seven years. It begins immediately after the departure of the Body of Christ.

His time is referred to as Daniel's Seventieth Week (see Daniel 9:26-27), which is a week of years. Therefore, it is a seven-year period of time—no more and no less.

The Antichrist will come to his end the same day that Christ returns to the earth to set up His earthly kingdom. (Revelation 19:1-20.)

Some of the following prophetic statements have been covered in preceding chapters a little differently, but they bear repeating in the context of 2 Thessalonians 2:6-11.

6 And now ye know what withholdeth that he might be revealed in his time.

Christians are to reflect Christ, Who is the light of the world. We are capable of reflecting His light to a sin-darkened world with such intensity that it restrains the Antichrist spirit. The Body of Christ will hold back the Antichrist until we are taken out of the earth.

It seems that God turned His time clock off concerning Israel after the sixty-nine weeks prophesied in Daniel 9:25-26. Daniel's Seventieth Week must begin after the Rapture. The true Church (Body of Christ) is what withholds and restrains the Antichrist until his time period arrives.

HE WHO RESTRAINS

Second Thessalonians 2:7 states, **"...only he who now letteth will let, until he be taken out of the way."** According to *Strong's Concordance* the word translated as both "letteth" and "let" in this verse means to "hold down." It is the same word translated "withholdeth" in verse 6. So we could say, *He who*

> The true Church... is what withholds and restrains the Antichrist until his time period arrives.

withholds will hold down the Antichrist spirit until he be taken out of the way.[2]

The Interlinear Greek-English New Testament renders this verse:

7 For the mystery already is working of lawlessness: only (there is) he who restrains at present, until out of (the) midst he be (gone), and then will be revealed the lawless (one); whom the Lord will consume with the breath of His mouth.*

Now let's investigate verse 7 a little closer. Notice the pronoun "he": **"He who holds down will hold down until he be taken out of the way."** The pronoun "he" which is in reference to the one who **"restrains or holds down"** in verse 7, is the same referred to in verse 3, which will *fall away or depart*.

We certainly couldn't apply the pronoun "he" to a falling away or a backsliding. However, the pronoun "he" can be applied to the Church. I believe these Scriptures reveal that He who restrains, or withholds, the Antichrist from being revealed is the true Church, the Body of Christ. *God has the Antichrist zipped up in a short time slot, and he can't be revealed until after the departure of the Church.*

It is evident that what "withholds" in verse 6 is the same that "letteth," or "restrains," in verse 7, until *he* be taken out of the way. After the departure of the Church, then the wicked man of sin (Antichrist) will be revealed. The "Man of Sin" in verse 3 and the "wicked" in verse 8 are one and the same—the Antichrist.

There are some who believe the pronoun "he" in verse 7 is referring to the Holy Spirit. But let's do some scriptural thinking regarding that matter.

---

*The Word.

We know there will be multiplied millions of people saved during the seven years of tribulation. (Revelation 7:9-14.) One of the greatest revivals to ever hit planet Earth will continue into that time period. But if the Holy Ghost were to be taken out of the earth, then we must conclude that no one could be saved during that seven-year period. No one could be born again on the earth without the work of the Holy Spirit. The rebirth comes by the washing of regeneration and renewing of the Holy Ghost. (Titus 3:5.) The Holy Spirit came to the earth on the Day of Pentecost, and He will be here for the great harvest of souls even during the Tribulation. The Holy Spirit was here before you received Him, and He will be here when you leave, and He will bring in a great harvest of souls during that seven-year period.

Then the only scriptural conclusion seems to be that the pronoun "he" refers to the Church. This conclusion would fit in the context of these verses and still be in agreement with the other prophetic Scriptures. When the restrainer is removed, the Antichrist will begin his master plan to deceive all that dwell on the earth.

In 2 Thessalonians, Paul describes the Antichrist's coming:

2 Thessalonians 2:9 **Even him, whose coming is after the working of Satan with all power and signs and lying wonders,**
10 And with all deceivableness of unrighteousness in them that perish; because they received not the love of the truth, that they might be saved.
11 And for this cause God shall send them strong delusion, that they should believe a lie:
12 That they all might be damned who believed not the truth, but had pleasure in unrighteousness.

Paul seems to be saying that during the Tribulation everyone who does not have the truth of God's Holy Word will be deceived by the Man of Sin and his lying wonders.

But there is good news—God has provided better things for the Body of Christ through the *blessed hope*. God has made provisions for the resurrection of the righteous dead and for the redemption of the bodies of all who are alive in Christ at the time of that blessed event we refer to as the Rapture.

The Faith and Rapture Connection

Some of the great faith Scriptures which have given us much insight into the principles of faith are found in the tenth and eleventh chapters of Hebrews. It is these Scriptures and others which have given us great revelation concerning the law of faith and how to apply it in our everyday lives.

God's revelations are always progressive, and we have arrived at a segment of time in which the Holy Spirit is revealing deeper insight from these same Scriptures concerning their connection to the Rapture of the Church. The faith connection begins in the tenth chapter of Hebrews.

> **34 For ye had compassion of me in my bonds, and took joyfully the spoiling of your goods, knowing in yourselves that YE HAVE IN HEAVEN A BETTER AND AN ENDURING SUBSTANCE.**
> **35 Cast not away therefore your confidence, which hath great recompence of reward.**
> **36 For ye have need of patience, that, after ye have done the will of God, ye might receive the promise.**
> **37 For yet a little while, and HE THAT SHALL COME WILL COME, AND WILL NOT TARRY.**

Notice the context of these statements. **"Ye have in heaven a better and an enduring substance"** and **"He that shall come will come, and will not tarry."** I believe these verses can only be in reference to one event, and that is the coming of Christ to catch away the Church.

These Scriptures reveal that they were looking for Christ to come for the Church even in their generation. This seems to confirm the fact that there are no certain signs that must appear before the Rapture of the Church. I believe *only time itself establishes the date of the Rapture of the Church*. Since God has spoken the end from the beginning, that event must fit the scriptural profile of God's timetable.

DISCERNING THE INTENT

Allow me to arrange a few of the Scriptures in sequence for the purpose of revealing what I believe to be the intent of Paul's statements in Romans 8:24-25 concerning "being saved by hope that is not seen"—the hope that we have patience to wait for.

Hebrews 10:34 **For ye had compassion of me in my bonds, and took joyfully the spoiling of your goods, knowing in yourselves that ye have in heaven a better and an enduring** SUBSTANCE.
35 Cast not away therefore your confidence, which hath great RECOMPENCE OF REWARD.
36 For ye have need of patience, that, after ye have done the will of God, ye MIGHT RECEIVE THE PROMISE.
37 For yet a little while, and HE THAT SHALL COME WILL COME, AND WILL NOT TARRY.

Hebrews 11:1 **Now faith is the** SUBSTANCE OF THINGS HOPED FOR, **the evidence of things not seen.**

Romans 8:24 **For we are saved by hope: but hope that is seen is not hope: for what a man seeth, why doth he yet hope for?**
25 But if we hope for that we see not, then do we with patience wait for it.

The Rapture, as we have already seen, is referred to as the *blessed hope* in Titus 2:13. It is through faith in the time element of God's timetable that we have patience to wait for the fulfillment of that blessed hope. It is significant that Hebrews 10:34 states that we have in Heaven a better and an enduring *substance*. Hebrews 11:1 reveals that faith is the *substance* of things *hoped for*. Let's look at it this way: If faith is the substance of what you hope for and you have no hope, then there is nothing for faith to give substance to.

Let's ask ourselves some scriptural questions about this matter. Are there any promises of blessing in the New Covenant which you receive just because they are in the Bible? Generally speaking, no. You must first hear the promise. Then, you must make a decision to believe it. And finally, you must act on it in faith to receive it. It is because of these facts that I pose the following questions.

Will God's promise of a way to escape the seven years of tribulation be any different? Will those who don't believe in the catching away of the Church be partakers of the Rapture?

I don't intend to answer those questions, because I'm not sure I know the answer. I ask them simply to provoke you to scriptural thought concerning this matter.

I know there are many who say they have been born again and don't believe in the Rapture. But to not believe in the Rapture is like saying, "I don't believe in yesterday; yesterday never happened." But yesterday did happen, and three raptures have already taken place. Enoch and Elijah were caught up alive to Heaven as natural people. (Genesis 5:24; 2 Kings 2:11.) Jesus was also caught up, and the disciples watched as a cloud received Him out of their sight. (Acts 1:9.)

There are some who call the Rapture an escape theory. But it has been proven in Scripture to be a supernatural event that transported living people from the earth to Heaven.

The Scriptures reveal that even when there is tremendous power available to do supernatural things, it is not always apparent in the natural realm.

Hebrews 11:3 **Through faith we understand that the worlds were framed by the word of God, so that things which are seen were not made of things which do appear.**

The Rapture has also been framed and woven into the fabric of God's Word, yet it isn't apparent to everyone. The Scriptures reveal that not everyone will see Him when He appears for the Church. (Hebrews 9:28.) Some call the Rapture "The Pie in the Sky." Others call it "The Great Snatch." It has even been labeled "The Great Escape" by some.

There are many people scoffing at the very event that could save them from the wrath to come. This is not a time to scoff at or discredit God's promised deliverance, for we can already see signs of the coming Tribulation on the horizon.

ENOCH RAPTURED

Bible history gives us positive proof of three separate supernatural events in which living people were physically taken from the earth to Heaven. The first such event is recorded in Genesis 5:24: **"And Enoch walked with God: and he was not; for God took him."**

The Book of Hebrews also gives witness of Enoch's rapture:

Hebrews 11:5 **By faith Enoch was translated that he should not see death; and was not found, because God had translated him: for before his translation he had this testimony, that he pleased God.**
6 But without faith it is impossible to please him: for he that cometh to God must believe that he is, and that he is a rewarder of them that diligently seek him.

What is our reward for diligently seeking Him? Our reward is a *better* and *enduring substance* in Heaven. (Hebrews 10:34.) If we are not going to Heaven, as some teach, then what possible benefit would we receive from that *better* and *enduring substance* that is in *Heaven*?

Peter gives us more revelation concerning our inheritance:

> 1 Peter 1:3 **Blessed be the God and Father of our Lord Jesus Christ, which according to his abundant mercy hath begotten us again unto a lively hope by the resurrection of Jesus Christ from the dead,**
> **4 To an INHERITANCE INCORRUPTIBLE, and undefiled, and that fadeth not away, RESERVED IN HEAVEN FOR YOU,**
> **5 Who are kept by the power of God through faith unto salvation ready to be revealed in the last time.**
> **9 Receiving the end of your faith, *even* the salvation of *your* souls.**
> **13 Wherefore gird up the loins of your mind, be sober, and hope to the end for the grace that is to be brought unto you at the revelation of Jesus Christ.**

An inheritance reserved in Heaven wouldn't be of any benefit to us if we were not going there. I grant you, we will only be there for a period of seven years. But during that time, we will receive that inheritance and be taught how to rule and reign with Christ. Then we will come back with Him to end the Tribulation on the earth. We will then rule and reign with Him in His earthly kingdom. (Revelation 19:11-20; 20:1-6.)

ENOCH RAPTURED THROUGH FAITH

The context of Hebrews 10:34 and most of chapter 11 corresponds with or points toward the Rapture of the Church and the resurrection of the righteous dead.

Let's take a closer look at the Scripture concerning Enoch's rapture:

Hebrews 11:5 **By faith Enoch was translated that he should not see death; and was not found, because God had translated him: for before his translation he had this testimony, that he pleased God.**
6 But without faith it is impossible to please him: for he that cometh to God must believe that he is, and that he is a rewarder of them that diligently seek him.

The English word "translated" comes from the Greek word *metatithemi*[1] which has a very similar meaning to the Greek word *apostasia*[2] used in 2 Thessalonians 2:3, which is translated, "falling away." As you compare these two words, you can't help but notice their similarity. The Greek word *metatithemi*, which is interpreted in the *King James Version* as "translated," means *to remove, to change, to carry over, to transpose, to transfer, to suffer oneself, to be transferred;* i.e., *to go or pass over; to fall away or desert from one person or thing to another.*

In studying the meaning of this word, you will notice that it corresponds closely in some ways with the word *apostasia*,[3] which the *King James Version* has translated "a falling away" in 2 Thessalonians 2:3. It is very obvious that the words "translated" and "translation" in Hebrews 11:5-6 mean the catching away of Enoch from earth to Heaven. It is also clear that these words are not in any way associated with backsliding or a falling away from God. The word emphatically refers to Enoch's removal or departure from the earth to Heaven.

In comparison, here are some of the meanings of the word *apostasia:* "to forsake," "falling away," "defection," or "apostasy." This gives us some insight into why Paul used the word *apostasia* in 2 Thessalonians 2:3. Some of the same expressions are used to define the word *translate,* such as "a falling away" or "to desert from one person or thing to another."

Possibly the reason Paul used the word *apostasia* (which must be considered in this context in order to know exactly what it means) was that the context in which it was used leaves no doubt about the meaning. In the first verse, Paul refers to "**...our gathering together unto him,**" which clearly establishes the context as being the Rapture of the Church.

Again, a footnote in *The Amplified Bible* concerning the word *apostasia* states, "A possible rendering of the Greek *apostasia* is '**departure**' (of the Church)."

So it is evident that it could be interpreted "departure" in reference to the Church, especially within the context that Paul used it.

ENOCH'S PROPHECY

The Book of Jude reveals that Enoch was the one who prophesied that Christ would come with *ten thousands of his saints:*

Jude 1:14 **And Enoch also, the seventh from Adam, prophesied of these, saying, Behold, the Lord cometh with ten thousands of his saints,**
15 To execute judgment upon all, and to convince all that are ungodly among them of their ungodly deeds which they have ungodly committed, and of all their hard speeches which ungodly sinners have spoken against him.

Enoch's prophecy brings us to a very obvious conclusion— the saints must first be "caught up to Heaven...."

Enoch's prophecy brings us to a very obvious conclusion— the saints must first be "caught up to Heaven" before they can come back with Christ from Heaven, as revealed in Revelation 19:11-20 and Zechariah 14:1-5.

Although the Rapture was not for Enoch's dispensation, God revealed it to him. He was so completely captivated by it that through faith he experienced his own private rapture.

Enoch proved that faith gives substance to that blessed hope. He also proved that faith *is our evidence of the Rapture that has not yet been seen in our day.* It is significant that Hebrews 11:5-6 reveals that Enoch's faith pleased God so much that He translated him, and then emphatically states that without faith it is impossible to please God. Could this be implying that we must have faith in the blessed hope of the Rapture in order to experience it?

NOAH PREPARED AND ESCAPED

Hebrews 11:7 **By faith Noah, being warned of God of things not seen as yet, moved with fear, prepared an ark to the saving of his house; by the which he condemned the world, and became heir of the righteousness which is by faith.**

The fact that Noah obeyed God by preparing to escape and was lifted above the Flood to safety at the time when God's judgment came on a wicked world seems to be a perfect parallel of the Church that must be prepared for the Rapture before the wrath of God comes upon the earth. Just as God made a way of escape for Noah, He has made a way for us to escape that seven-year period of tribulation which is coming upon the earth.

ABRAHAM LOOKED FOR A CITY

Hebrews 11:8 **By faith Abraham, when he was called to go out into a place which he should after receive for an inheritance, obeyed; and he went out, not knowing whither he went.**

What inheritance was Abraham looking for? A *better* and *enduring substance* (inheritance) that is reserved in Heaven for both Old and New Testament saints (Hebrews 10:36; 1 Peter 1:3-5.) Verse 9 continues with the same thought.

Hebrews 11:9 **By faith he sojourned in the land of promise, as in a strange country, dwelling in tabernacles with Isaac and Jacob, the heirs with him of the same promise:**
10 For he looked for A CITY which hath foundations, WHOSE BUILDER AND MAKER IS GOD.

Abraham was looking for a different city than those found on the earth. John gave us a glimpse in Revelation of such a city, whose Builder and Maker is God.

Revelation 21:2 **And I John saw the holy city, new Jerusalem, coming down from God out of heaven, prepared as a bride adorned for her husband.**
10 And he carried me away in the spirit to a great and high mountain, and shewed me that great city, the holy Jerusalem, descending out of heaven from God.

It seems that nearly every verse of Hebrews 11 either parallels in some way, or is in direct reference to, the catching away of the righteous to obtain their inheritance in a city not made with hands.

SARAH JUDGED GOD FAITHFUL TO HIS PROMISE

Hebrews 11:11 **Through faith also Sarah herself received strength to conceive seed, and was delivered of a child when she was past age, because she judged him faithful who had promised.**

God was faithful in His promise concerning Abraham, that through Isaac, He would send His Son to deliver mankind. Jesus Christ will also be faithful to His promise recorded in John 14.

2 In my Father's house are many mansions: if it were not so, I would have told you. I go to prepare a place for you.

3 And if I go and prepare a place for you, I will come again, and receive you unto myself; that where I am, there ye may be also.

What a glorious promise this is, and yet, it is so simple that even a child could understand the intent of these statements.

Jesus gave us a very simple sequence. First, He will prepare a place for us in the Father's house. Second, He will come to receive the Church (Body of Christ) unto Himself so the Church will be with Him in Heaven during the time of tribulation on the earth.

The Tribulation is referred to by Paul as the "time of the Antichrist." I believe that seven-year period begins the day the Church is taken out of the earth.

All things concerning the Church will be brought to an appropriate conclusion; then God will begin the final chapter of contending with fallen humanity.

Romans 9:28 AMP **For the Lord will execute His sentence upon the earth [He will conclude and close His account with men completely and without delay], rigorously cutting it short in His justice.**

THEY WERE PERSUADED

Hebrews 11:13 **These all died in faith, not having received the promises, but having seen them afar off, and were persuaded of them, and embraced them, and confessed that they were strangers and pilgrims on the earth.**
16 But now they desire a better country, that is, an heavenly: wherefore God is not ashamed to be called their God: for he hath prepared for them a city.

Revelation 21:2 reveals that the city that God has prepared is the New Jerusalem.

FAITH FOR A RESURRECTION

Abraham proved he had faith for a bodily resurrection:

Hebrews 11:17 **By faith Abraham, when he was tried, offered up Isaac: and he that had received the promises offered up his only begotten son,**
18 Of whom it was said, That in Isaac shall thy seed be called:
19 Accounting that God was able to raise him up, even from the dead; from whence also he received him in a figure.

It is obvious that Abraham believed that God was able to resurrect Isaac from the dead, if necessary, to fulfill His promise.

So again, as one follows the flow of thought in the eleventh chapter of Hebrews, it seems to be slanted toward the departure of the righteous from the earth and the eternal bliss to be revealed. The Old Testament saints saw it afar off. Through faith they saw the promises of the Messiah, but they didn't have a revelation of the New Covenant of better promises.

Revelation 21:2 reveals that the city that God has prepared is the New Jerusalem.

There were many things they didn't understand about the first coming of the Messiah. But notice that the last six verses of Hebrews 10, and a major portion of chapter 11, give us a parallel pointing toward the Resurrection, the Rapture, recompense of reward, and the New Jerusalem.

JOSEPH'S BONES

Hebrews 11:22 **By faith Joseph, when he died, made mention of the departing of the children of Israel; and gave commandment concerning his bones.**

The fact that Joseph's bones were brought out of Egypt seems to be symbolic of the dead bodies of both the Old and New Testament saints which will not be left behind when the Church departs this earth.

"...The dead in Christ shall rise first: Then we which are alive and remain shall be caught up together with them..." (1 Thessalonians 4:16-17). The bodies of those who have died being *in Christ*, will not be left in the earth.

Christ paid the full price and redeemed the whole man— spirit, soul, *and body;* and He will not lose any part of that which He has purchased with His own blood.

RESPECT UNTO THE RECOMPENCE OF REWARD

Hebrews 11:23 **By faith Moses, when he was born, was hid three months of his parents, because they saw he was a proper child; and they were not afraid of the king's commandment.**
26 Esteeming the reproach of Christ greater riches than the treasures in Egypt: for he had respect unto the RECOMPENCE OF THE REWARD.

This phrase "recompence of reward" should be familiar by now. It's easy to see why Moses had respect unto the recompence and reward of his faith. He was born with a death sentence on him. He represented the righteous dead of all ages whose bodies will not be found (left) in the earth. This phrase, "recompence of reward," seems to refer to the time when Christ will catch away the righteous, both dead and alive, to be rewarded in Heaven at the judgment seat of Christ. (2 Corinthians 5:10; Matthew 16:27.)

Hebrews 11:29 **By faith they passed through the Red sea as by dry land: which the Egyptians assaying to do were drowned.**

30 By faith the walls of Jericho fell down, after they were compassed about seven days.

The city of Jericho is a type of the wicked world. After Joshua crossed over the Jordan, he marched around the city once a day for six days with seven priests out front blowing seven trumpets. I believe the trumpets represent a prophetic warning God has issued to the wicked world for a period of 6000 years. Remember, **"...one day is with the Lord as a thousand years, and a thousand years as one day"** (2 Peter 3:8).

Just as Jericho was warned six days by seven priests sounding their trumpets, the earth has also been warned by God's prophetic word for nearly 6000 years of His coming wrath.

Joshua marched around Jericho seven times on the seventh day, which represents God's number of completion.

There was a great shout at the end of the seventh day, and the walls of the wicked came down. All of the people in Jericho were destroyed, except Rahab and her family, who represents the remnant of Israel that will be saved.

This seems to be another scriptural profile revealing that at the end of 7000 years of human history, all wickedness will be destroyed from the earth.

GOD PROVIDED BETTER THINGS FOR US

It is evident from the New Covenant that God has provided better things for the Church in this age.

Hebrews 11:39 **And these all, having obtained a good report through faith, received not the promise:**
40 **God having provided some better thing for us, that they without us should not be made perfect.**

Why didn't they receive the things promised? Because they did not live in the segment of time to which God had assigned the fulfillment of these promises. Yet, God has provided *better things for us,* that *they without us should not be made perfect.*

The dead in Christ, which would also include the Old Testament saints who have gone on before us, will not be made perfect (glorified, made immortal) without us. But at His appearing (time of the Rapture), the dead in Christ shall rise first. Then we who are alive shall be caught up together with them in the clouds, and *we will all be made perfect and glorified together in the same instant of time.*

> *...we will all be made perfect and glorified together in the same instant of time.*

We are fortunate to live in a time when the Holy Spirit is illuminating prophetic Scriptures as never before. God has not only told us directly what is about to happen at the end of the age, but He has clearly revealed in scriptural profiles the events that are about to transpire.

He prophesied it in Genesis. He preached it through His prophets. He revealed it to His apostles. He painted us scriptural pictorials through Enoch, Abraham, Noah, Moses, and Joshua.

Throughout the Bible, we have seen that God will warn the residents of planet Earth for 6000 years. This seems to represent the time span of the earth lease, in which man has the God-given right to exercise dominion on planet Earth. That lease seems to be divided into three segments of time.

- 2000 years from Adam to Abraham,

- 2000 years from Abraham to Christ,

- 2000 years from Christ to the end of the Church Age.

Just as the priests blew seven trumpets at Jericho, today godly men and women are sounding a prophetic warning from pulpits, radio, television, cassette tapes, and the printed page. The warning is circling the globe. The 2000-year the Church Age is drawing to a close. The prophetic implications are now quite clear.

The 6000-year lease on planet Earth is about to expire, and at that time wicked men will lose their dominion. Then God the Father, the Holy Spirit and Jesus will take control of planet Earth. A flood of anointing will come over the Body of Christ such as has never been in 6000 years of human history. I believe the anointing will be turned up sevenfold. The world will experience an awesome outpouring of the Holy Spirit with miracles, signs, and wonders through the Body of Christ before we rise to meet the Lord in the air.

The Parable of the Ten Virgins

As mentioned in the preface, many different views have been taught through the years on the subject of prophecy. And this is especially true concerning the parable of the ten virgins.

So, again, I encourage you to lay aside your preconceived ideas while we take a fresh look at this end-time parable as we investigate the prophetic Word of God.

> Matthew 25:1 **Then shall the kingdom of heaven be likened unto ten virgins, which took their lamps, and went forth to meet the bridegroom.**
> **2 And five of them were wise, and five were foolish.**
> **3 They that were foolish took their lamps, and took no oil with them:**
> **4 But the wise took oil in their vessels with their lamps.**
> **5 While the bridegroom tarried, they all slumbered and slept.**
> **6 And at midnight there was a cry made, Behold, the bridegroom cometh; go ye out to meet him.**
> **7 Then all those virgins arose, and trimmed their lamps.**

There are three keys in these verses that are very beneficial to understanding this parable.

First, notice that all ten were called virgins. Second, they all had lamps while they waited for the bridegroom. Thirdly, none of the ten virgins in this parable were brides. The reason for the marriage was that the bridegroom already had a bride.

Many have assumed that the five wise virgins represent the Bride of Christ, but they were friends of the bridegroom, or children of the bride chamber, as mentioned in Matthew 9:15. The five wise virgins do seem to represent the Body of Christ, which the apostle Paul identified in Scripture as a perfect man, not a bride. (Ephesians 4:13.)

In Jewish weddings, the bridegroom usually arrived around midnight. Someone accompanying the bridegroom would run ahead and cry out, "Behold, the bridegroom cometh!" Then they would arise, trim their lamps, go out to meet Him, and accompany him to the bride's place.

In this parable, they all had lamps. Evidently, they were all burning at one time, because the unwise virgins said, "Our lamps are gone out."

THIS PARABLE REVEALS AN END-TIME EVENT

The five foolish virgins had failed to prepare for the bridegroom's coming.

> Matthew 25:8 **And the foolish said unto the wise, Give us of your oil; for our lamps are gone out.**
> **9 But the wise answered, saying, Not so; lest there be not enough for us and you: but go ye rather to them that sell, and buy for yourselves.**
> **10 And while they went to buy, the bridegroom came; and they that were ready went in with him to the marriage: and the door was shut.**

These verses leave no doubt that this parable is revealing an end-time event, for which some have failed to make preparations. This story clearly parallels the catching away of the Church for the Marriage Supper of the Lamb, which will take place in

Heaven during the time frame of the Great Tribulation on the earth. The Church (Body of Christ), being caught up to Heaven, will escape the wrath of God that will be poured out on the earth during that seven-year period. (Revelation 4:1; 5:9-11; 1 Thessalonians 4:16-17.)

It is evident from verse 10 that half of those waiting for the bridegroom were not prepared at the time of His appearance. Therefore, they were not recognized as guests for the marriage.

> Matthew 25:11 **Afterward came also the other virgins, saying, Lord, Lord, open to us.**
> **12 But he answered and said, Verily l say unto you, I know you not.**
> **13 Watch therefore, for ye know neither the day nor the hour wherein the Son of man cometh.**

It is significant that the bridegroom said, **"I know you not,"** rather than, **"I never knew you,"** as is stated on another occasion in Matthew 7:23.

Verse 12 seems to imply that He had known them at one time. However, He did not recognize them as guests for the marriage, because they were unprepared—the problem being they had no oil, which in this parable, represents the Source of their

The Church (Body of Christ), being caught up to Heaven, will escape the wrath of God....

Light. This seems to be a minor problem until we do some scriptural investigation into the matter. Then we find it to be a problem of major consequence.

YOUR LAMP MUST BE BURNING

The following scriptural references lay a foundation that will give you a better understanding of this parable.

Proverbs 20:27 **The spirit of man is the candle of the Lord, searching all the inward parts of the belly.**

If you have a Bible with a center-column reference, it may have a footnote by the word "candle" which says *lamp* (of the Lord). Today, we would say it this way: The spirit of man is the lightbulb which God uses to enlighten man and to bring him out of spiritual darkness. This seems to be indicative of the reborn human spirit.

Proverbs 13:9 **The light of the righteous rejoiceth: but the lamp of the wicked shall be put out.**

When the bridegroom came, the lamps of the five foolish virgins had gone out.

JESUS IS THE LIGHT

The following Scriptures give us a strong indication of the reason that their lamps had gone out:

John 1:3 **All things were made by him; and without him was not any thing made that was made.**
4 In him was life; and the life was the light of men.

John 12:35 **Then Jesus said unto them, Yet a little while is the light with you. Walk while ye have the light, lest darkness come upon you: for he that walketh in darkness knoweth not whither he goeth.**
36 While ye have light, believe in the light, that ye may be the children of light.

Jesus Christ was **"the true Light, which lighteth every man that cometh into the world"** (John 1:9). These Scriptures help us understand this statement in Proverbs 13:9: **"...the lamp of the wicked shall be put out."**

ISRAEL–THE FALLEN VIRGIN

The Books of Amos and Jeremiah both refer to Israel as a virgin.

Amos 5:1 **Hear ye this word which I take up against you, even a lamentation, O house of Israel.**
2 THE VIRGIN OF ISRAEL IS FALLEN; she shall no more rise: she is forsaken upon her land; there is none to raise her up.
4 For thus saith the Lord unto the house of Israel, Seek ye me, and ye shall live.

Then the prophecy of Jeremiah states:

Jeremiah 31:4 **Again I will build thee, and thou shalt be built, O VIRGIN OF ISRAEL: thou shalt again be adorned with thy tabrets, and shalt go forth in the dances of them that make merry.**
21 Set thee up waymarks, make thee high heaps: set thine heart toward the highway, even the way which thou wentest: turn again, O VIRGIN OF ISRAEL, turn again to these thy cities.

There is no doubt that these prophetic Scriptures are referring to Israel as the virgin, stating that the virgin has fallen. Then from these verses it seems obvious that the five foolish virgins could represent the Jewish people (Israel) as well as Gentiles who have not received Christ (the Messiah) as the true Light.

However, in general terms, Matthew 24:1-13 seems to be in one sense a parable of contrast between the Jews who have not received Christ as the Messiah, and the Gentiles.

Proverbs gives us another clue as to why their lamps had gone out.

Proverbs 6:23 **For the commandment is a lamp; and the law is light; and reproofs of instruction are the way of life.**

What a revealing statement—**"The commandment is a lamp; and the law is light."** To the Jews, the Law was their light. When Jesus fulfilled the Law, it passed away and their light went out. Both David and John make some revealing statements concerning this matter.

Psalm 18:28 **For thou wilt light my candle: the Lord my God will enlighten my darkness.**

John 1:17 **For the law was given by Moses, but grace and truth came by Jesus Christ.**

The revelation of the New Covenant came by Jesus Christ. If the commandment was their lamp, and they all had lamps, it is clear from combining information from several previous Scriptures that the lamps represent the human spirit, which enlightens men.

It is God's Spirit bearing witness with our spirit that gives us the light of salvation. (Romans 8:16-17.)

JESUS CAME TO FULFILL

Jesus Himself said that He didn't come to destroy the Law but to fulfill it. (Matthew 5:17-18.) Jesus had indeed fulfilled the Law to the letter, and it passed away, as Paul reveals in Romans chapter 10:

4 For Christ is the end of the law for righteousness to every one that believeth.

But the Law was more than just the Ten Commandments. We don't keep the letter of the Law today, but we keep the spirit of the Law. Paul said, **"For all the law is fulfilled in one word, even in this; Thou shalt love thy neighbour as thyself"** (Galatians 5:14). If we love our neighbor, we won't steal from him; and if we love him, we certainly won't kill him. So, righteous people don't need the Law (except to show what sin is [Romans 3:20]); spiritually dead people can't keep the Law. Paul said,

"**The letter** [of the law] **killeth, but the spirit giveth life**" (2 Corinthians 3:6).

THEIR LIGHT WENT OUT

When Christ came, Israel, generally speaking, closed their eyes to Him and His redemptive work. They refused to believe He was the Messiah. Since the Law was the source of their light, when it passed away, their light was put out. (Proverbs 13:9.)

...the majority of the nation of Israel will go through the seven years of tribulation.

Jesus stated in John's gospel that He was "**the light of the world**" (John 8:12). It seems clear from the Scriptures that the Jews had no light, because they rejected the Messiah, Who is the Source of all spiritual light. This is the contrast typified by the five foolish virgins whose lamps had gone out. The five wise virgins represent those who recognized Christ as their Light and received Him as their Savior. The oil represents eternal salvation, which is the source of spiritual light in the reborn human spirit.

In John 3:3, Jesus said to Nicodemus, "**Except a man be born again, he cannot see the kingdom of God.**" In this parable, all the virgins were friends of the bridegroom and probably had received an invitation. But they didn't all qualify as guests for the marriage when the bridegroom came, revealing that it was because their relationship with God was not maintained through His Son, Jesus, after the Law passed away.

Paul reveals in Galatians that those who are trying to be justified through the Law are fallen from grace.

Galatians 5:4 **Christ is become of no effect unto you, whosoever of you are justified by the law; ye are fallen from grace.**

It is true that there are many Jewish people who have received Christ and have the Light of Life. However, the majority of the nation of Israel will go through the seven years of tribulation. The Scripture states that a remnant shall be saved.

Romans 9:27 **Esaias also crieth concerning Israel, Though the number of the children of Israel be as the sand of the sea, a remnant shall be saved.**

ISRAEL IGNORED GOD'S RIGHTEOUSNESS

Romans 10:1 **Brethren, my heart's desire and prayer to God for Israel is, that they might be saved.**
2 For I bear them record that they have a zeal of God, but not according to knowledge.
3 For they being ignorant of God's righteousness, and going about to establish their own righteousness, have not submitted themselves unto the righteousness of God.

To bring righteousness into the earth, God sent His Son as the Seed of righteousness. God's righteousness was imparted to us because of our faith in Jesus Christ and His substitutionary sacrifice—but Israel would not submit to God's righteousness, which was personified in Christ.

Romans 10:4 **For Christ is the end of the law for righteousness to every one that believeth.**

This statement should be proof enough that Christ put an end to the Law for righteousness. In this dispensation, you must be born again to obtain eternal salvation.

PURE OIL FOR LIGHT

The lamps of the five foolish virgins burned before the bridegroom came, but when he arrived, their lamps had gone out. In the final analysis, the lamps represent the human spirit, for it is the lamp of the Lord. (Proverbs 20:27.) Oil is the source of the light and represents the work of the Holy Spirit to bring salvation and light to the human spirit by the new birth. God gives us scriptural insight into this matter in the Book of Exodus:

> Exodus 27:20 **And thou shalt command the children of Israel, that they bring thee pure oil olive beaten for the light, to cause the lamp to burn always.**

This was a perpetual flame, or light, that was to burn continually in the tabernacle. It was to be fueled by oil from pure olives which were beaten and crushed—a perfect parallel of the Lord Jesus Christ being beaten and bruised for our sins to bring us salvation. This lamp was to burn continually in the tabernacle to represent eternal salvation, which came through the stripes, bruises, and blood of Jesus Christ.

The bridegroom in this parable seems to vividly foreshadow Jesus' coming for the Church. Those who reject His righteousness have no light of salvation. Jesus, in His own words said: **"Ye must be born again"** (John 3:7). There are many born-again Jewish people who have the Light of Life and are looking for Christ to appear for the Church. But generally speaking the Jews reject Christ as their Messiah.

KEEP YOUR LAMPS BURNING

The instructions which Jesus gave in Luke 12:35-46 seem to be for those who are not prepared when the Rapture takes place, but are saved during the last three-and-a-half years of the Tribulation. Those saved in the first three-and-a-half years seem to be raptured sometime after Mid-Tribulation. (Revelation 7:9-19.)

> Luke 12:35 **Let your loins be girded about, and your lights (lamps) burning;**
> **36 And ye yourselves like unto men that wait for their Lord, WHEN HE WILL RETURN FROM THE WEDDING; that when he cometh and knocketh, they may open unto him immediately.**

They are to gird their loins (which signifies being ready to run or to travel quickly) and to have their lamps (lights) burning. These verses seem to refer to the Second Advent of Revelation 19:11-21, where the Lord is returning from the Marriage Supper of the Lamb. Luke 12:36 reveals that they did not go with the other guests but were left behind.

I believe this is an admonition to the remnant of Israel and to all who survive the Tribulation to be born again and to keep their lamps burning. The burning lamps would be the light of salvation in the born-again human spirit. They are to be watching, girded with truth and ready to run. This implies that they must flee Jerusalem immediately when the Mount of Olives splits in half. (Zechariah 14:1-5; Matthew 24:29-31; Revelation 19:11-21.) They must obey the instructions of Jesus in Luke 17:31-33 to escape the armies of the Antichrist. They must watch and be prepared for Christ when He returns from the Wedding of the Lamb.

> Luke 12:37 **Blessed are those servants, whom the Lord when he cometh shall find watching: verily I say unto you, that he shall gird himself, and make them to sit down to meat, and will come forth and serve them.**
> **38 And if he shall come in the second watch, or come in the third watch, and find them so, blessed are those servants.**
> **39 And this know, that if the goodman of the house had known what hour the thief would come, he would have watched, and not have suffered his house to be broken through.**
> **40 Be ye therefore ready also: for the Son of man cometh at an hour when ye think not.**

These verses refer to the Second Advent, for it is the only event referred to in the Scriptures by the phrase coming AS A THIEF IN THE NIGHT. (1 Thessalonians 5:2; 2 Peter 3:10; Revelation 16:15.)

ISRAEL'S EYES ARE CLOSED

In Matthew 13, Jesus gives us more insight into why Israel is blind to the truth that salvation is in the person of Jesus Christ, the Messiah.

> Matthew 13:14 **And in them is fulfilled the prophecy of Esaias, which saith, By hearing ye shall hear, and shall not understand; and seeing ye shall see, and shall not perceive:**
> **15 For this people's heart is waxed gross, and their ears are dull of hearing, and THEIR EYES THEY HAVE CLOSED; lest at any time they should see with their eyes, and hear with their ears, and should understand with their heart, and should be converted, and I should heal them.**

Jesus was referring to the Jews closing their eyes to the fact that Jesus was the Messiah. Because of the way the Old Testament is written, Isaiah's account makes it sound as if God had closed their eyes. But Jesus said, **"Their eyes they have closed."**

In this parable of the ten virgins, the burning lamps represent salvation. When speaking to Nicodemus, Jesus referred to salvation as being "born again."

The statement referring to the born-again spirit of man in Proverbs 20:27, **"The spirit of man is the candle (lamp) of the Lord,"** becomes much clearer when viewed in the light of the words of David in Psalm 18:28, **"For thou wilt light my candle: the Lord my God will enlighten my darkness."** The rebirth will light our candle (lamp of the human spirit) with the light of salvation.

CHILDREN OF THE BRIDECHAMBER

To fully understand the parable of the ten virgins, we need to review some information concerning the "children of the bridechamber" mentioned by Jesus in Matthew, chapter 9.

15 And Jesus said unto them, Can the children of the bridechamber mourn, as long as the bridegroom is with them? but the days will come, when the bridegroom shall be taken from them, and then shall they fast.

Don't be misled by the word *children* in this phrase. *Children of the bridechamber* refers to people who are friends of the bridegroom.

The Greek word used in this verse for children is *huios*.[1] This word is used in Scripture as "sons," "son of David," "his son," "son of man," and "offspring," such as "sons of Abraham" and "children of Israel."

So they were not little children as some suppose. They were to take care of whatever was needed for the bridechamber and to decorate the room in which marriage ceremonies were to be held.

The ten virgins were friends of the bridegroom, as well as the children of the bridechamber referred to in Matthew 9:15.

The bridegroom usually came about midnight. Someone in the bridegroom's company would cry, "Behold, the bridegroom cometh!" Then they would go with him to the bride's place and would eventually escort her back to his place.

IDENTITY OF THE BRIDE

We have been taught for many years that the Church is the Bride of Christ, but there is no scriptural evidence to identify the Church as the Bride of Christ. It's all right to use the Church as a parallel or illustration of a bride, for Jesus is coming for the Church as a bridegroom would come for a bride. But, for the sake of identity we must let God's Word settle the question.

Now don't turn me off or throw this book away. I know I am about to touch a sacred cow, so to speak, but hear me out. You don't have to believe it. But after we do a scriptural investigation, the Word of God might change your mind. For forty-five years I believed that the Church was the Bride, but a thorough study of God's Word concerning this matter changed my mind.

I find no scriptural evidence that would identify the Church as the Bride.

When we study the Scriptures carefully, they give us a true revelation of the identity of the bride. The parable of the ten virgins cannot be fully comprehended until we understand the scriptural identity of both the Church and the bride. Let's investigate a few scriptural facts concerning this matter. John makes mention of the Lamb's wife in Revelation 19:7-8. Then in Revelation 21 John reveals the bride, the Lamb's wife, to be the New Jerusalem.

> Revelation 19:7 **Let us be glad and rejoice, and give honour to him: for the marriage of the Lamb is come, and his wife hath made herself ready.**
> **8 And to her was granted that she should be arrayed in fine linen, clean and white: for the fine linen is the righteousness of saints.**

Notice that the "fine linen" in which the bride was "arrayed" was the righteousness of the saints. Ask yourself this question: If you saw a bridal gown hanging in the closet, would you call it the bride? Would you say that the bride was hanging in the closet? The answer is obvious. The bride is the one who will be adorned with the bridal gown, but the bridal gown would never be identified as the bride.

In the same manner, the Church (Body of Christ) will adorn that city with white robes of righteousness as Christ and His Body (Church) live in the New Jerusalem.

Contrary to what many believe, I find no scriptural evidence that would identify the Church as the Bride. I know many of you reading this book believe there are such Scriptures and you are going to stay up late tonight trying to find them. But first let's do some more Scripture investigation.

THE QUESTION OF GENDER

There is a vast difference between a parallel of the Body of Christ and the true identity of the Church. For instance, the phrases *children of the bridechamber* and *five wise virgins* both seem to represent the Body of Christ. In each case, they represent both the male and female genders. When we find the true identity of the Church—of which Christ is the Head—the word used must be the same gender as the Head (Christ), which is male.

The word *numphe*,[2] translated "bride," is never used for both male and female. It is only used in Scripture to describe the female gender.

However, the word *huios,* which is translated "children" (of the bridechamber) in Matthew 9:15, is used for both genders. Examples include the *children of Israel* (Revelation 2:14; 21:12) and the *children of God.* (Matthew 5:9; Luke 20:36; Galatians 3:26.)

This Greek word translated "children" includes male and female. This fits with the intent of the parable of the ten virgins, in which the five wise virgins represent the Body of Christ (the Church).

We also find that the Greek word *parthenos,*[3] translated "virgin," is used for both male and female.

Consequently, if the Church were identified as a bride, then the word itself would seem to exclude the male gender from the Body. And we know that would be contrary to the Scriptures, for the Church is composed of both male and female.

John identifies the bride in the Book of Revelation as the new Jerusalem.

> Revelation 21:2 **And I John saw the holy city, new Jerusalem, coming down from God out of heaven, prepared** AS A BRIDE ADORNED FOR HER HUSBAND.
>
> **9 And there came unto me one of the seven angels which had the seven vials full of the seven last plagues, and talked with me, saying, Come hither, I** WILL SHEW THEE THE BRIDE, THE LAMB'S WIFE.
>
> **10 And he carried me away in the spirit to a great and high mountain, and shewed me that great city, the holy Jerusalem, descending out of heaven from God.**

A PERFECT MAN

In Ephesians 4:11-13 we learn from Paul that Christ has given a fivefold ministry of apostles, prophets, evangelists, pastors, and teachers **"For the perfecting of the saints, for the work of the ministry, for the edifying of the body of Christ: Till we all come in the unity of the faith, and of the knowledge of the Son of God, unto a perfect MAN, unto the measure of the stature of the fulness of Christ"** (vv. 12-13).

Here Paul calls the Church, (when matured), *a perfect man*. The Greek word translated "man" in this verse is *aner*,[4] which refers only to the male gender, which fits perfectly with other Scriptures.

The Greek word being used most often in the Scripture referring either to mankind or both male and female is the word *anthropos*.[5] But the word *aner* is only used in reference to the male gender.

Then for the sake of scriptural identity of the Church, the word used must represent the Head (Christ). Therefore, the Body (Church) must of necessity also be identified as the same gender as Christ.

As we have seen in Ephesians 4:13, Paul refers to the Church as *a perfect man*. Yet we know that those in Christ are both male and female. The identity of the Church as the corporate Body of Christ seems to always be referred by the personal pronoun "He," or "His body." The Greek word *aner* would seem to clearly establish the identity of the Body of Christ as being a mature man, rather than a bride.

Now let me reiterate the fact that we see some parallels of relationship between Christ coming for the Church as a bridegroom comes for a bride. And it makes a wonderful allegory, but for the sake of scriptural identity, we must allow God's Word to be the final authority.

THE "BODY" OF CHRIST

Paul reveals in Ephesians 1:22-23 that Jesus is the Head and the Church is His Body. The Head can't be male and the body female, for the body is always referred to as the same gender as the Head. This will become much clearer as we look at Paul's statement in Galatians 3:27: **"For as many of you as have been baptized into Christ have put on Christ."**

In other words, you have taken on His gender identity. Paul put it this way in Galatians 3:28: **"There is neither Jew nor Greek, there is neither bond nor free, there is neither male nor female: for ye are all one in Christ Jesus."**

Even though there are both genders *in the Church*, there is neither male nor female in Christ (no gender identity but His); for we are one with Him. (John 17:21-23.)

Then in Ephesians 5 Paul makes it very clear that the Body of Christ is of His body, His flesh, and His bones. If Jesus has a bride, then we (the Church) also have a bride, for we are one with Him now.

Ephesians 5:29 **For no man ever yet hated his own flesh; but nourisheth and cherisheth it, even as the Lord the church:**
30 For we are members of his body, of his flesh, and of his bones.
31 For this cause shall a man leave his father and mother, and shall be joined unto his wife, and they two shall be one flesh.
32 This is a great mystery: but I speak concerning Christ and the church.

In these verses Paul leaves no doubt that we take on Christ's gender for identity's sake as we become *one with Him,* much the same as a woman takes the name of her husband when they become one in marriage. The ultimate confirmation of this is found in Revelation 3:

Revelation 3:12 **Him that overcometh will I make a pillar in the temple of my God, and he shall go no more out: and I WILL WRITE UPON HIM THE NAME OF MY GOD, and the name of the city of my God, which is NEW JERUSALEM, which cometh down out of heaven from my God: and I will write upon him my new name.**

This verse seems to confirm that Christ and His Body (the Church) will become one with the holy city, the New Jerusalem.

THE NEW JERUSALEM IDENTIFIED AS THE BRIDE

In the following verses, John gives us biblical insight into the identity of the bride.

Revelation 21:2 **And I John saw the holy city, new Jerusalem, coming down from God out of heaven, prepared as a BRIDE adorned for her husband.**
3 And I heard a great voice out of heaven saying, Behold, the tabernacle of God is with men, and he

will dwell with them, and they shall be his people, and
God himself shall be with them, and be their God.
9 And there came unto me one of the seven angels...
and talked with me, saying, Come hither, I will shew
thee the BRIDE, THE LAMB'S WIFE.
10 And he carried me away in the spirit to a great and
high mountain, and shewed me THAT GREAT CITY, THE
HOLY JERUSALEM, descending out of heaven from God.

We would have to have help to misunderstand these statements! However, for many years, we've had a lot of help, and it
is called "indoctrination."

In Acts chapter 9, we find a passage of Scripture that will lend
support to the fact that the Church is Christ's Body and not the
bride. Let's say it another way—the Church is considered to be
Him because the body and head make the whole perfect man.

The account of Paul's experience on the road to Damascus
verifies that the Church is considered to be Him (Christ) for
identity's sake:

Acts 9:3 And as he journeyed, he came near Damascus:
and suddenly there shined round about him a light
from heaven:
4 And he fell to the earth, and heard a voice saying
unto him, Saul, Saul, why persecutest thou ME?

Notice that Jesus didn't question why Saul was persecuting
His bride. Instead, His question was, "...why persecutest thou
ME?" The Church is His Body; He considered it to be Him. In
John chapter 3, we have another Scripture that seems to lend sup-
port to the position that the Church should not be considered
the bride.

John 3:29 He that hath the bride is the bridegroom:
but the friend of the bridegroom, which standeth and

heareth him, rejoiceth greatly because of the bridegroom's voice: this my joy therefore is fulfilled.

The Church had not been officially established at that time, but John was a prophet and referred to himself as "the friend of the bridegroom."

There is no indication here that he thought the disciples or those who followed Christ would be the Bride. He describes himself as being a "friend of the bridegroom." Then Revelation 22:17 gives another reference revealing that the bride was considered to be separate from the Church.

> Revelation 22:17. **And the Spirit and** THE BRIDE SAY, COME. **And let** HIM THAT HEARETH SAY, **Come. And let him that is athirst come. And whosoever will, let him come and take the water of life freely.**

If the Church...were identified as the Bride...we would not have the legal right to...use His name until after our marriage actually took place.

The Book of Revelation was written to the Church. (Revelation 22:16.) So from verse 17 we must conclude that *he that heareth* is the Church and is not the same as the bride.

A BRIDE HAS NO AUTHORITY TO USE
THE GROOM'S NAME

One last point of major importance concerning the identity of the Church (this is the main reason I have belabored this matter): If the Church, the Body of Christ, were identified as the Bride of Christ in Scripture, then it seems that we would not have the legal right to take on His identity and use His name until after the marriage actually took place. So you can see the far-reaching implication of a simple misunderstanding of the identity of the Church of Jesus Christ. The Scriptures plainly reveal He has already given us His name to use. (John 16:23-26; Mark 16:17-18.)

I rest my case concerning that matter. Now let's get back to the parable.

THE UNPREPARED SHUT OUT

It is evident from the parable of the ten virgins that the five foolish virgins were not prepared when the bridegroom came and were not recognized as guests for the marriage.

Matthew 25:8 **And the foolish said unto the wise, Give us of your oil; for our lamps are gone out. 10 And while they went to buy, the bridegroom came; and they that were ready went in with him to the marriage: and the door was shut.**

When the bridegroom arrived, the five foolish virgins found themselves with a severe problem at a very critical time, because they hadn't made the proper preparations. They needed oil, which represented the source of light.

Some might ask, "How could oil represent salvation since we know that no one can buy salvation?" However, the prophetic utterance found in Isaiah 55 and the statements of Jesus in John 6:56-58 give us the answer and bring the whole matter into biblical perspective. As we compare the following verse in Isaiah to the statements of the five who were wise virgins, we will be able to see the intent of those words.

Isaiah 55:1 **Ho, every one that thirsteth, come ye to the waters, and he that hath no money; come ye, buy, and eat; yea, come, buy wine and milk without money and without price. 2 Wherefore do ye spend money for that which is not bread? and your labour for that which satisfieth not? hearken diligently unto me, and eat ye that which is good, and let your soul delight itself in fatness.**

John 6:56 **He that eateth my flesh, and drinketh my blood, dwelleth in me, and I in him.**
57 As the living Father hath sent me, and I live by the Father: so he that eateth me, even he shall live by me.
58 This is that bread which came down from heaven: not as your fathers did eat manna, and are dead: he that eateth of this bread shall live for ever.

Jesus is the Bread of Life *which came down from Heaven.* God is saying, "Come and buy Living Bread without money."

This would seem to reveal the intent of the reference in Matthew 25:9 when the five wise virgins said to the five foolish, "Go to those that sell and buy." In other words, go and obtain from the One Who is the Source of supply.

This is a major point in this parable, revealing that those whose lamps were not burning could not borrow what they lacked from others, but were required to obtain from the One Who is the Source of supply. The Scriptures reveal that Source to be Jesus Christ, for He said, "I am the Bread of Life and the Light of Life." (John 6:35; 8:12.) He is the only Source of true spiritual light and life.

The following verses give us more insight into why the five foolish virgins were shut out from the marriage and were not recognized as guests.

1 John 5:11 **And this is the record, that God hath given to us eternal life, and this life is in his Son.**
12 He that hath the Son hath life; and he that hath not the Son of God hath not life.

John 8:12 **Then spake Jesus again unto them, saying, I am the light of the world: he that followeth me shall not walk in darkness, but shall have the light of life.**

The implications are that the foolish virgins did not accept the Son; therefore, they did not have the light of life.

SEVEN DAYS REPRESENT SEVEN YEARS

It is quite significant that the Jewish marriage feast lasted for seven days, in view of the fact that Daniel's Seventieth Week is a week of years, an exact period of seven years. That will be the exact time period the Church will be in Heaven for the Marriage Supper before coming back with Christ at the Second Advent.

No doubt they will at that time say, "Blessed is he that cometh in the name of the Lord"....

The Marriage Feast will take place in Heaven during that same seven-year period, which is the exact time allotted to the Man of Sin (Antichrist) on earth. (2 Thessalonians 2:6; Daniel 9:20-27.)

Before Jesus finished His ministry here on the earth, He made these statements to the Jews:

Matthew 23:38 **Behold, your house is left unto you desolate.**
39 For I say unto you, Ye shall not see me henceforth, till ye shall say, Blessed is he that cometh in the name of the Lord.

Even though many of the Jews have rejected Jesus for nearly 2000 years, at the end of the Tribulation they will see Him descend from Heaven to the Mount of Olives. He will be accompanied by the saints and will deliver Israel and save them from total destruction. No doubt they will at that time say, **"Blessed is he that cometh in the name of the Lord,"** as revealed by the scriptural composite found in Matthew 21:1-14.

Many of the Jewish people will receive Christ as their Messiah during the Tribulation and will be caught up to Heaven shortly after Mid-Tribulation in time for the Marriage Supper of the Lamb. (Revelation 7:14.)

THEY WILL SEE THE MESSIAH COME

The Rabbis are still looking for their Messiah to come—not knowing that He has already come. However, He will come again, and those who survive the Tribulation will recognize Him. Zechariah 12 reveals some details of the Second Advent and states that they will look upon Him Whom they have pierced. (Zechariah 12:10.)

In the first three-and-one-half years of the Tribulation Period, the 144,000 Jewish men who are sealed in their foreheads will have supernatural protection from the Antichrist, and they will preach the Gospel to the nation of Israel and the Gentiles. It seems the 144,000 will be born again immediately after the Rapture of the Church. When they realize that the Messiah has come and taken the Church to Heaven, they will become jealous as well as zealous for the Lord.

God spoke through the prophet Moses that He would move the Jews to jealousy by those who were not his people. He fulfilled this by making salvation available to the Gentiles. I believe they will be moved even more when they discover that Jesus, the Messiah, came for the Church and that they were left on earth to experience the fulfillment of the Seventieth Week of Daniel's prophecy.

THE CURE FOR ISRAEL'S BLINDNESS

We find in the ninth chapter of John another event which reveals prophetic insight concerning Israel. It is an incident in the life of a man who was blind from his birth.

John 9:1 **And as Jesus passed by, he saw a man which was blind from his birth.**
2 And his disciples asked him, saying, Master, who did sin, this man, or his parents, that he was born blind?

3 Jesus answered, Neither hath this man sinned, nor his parents: but that the works of God should be made manifest in him.
4 I must work the works of him that sent me....

Jesus said that neither of their suggested answers was correct. He didn't reveal to them the cause of the blindness, but rather He told them that He was going to work the works of God so that God's work would be manifest in the blind man.

John 9:6 When he had thus spoken, he spat on the ground, and made clay of the spittle, and he anointed the eyes of the blind man with the clay,
7 And said unto him, Go, wash in the pool of Siloam, (which is by interpretation, Sent.) He went his way therefore, and washed, and came seeing.

Now, let's allow the Scriptures to reveal the prophetic implications concerning these verses by letting them give the interpretation. The apostle Paul, when referring to the Church, said:

Ephesians 5:25 Husbands, love your wives, even as Christ also loved the church, and gave himself for it;
26 That he might sanctify and cleanse it WITH THE WASHING OF WATER BY THE WORD.

Then in John 15:3, Jesus said to the disciples, **"Now ye are clean through the word which I have spoken unto you."** These verses give an excellent illustration of God's Word being a cleansing agent much the same as water. The blind man seems to be a parallel of the nation of Israel. When Jesus came, they closed their eyes to truth and became spiritually blind. They did not recognize Him as their Messiah. So Jesus made clay (the same substance God had used in Genesis to create man) and anointed the blind man's eyes. In the natural, this would seem to make things worse and necessitate his washing in water. The water represents the water of God's Word, which has the ability to cleanse and restore.

HEALING WATER OF THE WORD

Jesus told the blind man to go and wash in the pool, which was called *Sent*. The word "sent" here gives us a clue, for Psalm 107:20 states, **"He [God] sent his word, and healed them, and delivered them from their destructions."**

The pool named "sent" represented the water of the Word, which God sent to open the eyes of those who are blind to the truth of the Gospel.

When Israel hears God's Word without the veil on their hearts, their eyes will be opened.

Paul reveals when the children of Israel turn to the Lord the veil will be taken away.

2 Corinthians 3:14 **But their minds were blinded: for until this day remaineth the same vail untaken away in the reading of the old testament; which vail is done away in Christ.**
15 But even unto this day, when Moses is read, the vail is upon their heart.
16 Nevertheless when it shall turn to the Lord, the vail shall be taken away.
17 Now the Lord is that Spirit: and where the Spirit of the Lord is, there is liberty.
18 But we all, with open face beholding as in a glass the glory of the Lord, are changed into the same image from glory to glory, even as by the Spirit of the Lord.

When Israel hears God's Word without the veil on their hearts, their eyes will be opened, just as the blind man that "washed and came seeing." It seems that John 9:1-7 fits as a parallel of the remnant of Israel being healed of their spiritual blindness.

Even though the majority of the Jews closed their eyes and their hearts to Christ nearly 2000 years ago, when they turn their hearts to the Word, their eyes will behold with great revelation their

Messiah. When Christ appears at His Second Advent, they will recognize Him and accept Him as their Messiah. (Zechariah 12:9-10.)

Many in Israel will accept Him during the first half of the Tribulation Period because of the ministry of the 144,000, who will point them to Christ. I believe they will be preaching, from the Old Testament, Jesus Christ and Him crucified.

RESTORATION

The prophet Isaiah gives us marvelous insight to the results of the ministry of the 144,000.

Isaiah 60:1 **Arise, shine; for thy light is come, and the glory of the Lord is risen upon thee.**
2 For, behold, the darkness shall cover the earth, and gross darkness the people: but the Lord shall arise upon thee, and his glory shall be seen upon thee.

In this verse Isaiah is referring to the future Israel as well as Zion, the church of the firstborn—at a time when their Light has truly been increased. For God will light their candle with an everlasting oil of salvation that will be a perpetual light into eternity to come.

Isaiah 60:3 **And the Gentiles shall come to thy light, and kings to the brightness of thy rising.**

This verse in one sense seems to be referring to the time of the millennial reign when their eyes will be opened. The nations will come to the Jews for the light and revelation that they will have in that day.

I believe these verses also reveal that there is coming a flood of revelation and glory upon the Church before the final harvest, just before the Rapture.

BURNING LAMP REPRESENTS SALVATION

Finally, Hosea and Isaiah gave us two separate prophecies which confirm the intent of the parable of the ten virgins.

> Hosea 6:1 **Come, and let us return unto the Lord: for he hath torn, and he will heal us; he hath smitten, and he will bind us up.**
> **2 After two days will he revive us: in the third day he will raise us up, and we shall live in his sight.**

> Isaiah 62:1 **For Zion's sake will I not hold my peace, and for Jerusalem's sake I will not rest, until the righteousness thereof go forth as** BRIGHTNESS**, and the** SALVATION **thereof** AS A LAMP THAT BURNETH.
> **2 And the Gentiles shall see thy righteousness, and all kings thy glory: and thou shalt be called by a new name, which the mouth of the Lord shall name.**

These prophecies should be proof enough that the parable of the ten virgins is a parable of contrast between the Jews and the Gentiles.

The five foolish virgins whose lamps had gone out represent the Jews, as well as others, who reject Christ.

Sequence of End-time Events

In Matthew, chapter 23, Jesus gave the Pharisees quite a tongue-lashing for being hypocritical. He ended His reprimand by saying that their house was left desolate and that they would not see Him again until the time when they would say, "Blessed is he that cometh in the name of the Lord!" This sets the stage for Matthew 24:

> 1 And Jesus went out, and departed from the temple: and his disciples came to him for to shew him the buildings of the temple.
> 2 And Jesus said unto them, See ye not all these things? verily I say unto you, There shall not be left here one stone upon another, that shall not be thrown down.
> 3 And as he sat upon the mount of Olives, the disciples came unto him privately, saying, Tell us, when shall these things be? and what shall be the sign of thy coming, and of the end of the world?

The phrase *end of the world* really means the end of the age, because the world will never end. The world will be renovated with fire, but it will be here forever as the new earth. (2 Peter 3:10; Revelation 21:1.)

These were Jewish questions, so Jesus gave them Jewish answers. It is interesting to note that the discourse by Jesus in Matthew 24 seems to parallel the opening of the six seals of Revelation 6.

THE OPENING OF THE SIX SEALS

It is important to review the events that immediately precede the opening of the six seals. First, in Revelation 4:1, John both witnessed and experienced an event that is a perfect parallel of the Rapture. He heard a voice as a trumpet say to him, **"Come up hither,"** and immediately he was in Heaven before God's throne.

They will return to earth with Christ after the Tribulation to set up His kingdom.

Then in Revelation 5:9-10, the saints are singing a new song of the redeemed. They have just been made kings and priests. They will return to earth with Christ after the Tribulation to set up His kingdom.

Then, at the beginning of Revelation 6, the Lamb opens the first seal. You will notice that when John starts revealing the opening of these seals, he carries it through to the end. He will fill in many of the details in parenthetical chapters to follow.

MATTHEW 24 AND THE SIX SEALS

Compare the following Scriptures from Matthew 24 with Revelation 6 concerning the six seals.

JESUS' REFERENCE TO THE FIRST SEAL

**Matthew 24:4 And Jesus answered and said unto them, Take heed that no man deceive you.
5 For many shall come in my name, saying, I am Christ; and shall deceive many.**

It is evident that one of those who will claim to be the Christ will be the Man of Sin (the Antichrist).

JOHN'S REFERENCE TO THE FIRST SEAL

Revelation 6:1 And I saw when the Lamb opened one of the seals, and I heard, as it were the noise of thunder, one of the four beasts saying, Come and see.

2 And I saw, and behold a white horse: and he that sat on him had a bow; and a crown was given unto him: and he went forth conquering, and to conquer.

When the first seal was opened, the Antichrist was revealed riding a white horse. He had a bow but no arrows, and someone had to give him a crown. These are some of the reasons that we can be sure that this refers to the Antichrist and not Jesus, as some have supposed.

JESUS' REFERENCE TO THE SECOND SEAL

**Matthew 24:6 And ye shall hear of wars and rumours of wars: see that ye be not troubled: for all these things must come to pass, but the end is not yet.
7 For nation shall rise against nation, and kingdom against kingdom.**

JOHN'S REFERENCE TO THE SECOND SEAL

Revelation 6:3 **And when he had opened the second seal, I heard the second beast say, Come and see.
4 And there went out another horse that was red: and power was given to him that sat thereon to take peace from the earth, and that they should kill one another: and there was given unto him a great sword.**

As the second seal is opened, the red horse rider, which will take peace from the earth, is revealed. It seems that war will break out almost immediately after the Church is raptured. This will most likely be Russia's move toward Israel, as prophesied in Ezekiel 38 and 39.

JESUS' REFERENCE TO THE THIRD SEAL

Matthew 24:7 **...and there shall be famines, and pestilences, and earthquakes, in divers places.**

8 All these are the beginning of sorrows.

JOHN'S REFERENCE TO THE THIRD SEAL

Revelation 6:5 **And when he had opened the third seal, I heard the third beast say, Come and see. And I beheld, and lo a black horse; and he that sat on him had a pair of balances in his hand.**
6 And I heard a voice in the midst of the four beasts say, A measure of wheat for a penny, and three measures of barley for a penny; and see thou hurt not the oil and the wine.

When the third seal is opened, the black horse rider is revealed, which represents famine, for famine always follows war. The opening of the third seal seems to occur about Mid-Tribulation.

JESUS' REFERENCE TO THE FOURTH SEAL

The opening of the fourth seal seems to reveal things that happen right after Mid-Tribulation, and corresponds with Matthew 24:9-13.

9 Then shall they deliver you up to be afflicted, and shall kill you: and ye shall be hated of all nations for my name's sake.
10 And then shall many be offended, and shall betray one another, and shall hate one another.
11 And many false prophets shall rise, and shall deceive many.
12 And because iniquity shall abound, the love of many shall wax cold.
13 But he that shall endure unto the end, the same shall be saved.

JOHN'S REFERENCE TO THE FOURTH SEAL

Revelation 6:7 **And when he had opened the fourth seal, I heard the voice of the fourth beast say, Come and see.**
8 And I looked, and behold a pale horse: and his name that sat on him was Death, and Hell followed with him. And power was given unto them over the fourth part of the earth, to kill with sword, and with hunger, and with death, and with the beasts of the earth.

When the fourth seal is opened, the pale horse rider (death) shows up and Hell follows him, giving those on earth a taste of what Hell is like.

JESUS' REFERENCE TO THE FIFTH SEAL

Matthew 24:14 **And this gospel of the kingdom shall be preached in all the world for a witness unto all nations; and then shall the end come.**
15 When ye therefore shall see the abomination of desolation, spoken of by Daniel the prophet, stand in the holy place, (whoso readeth, let him understand).

JOHN'S REFERENCE TO THE FIFTH SEAL

Revelation 6:9 **And when he had opened the fifth seal, I saw under the altar the souls of them that were slain for the word of God, and for the testimony which they held:**
10 And they cried with a loud voice, saying, How long, O Lord, holy and true, dost thou not judge and avenge our blood on them that dwell on the earth?

The fifth seal reveals Christian martyrs who give their lives for a testimony. These are Tribulation saints, people who were born again after the Rapture. Many will be slain for their profession of faith in Christ and refusal to worship the image of the beast.

Many will be slain for their profession of faith in Christ and refusal to worship the image of beast.

Revelation 6:11 **And white robes were given unto every one of them; and it was said unto them, that they should rest yet for a little season, until their fellowservants also and their brethren, that should be killed as they were, should be fulfilled.**

Not every person who is born again during the Tribulation will be martyred, but many will give their lives for their testimony of Jesus Christ. The Antichrist will wage unmerciful war against those who refuse to worship him after Mid-Tribulation, when he sets himself up in the temple as god.

JESUS' REFERENCE TO THE SIXTH SEAL

Matthew 24:29 **Immediately after the tribulation of those days shall the sun be darkened, and the moon shall not give her light, and the stars shall fall from heaven, and the powers of the heavens shall be shaken: 30 And then shall appear the sign of the Son of man in heaven: and then shall all the tribes of the earth mourn, and they shall see the Son of man coming in the clouds of heaven with power and great glory. 31 And he shall send his angels with a great sound of a trumpet, and they shall gather together his elect from the four winds, from one end of heaven to the other.**

JOHN'S REFERENCE TO THE SIXTH SEAL

With the opening of this sixth seal, we recognize the events revealing the Second Advent. Matthew 24:29-30, Isaiah 34:1-8, Revelation 19:11-19, and Zechariah 14:1-14 describe this same event with other details. It is referred to by Isaiah as "**...the day of the Lord's vengeance, and the year of recompences for the controversy of Zion**" (Isaiah 34:8).

> Revelation 6:12 **And I beheld when he had opened the sixth seal, and, lo, there was a great earthquake; and the sun became black as sackcloth of hair, and the moon became as blood;**
> 13 And the stars of heaven fell unto the earth, even as a fig tree casteth her untimely figs, when she is shaken of a mighty wind.
> 14 And the heaven departed as a scroll when it is rolled together; and every mountain and island were moved out of their places.
> 15 And the kings of the earth, and the great men, and the rich men, and the chief captains, and the mighty men, and every bondman, and every free man, hid themselves in the dens and in the rocks of the mountains;
> 16 And said to the mountains and rocks, Fall on us, and hide us from the face of him that sitteth on the throne, and from the wrath of the Lamb:
> 17 For the great day of his wrath is come; and who shall be able to stand?

When Heaven is rolled back as a scroll (v. 14), it is possible that the Hubble Telescope will be used to give the world advance notice of Christ's return to the earth to set up His kingdom. Then, by way of satellite, all the earth will be able to see Jesus as He descends from Heaven to the earth accompanied by the saints. (Matthew 24:29-30; Revelation 19:11-20; Zechariah 14:1-5.) What a tremendous day of victory that will be for Christ and His saints. But it will be a day of darkness for the wicked of the earth who have followed the Antichrist into his very last battle.

In Revelation 6, John gives us a synopsis of end-time events from the opening of the first seal, when the Antichrist is revealed, right up to the Second Advent. He stops just short of Christ's actual appearance on earth. He simply gives a short version of the whole picture.

Then, in chapter 7, John begins to fill in many of the details that occurred from the time the first seal was opened.

144,000 JEWISH BELIEVERS SEALED BY GOD

Revelation 7:2 And I saw another angel ascending from the east, having the seal of the living God: and he cried with a loud voice to the four angels, to whom it was given to hurt the earth and the sea,
3 Saying, Hurt not the earth, neither the sea, nor the trees, till we have sealed the servants of our God in their foreheads.
4 And I heard the number of them which were sealed: and there were sealed an hundred and forty and four thousand of all the tribes of the children of Israel.

Before God allows the angels to release judgment upon the earth, He will seal 144,000 Jewish men. Because of these Jewish men, the revival that started on the earth before the Rapture will continue through the Tribulation Period. There will be a great multitude saved out of all nations. (Revelation 7:9-17.)

Twelve thousand men from each of the twelve tribes of Israel will be sealed in their foreheads so the Antichrist can't harm them. They will preach the everlasting Gospel to Israel and the Gentiles.

Their spiritual eyes will have been opened to the fact that the true Messiah came and they missed Him. The truth of God's Word will set them free, and they will realize that the Antichrist is an impostor. This will make them both jealous and zealous for Christ.

They will create a major problem for the Antichrist until they are caught up to Heaven. It seems they are raptured possibly about five years into the Tribulation Period.

ENDURING THE TRIBULATION

Matthew 24:13 **But he that shall endure unto the end, the same shall be saved.**
14 And this gospel of the kingdom shall be preached in all the world for a witness unto all nations; and then shall the end come.

These verses are referring to the end of the Tribulation. Verses 15-22 are referring to the time when the Antichrist breaks the peace covenant with Israel. He will break that agreement in the middle of the Tribulation Period. He will set himself up in the temple as god, and there will be idol worship in the temple. The Antichrist will cause them to worship the image of the beast.

Jesus calls this period the "Abomination of Desolation." (Matthew 24:15.) In other words, it will set into motion God's prophetic Word, spoken in Daniel 9:27, that will bring an end to the Antichrist and to all those who follow him.

Matthew 24:16 **Then let them which be in Judaea flee into the mountains:**
17 Let him which is on the housetop not come down to take any thing out of his house:
18 Neither let him which is in the field return back to take his clothes.
19 And woe unto them that are with child, and to them that give suck in those days!
20 But pray ye that your flight be not in the winter, neither on the sabbath day:
21 For then shall be great tribulation, such as was not since the beginning of the world to this time, no, nor ever shall be.
22 And except those days should be shortened, there should no flesh be saved: but for the elect's sake those days shall be shortened.

The first three-and-one-half years of the Tribulation will be relatively mild compared to the last three-and-one-half years. It will be during the last half that the Antichrist will set himself up as god, forcing people to worship him. He will then wage war against those who have been saved and refuse to worship him. Yet, he will not be able to destroy the Jews, for a remnant will be hid away in the wilderness by the *wings of a great eagle*. (Revelation 12:14.) This could possibly refer to a U.S. airlift.

THE ELECT

There are those who believe Matthew 24:22 proves that the Church will go through the Tribulation, because it states, **"...for the elect's sake those days shall be shortened."** But the elect which Jesus refers to are the elect of Israel, not the Church as many have supposed. In fact, there are four called "elect" in Scripture. So one must determine which elect is being referred to from the context. The references are Jesus, in 1 Peter 2:6; the saints, in 1 Peter 1:2; angels, in 1 Timothy 5:21; and Israel, in Isaiah 45:4 and 65:9,22. So the elect in Matthew 24:22 are Israelis and other Tribulation saints who will be saved after the Rapture.

> Matthew 24:23 **Then if any man shall say unto you, Lo, here is Christ, or there; believe it not.**
> **24 For there shall arise false Christs, and false prophets, and shall shew great signs and wonders; insomuch that, if it were possible, they shall deceive the very elect.**

This most likely refers to the last three-and-one-half years of the Tribulation Period. The elect of Israel cannot be deceived at that time because the 144,000 Jewish men will have preached the Gospel to them and their eyes will have been opened to the truth that Christ is the true Messiah.

Then, after Mid-Tribulation, the *angels* begin preaching the everlasting Gospel. The elect of Israel will have recognized that the Antichrist is an impostor, and they will not be deceived by the false signs and wonders brought about through witchcraft.

TRIBULATION SAINTS RAPTURED

As you read Revelation chapter 7, you will notice John states that 12,000 men from each of the twelve tribes of Israel are sealed. Then he skips from that revelation to the results of their evangelistic efforts, revealing that their harvest will be a multitude that no man can number.

9 After this I beheld, and, lo, a great multitude, which no man could number, of all nations, and kindreds, and people, and tongues, stood before the throne, and before the Lamb, clothed with white robes, and palms in their hands;

...after Mid-Tribulation, the angels begin preaching the everlasting Gospel.

10 And cried with a loud voice, saying, Salvation to our God which sitteth upon the throne, and unto the Lamb.
11 And ALL the angels stood round about the throne, and about the elders and the four beasts, and fell before the throne on their faces, and worshipped God,
13 And one of the elders answered, saying unto me, What are these which are arrayed in white robes? and whence came they?
14 And I said unto him, Sir, thou knowest. And he said to me, These are they which came out of the great tribulation, and have washed their robes, and made them white in the blood of the Lamb.

It is significant that in verse 11 *all* of the angels are back in Heaven. Hebrews 2:14 reveals that the angels are ministering spirits to minister for those who are heirs of salvation. Why are they all in Heaven? They are there because there has been another rapture and the angels have transported the Tribulation saints to Heaven. This seems to take place sometime after Mid-Tribulation. These are people who will have been born again because of the preaching of the 144,000 Jewish men.

It seems the angels will have gone back to earth after transporting the Church to Heaven. I believe they will escort this great multitude of Tribulation saints to Heaven just in time for the Marriage Supper of the Lamb. We have evidence in Luke 16:22 of angels being in charge of carrying the spiritual body of the beggar who died to Abraham's bosom after he died.

THE SEVENTH SEAL

Revelation 8:1 **And when he had opened the seventh seal, there was silence in heaven about the space of half an hour.**

Someone said, "The thirty minutes of silence in Heaven will be so all the Revelation teachers can get their charts straightened out." But really, it is one of the unknowns of the Book of Revelation.

When John started with the revelation, he carried it all the way to the time where the Tribulation saints show up in Heaven. He did this in the seals of chapter 6, and again in chapter 7.

The things related in chapter 7 seem to be a synopsis of the things that will happen through Mid-Tribulation. Then in later chapters, John fills in the details. But, as we have already seen, when chapter 7 closes, there are Tribulation saints in Heaven.

However, it was not until chapter 14 that John saw the 144,000 in Heaven. So this is a separate rapture quite some time after Mid-Tribulation. When the seventh seal is opened in chapter 8, all of Heaven stands in awe for thirty minutes of silence. The opening of the seventh seal reveals seven angels with seven trumpets, preparing themselves to sound.

Those seven angels with seven trumpets fit perfectly with the scriptural profile of Joshua marching around the city of Jericho for six days with seven priests blowing seven trumpets. I believe it foreshadowed the seven angelic trumpets that will bring the judgment of God upon the wicked world. As the first angelic trumpet sounds, it sets in motion a seven-stage progression of God's wrath upon a wicked, unbelieving world.

THE SECOND ADVENT, OR THE RAPTURE?

Matthew 24:26 **Wherefore if they shall say unto you, Behold, he is in the desert; go not forth: behold, he is in the secret chambers; believe it not.**
27 For as the lightning cometh out of the east, and shineth even unto the west; so shall also the coming of the Son of man be.
28 For wheresoever the carcase is, there will the eagles be gathered together.

Verse 28 is the key verse which reveals that the context of verses 28-29 are in reference to the Second Advent rather than the Rapture. Verse 28 is a preface to what Jesus is about to reveal in verses 29-31. This plainly reveals it to be the same event as described in Revelation 19:17-18, when the angel will cry with a loud voice for all of the fowls of the earth to come and feast on kings and great men of the earth. The carcass to which Jesus gives reference (v. 28) is of the Antichrist as well as the armies that follow him. These will all be slain when Christ comes back with His saints at the end of the Tribulation.

When comparing Matthew 24:29-30 with Revelation 19:11-13 and Isaiah 13:9-11,13, you will recognize that all of these Scriptures are describing the Second Advent—when Christ returns to earth to set up His kingdom.

Matthew 24:29 **Immediately after the tribulation of those days shall the sun be darkened, and the moon** shall not give her light, and the stars shall fall from heaven, and the powers of the heavens shall be shaken: 30 And then shall appear the sign of the Son of man in heaven: and then shall all the tribes of the earth mourn, and they shall see the Son of man coming in the clouds of heaven with power and great glory.

Revelation 19:11 And I saw heaven opened, and behold a white horse; and he that sat upon him was called Faithful and True, and in righteousness he doth judge and make war.
12 His eyes were as a flame of fire, and on his head were many crowns; and he had a name written, that no man knew, but he himself.
13 And he was clothed with a vesture dipped in blood: and his name is called The Word of God.

Isaiah 13:9 Behold, the day of the Lord cometh, cruel both with wrath and fierce anger, to lay the land desolate: and he shall destroy the sinners thereof out of it.
10 For the stars of heaven and the constellations thereof shall not give their light: the sun shall be darkened in his going forth, and the moon shall not cause her light to shine.
11 And I will punish the world for their evil, and the wicked for their iniquity; and I will cause the arrogancy of the proud to cease, and will lay low the haughtiness of the terrible.
13 Therefore I will shake the heavens, and the earth shall remove out of her place, in the wrath of the Lord of hosts, and in the day of his fierce anger.

It is obvious that Isaiah is describing the very same event that Jesus described in Matthew 24:29-30. There are some who interpret these verses to mean that Christ is coming to catch away the Church immediately after the Tribulation. But that is not the meaning portrayed in these verses. Many Scriptures confirm verses 29-30 to be the Second Advent rather than the Rapture. (Isaiah 34:1-4; Ezekiel 39:1-7; Joel 2:1-3; Revelation 11:15-19; 19:11-21.)

THE SECOND ADVENT: ALL ON EARTH SHALL SEE HIM

Matthew 24:30 **And then shall appear the sign of the Son of man in heaven: and then shall all the tribes of the earth mourn, and they shall see the Son of man coming in the clouds of heaven with power and great glory.**

This verse cannot possibly refer to the Rapture, for when the Rapture takes place, no one will see Him except those who are looking for Him to appear. **"So Christ was once offered to bear the sins of many; and unto them that look for him shall he appear the second time without sin unto salvation"** (Hebrews 9:28).

Matthew 24:29-30 is a vivid description of Christ's Second Advent. It signals the end of the Tribulation Period and the beginning of a 1000-year reign of peace on the earth. (See Zechariah 14:1-13.) The first time all who dwell on the earth will see Him will be at His Second Advent as He descends on the Mount of Olives.

Not many years ago, people were saying, "That couldn't happen! It's impossible for everyone to see Him!" But with satellite news coverage as competitive as it is today, I believe CNN as well as many other TV networks will be there to broadcast Christ's Second Advent live via satellite and it will be seen around the world.

Allow me to give my view of what will be happening at the time of Christ's return to set up His kingdom. The armies of the Antichrist will have joined forces with a 200 million-man army from the Orient and will be coming down the Valley of Megiddo against Israel. Their purpose will be to totally annihilate Israel before Christ comes to establish His kingdom. At the time of

Christ's return, angels will have been flying above the earth, preaching the Gospel for more than three years. (Revelation 14.)

I believe CNN as well as many other TV networks will be there to broadcast Christ's Second Advent....

It is also possible that as the angels fly through the heavens they will be proclaiming that Christ is coming to set up His kingdom.

If that happens, there is no doubt that there will be TV cameras all over the mountains and valleys around Jerusalem to broadcast Christ's return.

WHEN JESUS RETURNS TO EARTH

When Christ descends on Mount Olivet, the mountain will split in half from the east to the west. Then, half will shift north and the other half south, creating a valley all the way to Jerusalem. The people in the city will flee to the valley to avoid total destruction by the Antichrist and his armies. God will protect Israel from certain destruction and gather her together again.

Compare these accounts in the following Scriptures:

Matthew 24:31 **And he shall send his angels with a great sound of a trumpet, and they shall gather together his elect from the four winds, from one end of heaven to the other.**

Micah 4:6 **In that day, saith the Lord, will I assemble her that halteth, and I will gather her that is driven out, and her that I have afflicted;**
7 And I will make her that halted a remnant, and her that was cast far off a strong nation: and the Lord shall reign over them in mount Zion from henceforth, even for ever.

Compare the above Scriptures with Isaiah 11:11-12:

11 And it shall come to pass in that day, that the Lord shall set his hand again the second time to recover the remnant of his people, which shall be left, from Assyria, and from Egypt, and from Pathros, and from Cush, and from Elam, and from Shinar, and from Hamath, and from the islands of the sea.

12 And he shall set up an ensign for the nations, and shall assemble the outcasts of Israel, and gather together the dispersed of Judah from the four corners of the earth.

In Matthew 24:29-30 Jesus did a marvelous job of pointing us to Revelation 19:11-21 and Zechariah 14:1-4, which are other prophetic utterances of the same event He described. These verses should leave no doubt that it is the Day of the Lord. The prophet Zechariah gives an overall view of this event.

Zechariah 14:1 **Behold, the day of the Lord cometh, and thy spoil shall be divided in the midst of thee.**

2 For I will gather all nations against Jerusalem to battle; and the city shall be taken, and the houses rifled, and the women ravished; and half of the city shall go forth into captivity, and the residue of the people shall not be cut off from the city.

3 Then shall the Lord go forth, and fight against those nations, as when he fought in the day of battle.

4 And his feet shall stand in that day upon the mount of Olives, which is before Jerusalem on the east, and the mount of Olives shall cleave in the midst thereof toward the east and toward the west, and there shall be a very great valley; and half of the mountain shall remove toward the north, and half of it toward the south.

God will make a way of escape for the people of Israel as the Antichrist and the armies with him move toward Jerusalem to annihilate them. Christ's coming seems to be split-second timing to deliver the Jews who are still in the city. However, most of the Israelis will still be hid away in other nations in order to escape the fury of the Antichrist. Those in Jerusalem will have to be ready to flee to the valley quickly. This is the purpose of Jesus' warning in Matthew 24:16-18. If they are on the housetop, they are not to get anything out of the house before they flee for their lives. This plainly puts it at the Second Advent and the Battle of Armageddon.

GATHERING TOGETHER HIS ELECT

Many times in the prophetic Scriptures when the phrase *in that day* is used, it is referring to the Second Advent. It is the beginning of the 1000-year day, the millennial reign of Christ. Let's compare Matthew's account of the event with that of Mark.

Matthew 24:31 **And he shall send his angels with a great sound of a trumpet, and they shall gather together his elect from the four winds, from one end of heaven to the other.**

Mark 13:27 **And then shall he send his angels, and shall gather together his elect from the four winds, from the uttermost part of the earth to the uttermost part of heaven.**

Mark's account states that it is from the **"uttermost part of the earth to the uttermost part of heaven."** This has been construed by some to mean the Rapture of the Church. But that concept does not agree with the prophetic Word.

The prophetic Scriptures plainly reveal this to be the Second Advent. It is evident from Isaiah's account that God will gather the remnant of Israel who have survived the seven years of tribulation as well as those born-again Jews who were caught up in the Rapture. He will gather those who are scattered on earth, and He will also bring back with Him those who were with Him in Heaven.

Let's look once again at Isaiah's prophecy concerning this event.

> Isaiah 11:11 **And it shall come to pass in that day, that the Lord shall set his hand again the second time to recover the remnant of his people, which shall be left, from Assyria, and from Egypt, and from Pathros, and from Cush, and from Elam, and from Shinar, and from Hamath, and from the islands of the sea.**
> **12 And he shall set up an ensign for the nations, and shall assemble the outcasts of Israel, and gather together the dispersed of Judah from the four corners of the earth.**

Notice, in verse 12, the phrase **"four corners of the earth."** In the other Scriptures from Matthew and Mark's gospels, it uses the phrase *four winds* (Matthew 24:31, Mark 13:27), which means "from the earth." The same verse in Matthew says, **"...from one end of heaven to the other."** I believe the reference here is to the Jewish people who were already born again at the time of the Rapture. They will be in Heaven. He is going to gather them out of Heaven and bring them back to the earth with Him. He will bring both groups together here on earth. No doubt the angels will be involved in gathering together all of the Jews that have been hidden away in other nations at that same time.

These verses are not in reference to the Rapture, because the Church will have already been in Heaven for seven years. At the time of this event, they will be returning with Christ when He descends on the Mount of Olives. John confirms that the Church is in Heaven in Revelation 5:9-10 before the first seal is opened in Revelation 6:1.

Now let's compare Psalm 101:7-8 with 2 Thessalonians 2:8. Both of these are referring to the destruction of the wicked of the world and the Antichrist.

> Psalm 101:7 **He that worketh deceit shall not dwell within my house: he that telleth lies shall not tarry in my sight.**

8 I will early destroy all the wicked of the land; that I may cut off all wicked doers from the city of the Lord.

2 Thessalonians 2:8 **And then shall that Wicked be revealed, whom the Lord shall consume with the spirit of his mouth, and shall destroy with the brightness of his coming.**

This takes place when Christ comes back with all the armies of Heaven. As stated in Psalm 101:8, He will **"early destroy all the wicked of the land."** A major part of wickedness in the earth will be destroyed at the Second Advent, but not all wickedness will be removed until the end of the 1000-year reign of Christ on the earth. (Revelation 20.)

WHEN WILL ALL THESE THINGS OCCUR?

Matthew 24:36 **But of that day and hour knoweth no man, no, not the angels of heaven, but my Father only.**

At the time of this writing, no man knows the day or the hour of the Rapture or the Second Advent, for God has put this in His own power. If we knew the day and hour of the Second Advent, we could count back exactly seven years and know the exact date of the Rapture. Then, on the other hand, if we knew the time of the Rapture, we could add seven years and have the exact date of the Second Advent. The Rapture will take place seven years before Christ's return to the earth to set up His earthly kingdom.

JUDGMENT UPON THE WICKED

Matthew 24:37 **But as the days of Noe were, so shall also the coming of the Son of man be.**
38 **For as in the days that were before the flood they were eating and drinking, marrying and giving in marriage, until the day that Noe entered into the ark,**

39 And knew not until the flood came, and took them all away; so shall also the coming of the Son of man be.
40 Then shall two be in the field; the one shall be taken, and the other left.
41 Two women shall be grinding at the mill; the one shall be taken, and the other left.

Please take note of the emphasis in these verses, for herein lies another key. They **"knew not until the flood came, and took them all away..."** The main emphasis of verses 37-41 seems to be the fact that the wicked did not know the time of their impending doom until judgment came and they were destroyed.

The Rapture will take place seven years before Christ's return to the earth to set up His earthly kingdom.

It has been taught for years that verses 40-41 refer to one being raptured and the other left, but that is not the case at all. A closer examination of these verses prove that Jesus was referring to His Second Advent as recorded in Revelation 19:11-21 and Zechariah 14:1-5.

It sounds somewhat like the Rapture, but remember the statement of Psalm 101:8, **"I will early destroy all the wicked of the land."** Every person who follows the Antichrist and his armies or takes the mark of the beast will be destroyed at that time. However, there will also be people among them who have not rebelled against God. They will refuse to take the mark of the beast. Therefore, they will be spared from the judgment of God at that particular time.

THE ANTICHRIST'S EXPLANATION OF THE RAPTURE

Have you ever wondered how the Antichrist is going to explain what happened to all the missing people?

His message is being preached even now. His message is, "There is no Rapture. God is not going to take the righteous, but the *wicked* from the earth."

Therefore, the Antichrist's explanation of millions of people missing when the Rapture takes place will probably be, "God has taken the wicked out of the earth; and I am the one who will bring peace." The Scripture states that by peace he shall destroy many. (Daniel 8:25.)

But the truth is, God is going to take the righteous out of the earth seven years before He destroys a major part of the wicked at the Second Advent.

NOAH'S DAY REVISITED

In Matthew 24, Jesus refers to "Noah's day" because Noah and his family represented all of the righteous on the earth at that time. They were taken into the safety of the ark *before* the judgment of God was released on the earth. Notice that His emphasis is really on the fact that the wicked didn't know what was coming until after Noah had escaped to safety. Then the flood came and took the wicked away.

Luke, in his account, gives the clearest understanding of this discourse. In fact, I believe the keys to understanding this clearly are found in Luke 17. We will study them in detail in later chapters.

Let's look again at 2 Peter, chapter 3, so this information will be fresh in our minds. In these verses, we find some key statements that will help us understand how Jesus subtly revealed the Rapture and Second Advent in Luke 17.

2 Peter 3:3 **Knowing this first, that there shall come in the last days scoffers, walking after their own lusts,**
4 And saying, Where is the promise of his coming? for since the fathers fell asleep, all things continue as they were from the beginning of the creation.

5 For this they willingly are ignorant of, that by the word of God the heavens were of old, and the earth standing out of the water and in the water:
6 Whereby the world that then was, being overflowed with water, perished.

It seems that verse 5 has a double reference. In one sense it refers to the flood mentioned in Genesis 1:2. But it also refers to what we call "Noah's flood," which destroyed the wicked from the earth in his day.

Then verse 7 gives us a valuable key to understanding five end-time events.

2 Peter 3:7 **But the heavens and the earth, which are now, by the SAME WORD are kept in store, reserved unto fire against the day of judgment and perdition of ungodly men.**

The same instructions God gave to Noah just before the flood will give us great insight into the sequence and timing of the fire and destruction that will one day destroy a major part of the wicked of the earth. So let's look again at God's instructions to Noah:

Genesis 7:1 **And the Lord said unto Noah, Come thou and all thy house into the ark; for thee have I seen righteous before me in this generation.**

Noah's family, who were all the righteous in his generation, portray an excellent parallel of the Church (Body of Christ) being the righteous in this generation.

Genesis 7:4 **For yet seven days, and I will cause it to rain upon the earth forty days and forty nights; and every living substance that I have made will I destroy from off the face of the earth.**
10 And it came to pass after seven days, that the waters of the flood were upon the earth.

This same word that God gave Noah reveals five end-time events and their sequence and timing. Here is a quick synopsis of that revelation:

(1) The Rapture of the Church is revealed by the fact that Noah's family (the righteous) were lifted up above the earth before the flood destroyed all life.

(2) The Tribulation Period and its length is revealed by the fact that the flood began the day Noah entered into safety, and it took seven days for the flood to cover the earth (representing the Antichrist's flood of deception for seven years).

(3) The Second Advent is revealed in the fact that Noah came back to earth after the flood.

(4) The 1000-year reign of Christ is revealed by the fact that Noah and his righteous family ruled the earth after their return.

(5) The purging from the earth of all wickedness at the end of the seven thousandth year is revealed by the fact that after seven days (representing 7000 years of human history), the judgment of God destroyed all the wicked from the earth.

Genesis 7:4 contains what I call *layered* revelation.

First, it has a natural meaning concerning events that actually happened in Noah's day. Secondly, it is a prophetic revelation of future events. God gave Noah seven natural days to make preparation and get into the ark of safety before judgment came. In this verse, we see a parallel truth in the fact that mankind also has a total of seven days (7000 years) to get prepared to escape the White Throne Judgment. All the wicked of the earth will face this judgment at the end of the Seventh Millennium. (Revelation 20.)

It is also a prophetic revelation of the Rapture of the right-eous (Body of Christ) before the Antichrist releases a flood of deception upon the earth.

It reveals the Tribulation Period to be seven years long as in Daniel's Seventieth Week where a day represents a year by double reference. The sabbath, or Millennium of rest, will follow the Tribulation. Destruction of all wickedness from planet Earth will occur at the end of seven days, representing 7000 years of human history. (Revelation 20.)

These statements may seem vague at this point, but as we look at the revelation God gave Daniel, they will come into sharper focus.

DANIEL'S DREAM

The ninth chapter of Daniel records Daniel's dream, which is another prophetic Scripture that gives us a key to understanding this revelation. Daniel had a vision, or a dream, and the angel Gabriel came to explain it to him.

> **21 Yea, whiles I was speaking in prayer, even the man Gabriel, whom I had seen in the vision at the beginning, being caused to fly swiftly, touched me about the time of the evening oblation.**
> **22 And he informed me, and talked with me, and said, O Daniel, I am now come forth to give thee skill and understanding.**
> **24 Seventy weeks are determined upon thy people and upon thy holy city, to finish the transgression, and to make an end of sins, and to make reconciliation for iniquity, and to bring in everlasting righteousness, and to seal up the vision and prophecy, and to anoint the most Holy.**
> **25 Know therefore and understand, that from the going forth of the commandment to restore and to**

build Jerusalem unto the Messiah the Prince shall be seven weeks, and threescore and two weeks: the street shall be built again, and the wall, even in troublous times. 26 And after threescore and two weeks shall Messiah be cut off, but not for himself: and the people of the prince that shall come shall destroy the city and the sanctuary; and the end thereof shall be with a flood, and unto the end of the war desolations are determined.

The first prince referred to in verse 25 is Christ the Messiah. The *people of the prince* refers to the Romans who destroyed Jerusalem in A.D. 70. The spirit of the Antichrist was already operating through them. That is evident from the phrase *people of the prince*—in other words, people who were under the influence of the Antichrist's spirit. Remember also that Jesus said, **"The prince of this world** [shall] **be cast out"** (John 12:31).

Daniel continues to give us revelation in verse 27 of a "Covenant of Peace" which the Antichrist will confirm with many for seven years. But he will break this covenant after three-and-one-half years.

Daniel 9:27 **And he shall confirm the covenant with many for one week: and in the midst of the week he shall cause the sacrifice and the oblation to cease, and for the overspreading of abominations he shall make it desolate, even until the consummation, and that determined shall be poured upon the desolate.**

Let's compare *The Amplified Bible:*

Daniel 9:27 AMP **And he shall enter into a strong and firm covenant with the many for one week [seven years]. And in the midst of the week he shall cause the sacrifice and offering to cease [for the remaining three and one-half years]; and upon the wing or pinnacle of abominations [shall come] one who makes desolate, until the full determined end is poured out on the desolator.**

It is clear from the revelation the angel brought to Daniel that God had determined He would deal with Israel for a total of 490 years. Then at the end of that time period, sin would cease and He would bring everlasting righteousness to Jerusalem.

GOD IS THE TIMEKEEPER

When God gives His Word on a matter, you can rest assured that it is going to happen exactly that way. Since God Himself is the Timekeeper of all prophetic events, He has the ability to stop His time clock of dealing with Israel whenever He desires and shift His attention to another event for a period of time. Then after He has fulfilled other prophetic events, He can again start His time clock and pick up where He left off to continue on until complete fulfillment. That is exactly what happened concerning the Seventy Weeks of Daniel, which are weeks of years.

When the Jews closed their eyes to Christ and cried out for the Romans to crucify Him, God turned His time clock off and turned to the Gentiles for two days, or 2000 years, which are generally referred to as *the last days*. However, it seems that the last days might also include the 1000-year reign of Christ, for eternity will begin at the end of that millennial reign.

We are also aware that Daniel's Seventieth Week is a week of years—an exact period of seven years. The Hebrew word used for "week" comes from the word *heptad*,[1] which means seven years— just as the word "decade" means ten years. One week of years (seven years) remains in which God will deal with Israel. That seven-year period, which is also referred to as Jacob's Trouble and the Tribulation, is on God's time clock and seems to begin ticking again immediately after the Church is raptured.

That period of time, and especially the last three-and-one-half years, will be very devastating to Israel. However, all of Israel who survive the seven-year period will be saved along with multitudes of Gentiles.

When God gives His Word on a matter, you can rest assured that it is going to happen exactly that way.

Then, at the end of the Tribulation Period (Daniel's Seventieth Week), Christ will return to the earth with the saints that were raptured and set up His kingdom of righteous rule in Jerusalem. This will usher in 1000 years of peace—the last Millennium before eternity. In the next chapter we will look at how Daniel's weeks and Noah's flood fit into Jesus' end-time prophecy in Luke 17.

Fitting Prophetic Scriptures in Place

In the previous chapter, we covered some important information concerning the Seventieth Week of Daniel. The information was necessary to help understand the discourse given by Jesus in Luke 17. When it is fitted together into its proper place in Jesus' teaching, it causes other pieces of the prophetic puzzle to fall into place. The end result is marvelous insight into certain end-time events.

Luke 17:20 **And when he was demanded of the Pharisees, when the kingdom of God should come, he answered them and said, The kingdom of God cometh not with observation:**
21 Neither shall they say, Lo here! or, lo there! for, behold, the kingdom of God is within you.
22 And he said unto the disciples, The days will come, when ye shall desire to see one of the days of the Son of man, and ye shall not see it.
23 And they shall say to you, See here; or, see there: go not after them, nor follow them.
24 For as the lightning, that lighteneth out of the one part under heaven, shineth unto the other part under heaven; so shall also the Son of man be in his day.
25 But first must He suffer many things, and be rejected of this generation.

The phrase *his day* in verse 24 refers to the day of Christ's coming to earth (the Second Advent) at the end of the Tribulation. At that time, He will destroy the armies of the Antichrist and his armies and begin His 1000-year day of righteous rule. The Latin word *mille* means "one thousand." This is why we refer to it as the millennial reign of Christ.

This phrase **"But first must he suffer many things, and be rejected of this generation"** (v. 25) fits in place at the end of the sixty-ninth week of the period called Daniel's Seventy Weeks. It was at that time, when Christ was rejected by His generation and crucified, that God turned to the Gentiles. This leaves one week of the seventy-week prophecy of Daniel unfulfilled. (Daniel 9:25-26.)

Jesus Christ was the beginning of the Church Age, and He will end the Church Age and bring it to completion by catching away the Church (His Body) just before the Antichrist is revealed to the world. (Colossians 1:12-19; 2 Thessalonians 2:1-8; Revelation 4:1; 1:7-8.)

THE FLOOD OF THE ANTICHRIST

Jesus indicated that the same prosperity and social life that existed in the days of Noah will exist in the days of the coming of the Son of Man.

> Luke 17:26 **And as it was in the days of Noe, so shall it be also in the days of the Son of man.**
> **27 They did eat, they drank, they married wives, they were given in marriage, until the day that Noe entered into the ark, and the flood came, and destroyed them all.**

These verses have a double reference, or what we call "layered revelation." In other words, there are many revelations in these and other related verses. Let's look again at key verses in Genesis 7:

7 And Noah went in, and his sons, and his wife, and his sons' wives with him, into the ark, because of the waters of the flood.

10 And it came to pass after seven days, that the waters of the flood were upon the earth.

13 In the selfsame day entered Noah, and Shem, and Ham, and Japheth, the sons of Noah, and Noah's wife, and the three wives of his sons with them, into the ark.

God's words to Noah had their present fulfillment in Noah's day. But they will also have a prophetic fulfillment in the near future.

When the Church is taken out of the way, there will be nothing to restrain the ambition of the Antichrist.

The literal fulfillment came exactly seven days after Noah entered the ark. Seven days after God spoke those words to Noah, the flood covered the earth. According to verse 7, Noah and his family went into the ark because of the waters of the flood. It is obvious that the rain started the day they entered the ark of safety. I believe this subtly reveals that the Antichrist begins his flood of deception upon the earth immediately after the righteous are removed from the earth.

When the Church is taken out of the way, there will be nothing to restrain the ambition of the Antichrist. It is very likely he will make his move as soon as the newspaper headlines and television newscasts reveal that millions of people have suddenly disappeared from the earth without a trace. His explanation will probably be, "God has removed the wicked from the earth, and I am the man of peace. I have come to bring peace to the earth."

Just as literal rain covered the earth in seven days, so will the Antichrist (Man of Sin) release a flood of deception and unrestrained perversion upon the earth during the seven years of tribulation. Then Christ will return with the saints from Heaven and forever end the Antichrist's ungodly ambitions. This concept corresponds perfectly with Isaiah's prophecy.

> Isaiah 59:18 **According to their deeds, accordingly he will repay, fury to his adversaries, recompence to his enemies; to the islands he will repay recompence.**
> **19 So shall they fear the name of the Lord from the west, and his glory from the rising of the sun. When the enemy shall come in** LIKE A FLOOD**, the Spirit of the Lord shall lift up a standard against him.**
> **20 And the Redeemer shall come to Zion, and unto them that turn from transgression in Jacob, saith the Lord.**

The Redeemer coming to Zion is none other than Christ coming to Jerusalem at the end of the seven years of tribulation to begin His earthly rule and reign for 1000 years. For further confirmation see Isaiah 60.

TRANSITION FROM RAPTURE TO SECOND ADVENT

As we apply the key found in 2 Peter 3:8, "**...one day is with the Lord as a thousand years, and a thousand years as one day,**" we can see the revelation Peter revealed so subtly in 2 Peter 3:7. "**But the heavens and the earth, which are now, by the same word** (that God gave Noah) **are kept in store, reserved unto fire against the day of judgment....**" In other words, He gave Noah the same word with one exception, and that being that the judgment will be by fire instead of water.

When we apply this key to the same word God gave Noah, it reveals that after "seven days," representing 7000 years, God's judgment on the wicked of the earth will be by fire. This places that judgment at the end of the millennial reign, which corresponds perfectly with the prophetic Scriptures of Revelation, chapter 20. We have already discovered that this same time frame was subtly revealed in the Genesis account by the six days that

God labored over creation and rested on the seventh day, having finished (perfected) His work for that particular six-day period.

The prophetic seventh day will be the millennial reign. Then, after that 1000 years of rest (peace), all wickedness will be totally destroyed from the earth.

The prophetic implications of the Rapture are also obvious in the fact that Noah and his family (the righteous) were in safety when the flood began.

But if you don't catch the transition made in Luke 17:28-30 from the days of Noah to the days of Lot, you will most likely misinterpret which end-time event Jesus is referring to in verses 28-37.

The first parallel given was of Noah being caught up away from the judgment of God, which parallels the Rapture of the Church. Let's take a closer look at the transition verses.

> Luke 17:28 **Likewise also as it was in the days of Lot; they did eat, they drank, they bought, they sold, they planted, they builded;**
> **29 But THE SAME DAY that Lot went out of Sodom IT RAINED FIRE AND BRIMSTONE FROM HEAVEN, AND DESTROYED THEM ALL.**
> **30 Even thus shall it be in the day when the Son of man is revealed.**

In these verses Jesus refers to destruction which comes by fire and brimstone. This places it prophetically in Revelation 14:10, 19:11-21, and Psalm 11:6. We know that there was no fire or brimstone connected with the destruction in the days of Noah's flood. It is evident that Jesus changed the subject matter and gave details that have been left out of previous verses.

Luke 17:28-30 clearly reveals that Jesus is referring to the Second Advent, in which He will descend with the saints upon the Mount of Olives. (Zechariah 14:1-5.)

LOT, A TYPE OF THE REMNANT OF ISRAEL

In these verses, Lot represents the remnant of Israel that Christ will save from the armies of the Antichrist at the Second Advent. When His feet touch the Mount of Olives, there will be a great earthquake which will split the mountain in half from east to west. Then one half will shift north and the other half will shift south. This will create a great valley all the way to Jerusalem. (Zechariah 14:4.) At that time Christ's coming will be in split-second timing. The armies of the Antichrist and other armies with him will have come as a storm and as a flood upon the land in their last effort to destroy Israel.

The people in Jerusalem at that time will be able to flee to the valley created by the earthquake—just in the nick of time to escape. Fire and brimstone will rain from Heaven on the Antichrist and the armies that are with him, destroying them all. (Zechariah 14:1-5,12-13; Psalm 11:6; Luke 17:30; Isaiah 59:19-21.)

These verses make it clear that Jesus is *not* referring to the Rapture in Luke 17:28-30 but rather to the Second Advent. Every detail fits perfectly in place with the prophetic Scriptures.

Now, let's compare Jesus' statements in Luke 17:29-30 with Isaiah 66:15-16 and Psalm 11:6.

Luke 17:29 **But the same day that Lot went out of Sodom it rained fire and brimstone from heaven, and destroyed them all.**
30 Even thus shall it be in the day WHEN THE SON OF MAN IS REVEALED.

Isaiah 66:15 **For, behold, the Lord will come with fire, and with his chariots like a whirlwind, to render his anger with fury, and his rebuke with flames of fire.**
16 For by fire and by his sword will the Lord plead with all flesh: and the slain of the Lord shall be many.

Psalm 11:6 **Upon the wicked he shall rain snares, fire and brimstone, and an horrible tempest: this shall be the portion of their cup.**

In Luke 17:30 the phrase **"...when the Son of man is revealed"** must of necessity refer to His Second Advent, when He will be seen by all who dwell on the earth, as described in Matthew 24:30.

Several years ago, we could not have understood how that would be possible. But with today's inventions and high technology, we know that it can easily be done.

I believe the network crews from CNN, ABC, NBC, and CBS will be there to cover Christ's return to earth. I believe the angels will have proclaimed the message that "The Messiah is coming to set up His kingdom in Jerusalem!" I'm sure much of the world will scoff at their predictions, but *the world* will be watching via satellite as this event takes place before their eyes.

AFTER THE TRIBULATION IN THOSE DAYS

Comparing Matthew 24:29-30 with Zechariah 12:9-11 is confirmation that these Scriptures are describing the very same event, the Second Advent.

Matthew 24:29 **Immediately after the tribulation of those days shall the sun be darkened, and the moon shall not give her light, and the stars shall fall from heaven, and the powers of the heavens shall be shaken: 30 And then shall appear the sign of the Son of man in heaven: and then shall all the tribes of the earth mourn, and they shall see the Son of man coming in the clouds of heaven with power and great glory.**

Zechariah 12:9 **And it shall come to pass in that day, that I will seek to destroy all the nations that come against Jerusalem.**

10 And I will pour upon the house of David, and upon the inhabitants of Jerusalem, the spirit of grace and of supplications: AND THEY SHALL LOOK UPON ME WHOM THEY HAVE PIERCED, and they shall mourn for him, as one mourneth for his only son, and shall be in bitterness for him, as one that is in bitterness for his firstborn.
11 In that day shall there be a great mourning in Jerusalem, as the mourning of Hadadrimmon in the valley of Megiddon.

The prophet Joel also adds dimension to this event:

Joel 3:12 Let the heathen be wakened, and come up to the valley of Jehoshaphat: for there will I sit to judge all the heathen round about.
13 Put ye in the sickle, for the harvest is ripe: come, get you down; for the press is full, the vats overflow; for their wickedness is great.
14 Multitudes, multitudes in the valley of decision: for the day of the Lord is near in the valley of decision.
15 The sun and the moon shall be darkened, and the stars shall withdraw their shining.
16 The Lord also shall roar out of Zion, and utter his voice from Jerusalem; and the heavens and the earth shall shake: but the Lord will be the hope of his people, and the strength of the children of Israel.

It is evident from these Scriptures that all these prophecies are revealing the Second Advent, referred to as the Day of the Lord. Now we can understand why Jesus gave the warning found in Luke 17:31-32.

JESUS SOUNDS WARNING

"In that day, he which shall be upon the housetop, and his stuff in the house, let him not come down to take it away: and he that is in the field, let him likewise not return back. Remember Lot's wife."

LOT'S WIFE

The statement by Jesus **"Remember Lot's wife"** is another detail that fits perfectly into this end-time event.

Lot's wife hesitated for an instant to look back. As a result of her disobedience, she lost her life. (Genesis 19:26.) This warning should be heeded by those who will be in Jerusalem at the time of Christ's Second Advent.

Jesus is emphatic about this warning: "Don't go into the house to retrieve anything." In other words, don't take time to get food or clothing, for the Antichrist's armies will have already taken half the city and the 200 million-man army from the Orient of Revelation 9:16 will be coming down the Valley of Megiddo with weapons of mass destruction. It seems this will be a desperate attempt to totally destroy Israel.

Jesus warns those who will be present at the time of this event not to look back or to hesitate for any reason. Their lives will depend on their obedience in heeding His warnings.

> Luke 17:33 **Whosoever shall seek to save his life shall lose it; and whosoever shall lose his life shall preserve it.**
> **34 I tell you, in that night there shall be two men in one bed; the one shall be taken, and the other shall be left.**
> **35 Two women shall be grinding together; the one shall be taken, and the other left.**
> **36 Two men shall be in the field; the one shall be taken, and the other left.**
> **37 And they answered and said unto him, Where, Lord? And he said unto them, Wheresoever the body is, thither will the eagles be gathered together.**

When viewed in the light of Revelation 19:17-20, this verse plainly reveals the events Jesus described to be the Second Advent. Although many have supposed that these verses dealt with the Rapture, it does not fit into the right time slot in the prophetic Scriptures. The description given in verses 34-36 does sound somewhat similar to the Rapture, until we read verse 37. Then it's very clear that verses 28-37 are a description of the event referred to in Revelation 19:11-21—which is the Second Advent.

JUDGMENT COMES

The question is often asked, "Why would one be taken (destroyed) and the other be left?" The answer is that this describes an act of judgment. It could even be called a search and destory Mission. It is the destruction of the wicked who have followed the Antichrist. This corresponds perfectly with Revelation 19:17-18.

CRY OF THE ANGEL

Revelation 19:17 **And I saw an angel standing in the sun; and he cried with a loud voice, saying to all the fowls that fly in the midst of heaven, Come and gather yourselves together unto the supper of the great God;**
18 That ye may eat the flesh of kings, and the flesh of captains, and the flesh of mighty men, and the flesh of horses, and of them that sit on them, and the flesh of all men, both free and bond, both small and great.

Then Psalm 101:8 gives another prophetic view:

8 I will early destroy all the wicked of the land; that I may cut off all wicked doers from the city of the Lord.

It is evident from these Scriptures that the angels, as well as Christ Himself, will be involved in taking out the wicked that followed the Antichrist at the end of the Tribulation. This fits prophetically with the discourse of Jesus in Luke 17:29-37. Christ and His angels will destroy the Antichrist and his followers, including all those who take the mark of the beast. As you can see, the prophetic Scriptures reveal that a major part of the wicked will be removed from the earth (destroyed) as Christ returns with the saints as described in Revelation 19:11-21 and Joel 3:9-16.

These Scriptures should be enough evidence to conclude that Jesus' words in Luke 17:28-37 are in reference to the Second Advent, but let's compare other Scriptures. *The Amplified Bible* states, "...Wherever the dead body is, there will the vultures (or eagles) be gathered together" (Luke 17:37). "Wheresoever the* body is, thither will the eagles be gathered together"(KJV).*

> *Christ and His angels will destroy the Antichrist and his followers, including all those who take the mark of the beast.*

Job 39:27 **Doth the eagle mount up at thy command, and make her nest on high?**
28 She dwelleth and abideth on the rock, upon the crag of the rock, and the strong place.
29 From thence she seeketh the prey, and her eyes behold afar off.
30 Her young ones also suck up blood: and where the slain are, there is she.

TWO HARVESTS FROM THE EARTH

The Bible reveals that there are two harvests of the earth. First, the harvest of the good wheat (the righteous) in Matthew

---

*The Greek word *soma,* translated *body,* is also used of a group of people, large or small. Verse 37 is in reference to the body of the wicked (tares) that have been gathered together in groups of bundles to be destroyed.

13:30 and 1 Thessalonians 4:16-17. Second, the harvest of the tares (wicked) in Matthew 13:40-42 and Revelation 14:15-20.

The parable of the tares, given by Jesus in Matthew 13, is actually a double parable, much the same as the one given in John 10:1-10. In both of these instances, Jesus lays out the parable which contains progressive revelation. In both instances (Matthew 13 and John 10), when asked to explain the parable, Jesus gives progressive revelation in a different form which covers two different time periods.

Here is a bottom-line synopsis. When the tares, which had been planted by an enemy, were discovered, the servant wanted to gather them up immediately.

Matthew 13:29 **But he said, Nay; lest while ye gather up the tares, ye root up also the wheat with them.**
30 Let both grow together UNTIL **the harvest: and in the time of harvest I will say to the reapers, Gather ye together first the tares, and bind them in bundles to burn them....**

We know from the information that Jesus reveals later in verse 39 that the reapers are the angels. They were instructed to "gather together first the tares, and bind them in bundles to burn them."

I believe this plainly represents what we are seeing today. The homosexuals are coming out of the closet demanding special rights. The wicked all over the world are gravitating toward each other. Terrorist groups are being formed all over the world. Notice in the parable, the tares were first recognized during fruiting season. However, they were not gathered in groups until harvest season. This reveals that we have entered into the time of harvest. We are seeing a special bond between the wicked of the world as never before in any generation. I believe time and angelic influence are causing the wicked to gravitate into bundles to be bound so they don't pollute or hinder the harvest.

In the parable of the tares, Jesus reveals **"...He that soweth the good seed is the Son of man"** (Matthew 13:37). Jesus was the One Who planted the good wheat (righteous seed) in the earth expecting a bountiful harvest.

John 12:24 **Verily, verily, I say unto you, Except a corn of wheat fall into the ground and die, it abideth alone: but if it die, it bringeth forth much fruit.**

Jesus was the (wheat) seed that willfully died to be planted in the earth to bring forth a harvest of good wheat. The fact that the wicked are coming together reveals that we have entered into the harvest season. The revelation Jesus gave in verse 30 reveals a general time frame for the first harvest of the earth.

The first sign of harvest is the wicked being brought together in bundles or groups. They are being brought together to be bound so they can't hinder or pollute the harvest. The very next event is the gathering of the wheat into His barn. This is a prophetic revelation of the first harvest of the earth which I believe to include a great in-gathering of souls into the kingdom of God just before the Rapture of the Church. Allow me to reiterate that at the time of this writing we are in the time of harvest and the season of His appearing. However, the harvest may have taken place by the time some of you read this book.

Later the disciples asked Jesus to declare unto them the parable of the tares. His explanation is similar in many ways, but it adds progressive revelation of a second harvest of the wicked from the earth at a later date, which is not connected with gathering of the good wheat into His barn. In verse 38, He reveals the field to be the world. The good seed are the children of the kingdom, but the tares are the children of the wicked one.

Verses 39 and 40 reveal the enemy that sowed them to be the devil, and the harvest to be the end of the world (age). The reapers are the angels that gather the tares, but there is no mention of the wheat being gathered. Why? Because the wheat harvest (Rapture) took place in a different time frame, seven years before.

Verse 30 reveals the time of harvest in which two distinct events took place. First, the tares were gathered in bundles *to be burned* but were not burned at that time. I believe this indicates that when the earth lease expires the wicked lose their authority to hinder or pollute the harvest. The second event was the gathering of wheat into His barn, which is indicative of a great in-gathering of souls just before the Rapture.

Paul gives us more conclusive evidence that Jesus was the seed which would produce this good harvest:

1 Corinthians 15:22 **For as in Adam all die, even so in Christ shall all be made alive.**
23 But every man in his own order: Christ the first-fruits; afterward they that are Christ's at his coming.

This seems to confirm that the wheat which would be gathered into the barn would be gathered at the time of Christ's coming for the Church. Paul continues:

1 Corinthians 15:24 **Then cometh the end, when he shall have delivered up the kingdom to God, even the Father; when he shall have put down all rule and all authority and power.**
25 For he must reign, till he hath put all enemies under his feet.
26 The last enemy that shall be destroyed is death.

These verses correspond perfectly with the time frame of the end of the world (age) referred to in Matthew 13:39.

Jesus continues with progressive revelation:

Matthew 13:40 **As therefore the tares are gathered and burned in the fire; so shall it be in the end of this world.**

41 The Son of man shall send forth his angels, and they shall gather out of his kingdom all things that offend, and them which do iniquity;
42 And shall cast them into a furnace of fire: there shall be wailing and gnashing of teeth.

These verses reveal the prophetic time frame of these events to be after the millennial reign of Christ, at which time the wicked will be gathered out of *His earthly kingdom.*

Matthew 13:43 **Then shall the righteous shine forth as the sun in the kingdom of their Father....**

The preceding verses correspond perfectly with the time frame of events revealed by Paul in 1 Corinthians 15:

24 Then cometh the end, when he shall have delivered up the kingdom to God, even the Father; when he shall have put down all rule and all authority and power.
25 For he must reign, till he hath put all enemies under his feet.

What's the bottom line of this matter? We are now in the season of a great harvest which will soon be consummated with the Rapture. The tares are gathering together in one united bundle (group) against God. The very next event is the gathering of the wheat. Jesus was the kernel of wheat planted, and the Body of Christ will be the wheat harvest that is about to be gathered into the Father's house. John, when referring to Jesus in Matthew 3:12, also confirms that Jesus will separate the chaff from the wheat and gather the wheat into His garner, then burn up the chaff with unquenchable fire. The same stern warning delivered to the Pharisees and Sadducees would seem to be very appropriate for this generation.

What's the bottom line of this matter? We are now in the season of great harvest....

Matthew 3:7 **But when he saw many of the Pharisees and Sadducees come to his baptism, he said unto them, O generation of vipers, who hath warned you to flee from the wrath to come?**

8 Bring forth therefore fruits meet for repentance:

9 And think not to say within yourselves, We have Abraham to our father: for I say unto you, that God is able of these stones to raise up children unto Abraham.

10 And now also the axe is laid unto the root of the trees: therefore every tree which bringeth not forth good fruit is hewn down, and cast into the fire.

11 I indeed baptize you with water unto repentance: but he that cometh after me is mightier than I, whose shoes I am not worthy to bear: he shall baptize you with the Holy Ghost, and with fire:

12 Whose fan is in his hand, and he will thoroughly purge his floor, and gather his wheat into the garner; but he will burn up the chaff with unquenchable fire.

It is obvious that the separation of the chaff from the wheat (wicked from righteous) has already begun. The fan* being in Jesus' hand reveals that He is in complete control of the separating process. The prophetic implications are clear—while the wheat is up in the air, the winds of time itself will separate the chaff from the wheat. You can rest assured that it will be completed on time to gather the wheat (righteous) into His garner (Father's house). (Matthew 13:30; John 14:1-3.)†

---

*Winnowing shovel.

†A wooden winnowing fork or shovel was used to toss the grain into the air, allowing the wind to take away the chaff.

Insight Through Special Events

We all know that Jesus was a preacher and a teacher. However, many fail to recognize Him as a prophet. In the last two verses of Matthew 16, Jesus prophesied of an event which had a partial fulfillment six days later in the form of a vision. But, as many other prophecies in the Scripture, it also has a future prophetic fulfillment of major importance.

> Matthew 16:26 **For what is a man profited, if he shall gain the whole world, and lose his own soul? or what shall a man give in exchange for his soul?**
> **27 For the Son of man shall come in the glory of his Father with his angels; and then he shall reward every man according to his works.**
> **28 Verily I say unto you, There be some standing here, which shall not taste of death, till they see the Son of man coming in his kingdom.**

These verses are in direct reference to a literal event that took place six days later. However, the prophetic implications are profound.

> Matthew 17:1 **And after six days Jesus taketh Peter, James, and John his brother, and bringeth them up into an high mountain apart,**
> **2 And was transfigured before them: and his face did shine as the sun, and his raiment was white as the light.**
> **3 And, behold, there appeared unto them Moses and Elias talking with him.**

It is significant that Jesus waited exactly six days after He made these statements before taking Peter, James, and John up to a high mountain where He was transfigured before them.

The Church is the only body that Christ has on the earth today.

This is a scriptural profile of the Rapture of the Church. We recognize Peter, James, and John as those who were considered to be His closest associates. It is also significant that they were the very ones who accompanied Jesus on occasions when He raised the dead. This alone would give us a strong clue that this event is a scriptural pictorial of an event in which the righteous dead will be resurrected. Another strong factor is that Moses, who had been dead over 1500 years, appeared in that vision and talked with Jesus.

Then ask yourself this question: "What would be considered the first stage of the Son of Man's coming in His kingdom?" Jesus is called the Head of the Church, and we, as believers, are the Body of Christ. Paul states in First Corinthians 12:27, **"Now ye are the body of Christ, and members in particular."**

The Church is the only body that Christ has on the earth today. He dwells in us in the Person of the Holy Spirit. The Body of Christ does His work here on earth. Yet, He is the Head over all the Church and is in Heaven.

Ephesians 1:22 **And hath put all things under his feet, and gave him to be the head over all things to the church, 23 Which is his body, the fulness of him that filleth all in all.**

Paul's statements in these verses indicate that the first of several stages of Jesus' coming into His kingdom will be to gather His Body (the Church) together unto Him. This would constitute the fullness of Him, partially fulfilling His promise to the Church. (Ephesians 1:10.)

The statement made by Jesus in Matthew 16:28 gives us a strong scriptural profile of the Rapture of the Church. This corresponds perfectly with what John experienced in his vision in Revelation 4:1-3, which is also a parallel of the Rapture.

> Revelation 4:1 **After this I looked, and, behold, a door was opened in heaven: and the first voice which I heard was as it were of a trumpet talking with me; which said, Come up hither, and I will shew thee things which MUST BE HEREAFTER.**

Take note of the fact that the voice of the trumpet said, "I will show you what must be hereafter." This statement refers to what must take place after the Church Age, because it is obvious that the subject matter of the first three chapters was the churches.

> Revelation 4:2 **And immediately I was in the spirit: and, behold, a throne was set in heaven, and one sat on the throne.**
> **3 And he that sat was to look upon like a jasper and a sardine stone: and there was a rainbow round about the throne, in sight like unto an emerald.**

John said, "I heard a voice as it were a trumpet talking with me."

What did the trumpet say? "**Come up hither.**" And, immediately, he was at the throne of God. John's description of what he heard and experienced in that vision is a perfect parallel of the Rapture. It reveals the time frame of this glorious event to be before the first seal is opened in Revelation chapter 6.

THE TRANSFIGURATION

Sometimes when reading the Scriptures, chapter divisions break our thought pattern. So let's read the last verse of Matthew 16 together with the first few verses of chapter 17 to retain the continuity of thought that is being portrayed.

Matthew 16:28 **Verily I say unto you, There be some standing here, which shall not taste of death, till they see the Son of man coming in his kingdom.**

Matthew 17:1 AND AFTER SIX DAYS **Jesus taketh Peter, James, and John his brother, and bringeth them up into an high mountain apart,**
2 And was transfigured before them: and his face did shine as the sun, and his raiment was white as the light.
3 And, behold, there appeared unto them Moses and Elias talking with him.

I don't believe it was a coincidence that Jesus waited exactly six days before taking Peter, James, and John (those closest to him) up to a high mountain? There is no doubt in my mind that God inspired the writer to count the days that passed before Jesus took them up to that mountain.

This could have been God's way of setting a sign along the road to eternity. The scriptural implications seem to reveal that the event foreshadowed by these verses will take place after six days (6000 years) of human history.

Again, let me reiterate that I am not setting dates, because we aren't sure where we are on the time calendar. Due to the lack of verified records covering almost 6000 years, there is some confusion over which or whose calendar is right. Yet, we know that God is not confused about His timing for these end-time events. He is the Master Timekeeper, and you can rest assured that His timetable is correct. Each prophetic event will be fulfilled on time.

SHADOW OF THINGS TO COME

The prophetic events foreshadowed in the Genesis account fit perfectly in the 1000-years-as-a day interpretation of the framework of God's Word revealing the end of the Church Age. In six days God finished everything that pertained to the earth and a mature man. Man was in the image and likeness of God at the end of the sixth day, and God considered everything that He had made, and it was very good.

Concerning the Transfiguration, I'm aware that Luke's account states that it occurred after **"about eight days."** (Luke 9:28.) However, the word *about* reveals that he wasn't sure of the number of days.

Matthew and Mark state emphatically that this event occurred six days after Jesus made the statement, **"...There be some standing here, which shall not taste of death, till they see the Son of man coming in his kingdom."**

When you take into consideration Peter's statement that **"one day is with the Lord as a thousand years, and a thousand years as one day,"** this gives us insight into how clearly this event foreshadows the Rapture of the Church.

Let's compare the information in the Book of Revelation with Matthew 17:1-2.

Revelation 1:16 **And he had in his right hand seven stars: and out of his mouth went a sharp twoedged sword: and his countenance was as the sun shineth in his strength.**

Each prophetic event will be fulfilled on time.

Revelation 21:10 **And he carried me away in the spirit to a great and high mountain, and shewed me that great city, the holy Jerusalem, descending out of heaven from God.**
23 And the city had no need of the sun, neither of the moon, to shine in it: for the glory of God did lighten it, and the Lamb is the light thereof.

Matthew 17:1 **And after six days Jesus taketh Peter, James, and John his brother, and bringeth them up into an high mountain apart,**

2 And was transfigured before them: and his face did shine as the sun, and his raiment was white as the light.

Revelation 21:23 also mentions Jesus' face shining as the sun. This is a strong indication that the Transfiguration was a vision that happened in the Holy Mount, the *Heavenly* New Jerusalem.

GOD FORBADE MOSES TO ENTER THE PROMISED LAND

Some Bible scholars believe the mountain to be Mount Tabor between Zebulun and Issachar. However, we have three major scriptural problems with Moses' being on that mountain in that time frame. The first is found in Deuteronomy, chapter 34.

4 And the Lord said unto him, This is the land which I sware unto Abraham, unto Isaac, and unto Jacob, saying, I will give it unto thy seed: I have caused thee to see it with thine eyes, but THOU SHALT NOT GO OVER THITHER.

If Moses was on that *literal* mountain and had not yet been resurrected, it would seem to be a contradiction of this last statement in verse 4. This Scripture supports the possibility that this vision reveals an event that will take place in the New Jerusalem after the Rapture.

SPIRITUAL VISION

It is clear that Peter, James, and John experienced a *spiritual vision*. They no doubt went up to a literal mountain, but through a spiritual vision, they were caught up into a "Holy Mountain," which would seem to be the New Jerusalem.

Let's compare Matthew 17:1 with Revelation 21:10 and 2 Peter 1:18.

Matthew 17:1 **And after six days Jesus taketh Peter, James, and John his brother, and bringeth them up into an HIGH MOUNTAIN APART.**

Revelation 21:10 **And he carried me away in the spirit to a GREAT AND HIGH MOUNTAIN, and shewed me that great city, the holy Jerusalem, descending out of heaven from God.**

2 Peter 1:18 **And this voice which came from heaven we heard, when we were with him IN THE HOLY MOUNT.**

It would appear from these verses that, in this vision, they were caught up into the Holy Mountain—the New Jerusalem. If Moses had been on that mountain *on the earth,* he would have been in the Promised Land. I don't believe Moses was on a literal mountain in the Promised Land, as we shall discover later.

MOSES WAS DEAD AND HELD CAPTIVE

The second scriptural problem we have is the fact that Moses had been dead 1500 years. Under the Old Covenant, when the righteous died, they went down into Paradise, which at that time was in the heart of the earth (Matthew 12:40).

Paradise was referred to by the Jews as "Abraham's bosom" and was located across a great gulf from Hell. (Luke 16:26.) The wicked dead went into Hell when they died and were tormented in flames. But it was not possible for them to get out of either place, for there was a great gulf fixed between them. (See Luke 16:26.)

The wicked dead will not be brought out until the time of the Great White Throne Judgment. They will then be assigned to the lake of fire permanently. The spiritual bodies of the righteous dead seem to have been confined in their compartment in Paradise until Jesus paid the price for their sin through His death. When Jesus arose from the dead, the righteous dead were liberated. Paul makes reference to this in the Book of Ephesians.

Ephesians 4:8 **Wherefore he saith, When he ascended up on high, he led captivity captive, and gave gifts unto men.**
9 (Now that he ascended, what is it but that he also descended first into the lower parts of the earth?
10 He that descended is the same also that ascended up far above all heavens, that he might fill all things).

So during the time Jesus took Peter, James, and John up to a high mountain apart and was transfigured before them, Moses' spiritual body was confined to Paradise in the heart of the earth. It seems that the righteous were held captive until Jesus paid the sin debt for all mankind and led them out of captivity.

> *The wicked dead will not be brought out until the time of the Great White Throne Judgment.*

Jesus suffered for our sins and paid the penalty we should have paid. Then He crossed that great gulf, liberated the spiritual bodies of the righteous dead, and brought them out with Him. He then moved Paradise from the heart of the earth to Heaven. (2 Corinthians 5:8.)

VEIL RENT AND THE GRAVES WERE OPENED

The Scripture records in Matthew 27 some amazing events that took place when Jesus died.

51 And, behold, the veil of the temple was rent in twain from the top to the bottom; and the earth did quake, and the rocks rent;
52 And the graves were opened; and many bodies of the saints which slept arose,
53 And came out of the graves after his resurrection, and went into the holy city, and appeared unto many.

These Scriptures seem to confirm that it was not possible for Moses to be on that earthly mountain in the natural time frame in which Jesus took Peter, James, and John up to that mountain, unless He had been resurrected, for Christ had not yet died and Paradise in general had not yet been liberated.

THIRD SCRIPTURAL PROBLEM CONCERNING MOSES

The third problem we have with Jesus' having a conversation with Moses is the fact that God's Word forbids anyone from trying to communicate with the dead. (Deuteronomy 18:11-12) God had forbidden it, because it was a heathen practice. It was called an abomination to God.

We know that Moses had been dead 1500 years. Therefore, we must conclude that Jesus did not violate God's Word by carrying on a conversation with a dead man. There are two possibilities: Either Moses had to be resurrected, or this vision represented a time frame after the Rapture. Both may be true.

It seems that Jesus did take Peter, James, and John up to an earthly mountain with Him. However, these Scriptures have strong implications that this event was a spiritual vision which caused them to be transported in the Spirit into a future point in time which corresponds with the time of the Rapture. The time frame of the events in this vision had to be after Jesus was resurrected from the dead.

The prophetic implications reveal the time frame represented by these events in this vision to be after 6000 years of human history and at the time of the Rapture. We know at that time, Moses would be in Heaven in his glorified body and it would be perfectly scriptural for Jesus to talk with him. The reason I have belabored this point is to make it clear that Jesus never did anything against the Word of His Father. He said, "I do always those things that please Him" (John 8:29).

CLOUD OVERSHADOWED THEM

Matthew 17:5 While he yet spake, behold, a bright cloud overshadowed them: and behold a voice out of the cloud, which said, This is my beloved Son, in whom I am well pleased; hear ye him.
9 And as they came down from the mountain, Jesus charged them, saying, Tell the vision to no man, until the Son of man be risen again from the dead.

JESUS' WARNING

This statement seems to validate what has already been stated. Jesus said, **"Tell the vision to no man, until the Son of man be risen from the dead."** He gave them this warning because they could have been stoned to death for even trying to communicate with the dead. (Leviticus 20:27; 1 Samuel 28:9.) The Jews would not have understood that this had happened in a spiritual vision. They especially would not have understood that the disciples were projected by the Spirit into a vision which profiles the Rapture of the Church nearly 2000 years later.

PETER'S ACCOUNT OF THE EVENT

Peter wrote about this event, giving more details of the vision and of the voice which they heard.

2 Peter 1:16 **For we have not followed cunningly devised fables,** WHEN WE MADE KNOWN UNTO YOU THE POWER AND COMING OF OUR LORD JESUS CHRIST, **but were eyewitnesses of his majesty.**
17 **For he received from God the Father honour and glory, when there came such a voice to him from the excellent glory, This is my beloved Son, in whom I am well pleased.**

18 And THIS VOICE WHICH CAME FROM HEAVEN **we heard,** WHEN WE WERE WITH HIM IN THE HOLY MOUNT.

Notice Peter refers to the vision as a revelation of *the power and coming of our Lord Jesus Christ.* Allow me to point out two very significant points about his statement. First, he describes the place where they were with Him as being in the *holy mount,* or mountain.

One of the rules of Bible interpretation is that when the word "mountain" is used and its name or geographical location is not given, it is referring to a kingdom. This is the case in Daniel 2:34-35, where he speaks of a stone that was cut out without hands, which represented Jesus Christ.

This Stone smote the great image upon its feet and broke it to pieces, and that Stone became a great mountain and filled the whole earth. This mountain is referred to later in verse 44 as *the kingdom.* From that point on, Daniel refers to it as a kingdom.

The Rapture is the very first of several events that will usher in Christ's kingdom....

I believe this would validate the use of this rule of interpretation concerning the mountain in Matthew 17:1: **"After six days Jesus taketh Peter, James, and John his brother, and bringeth them up into an high mountain apart."** The word "apart" used here is from the Greek word *idios,*[1] which means "pertaining to self, or one's own," which in the context would seem to mean *his own.* So there are strong implications that this statement refers to a high **kingdom, of His own,** or in other words, separate from the earth. Notice those are almost the exact words of Jesus' statement in verse 28.

Matthew 16:28 **Verily I say unto you, There be some standing here, which shall not taste of death, till they see the Son of man coming in** HIS KINGDOM.

This whole event seems to be a perfect profile of the first of several events which must take place to consummate Christ's kingdom on earth. The Rapture is the very first of several events that will usher in His kingdom on earth during the next Millennium.

Let's take a closer look at Peter's account of what he saw and heard in that vision.

> 2 Peter 1:17 **For he received from God the Father honour and glory, when there came such a voice to him from the excellent glory, This is my beloved Son, in whom I am well pleased.**
> **18 And this voice which came from heaven we heard, when we were with him in the holy mount.**

Peter states that they were with Him **"in the holy mount."** This seems to imply that it was in the *holy kingdom,* which would be the New Jerusalem.

Matthew's account of this event states, **"...and behold a voice out of the cloud, which said, This is my beloved Son, in whom I am well pleased..."** (Matthew 17:5). This verse reveals that the voice came out of the cloud as the cloud overshadowed them.

When giving his own eyewitness account of this event, Peter said, **"This voice which came from heaven we heard"** (2 Peter 1:18). If the voice came from Heaven and the voice also came out of the cloud, as Matthew states, this implies they were also in Heaven when the cloud covered them.

It would seem from these Scriptures that they were transported in the Spirit into the New Jerusalem, where they talked with Moses and Elijah. We don't know whether they were in the body or out of the body. But it seems evident that Peter believed the Transfiguration took place in Heaven, because he referred to that event as **"the power and coming of our Lord Jesus Christ."**

SIGN ON THE ROAD TO ETERNITY

I believe the Transfiguration event was God's way of setting a signpost on the road to eternity revealing that after six days (6000 years) of human history, the Body of Christ will be taken up into a high kingdom of His own. The purpose of the Rapture seems to be threefold:

1. To fulfill His (Christ's) promise by keeping the Church (Body of Christ) out of the seven years of tribulation that are coming upon the earth.

2. To reward the righteous for their works.

3. And to prepare the saints (Church) to rule and reign with Him in His earthly kingdom. (2 Corinthians 5:10; 1 Thessalonians 5:9; Revelation 3:7-12.)

This corresponds perfectly with the 1000-years-as-a-day interpretation of the Genesis account. Man was in God's image and likeness at the end of the sixth day. (Genesis 1:27.) But some ask, "How will we ever come into the image and likeness of God?" Paul gives us the answer in First Corinthians:

1 Corinthians 15:51 **Behold, I shew you a mystery; We shall not all sleep, but we shall all be changed,**
52 In a moment, in the twinkling of an eye, at the last trump: for the trumpet shall sound, and the dead shall be raised incorruptible, and we shall be changed.

What is the meaning of the phrase *last trump*? Many Jews believe this refers to the last trumpet blast of the Feast of Trumpets which seems to correspond with the trump of God, the trumpet which will signal the rapture.

The "trump of God" in First Thessalonians 4:16 and Revelation 4:1 is not the same as the seventh angelic trumpet mentioned in Revelation 11:15. The trumpet of the seventh angel signals a series of events which will take place over several days. The trump of God signals an event which will take place in the twinkling of an eye.

After Peter explained what he saw with his own eyes and what he heard with his own ears, he gave this account:

> 2 Peter 1:19 **We have also a more sure word of prophecy; whereunto ye do well that ye take heed, as unto a light that shineth in a dark place, until the day dawn, and the day star arise in your hearts:**
> **20 Knowing this first, that no prophecy of the scripture is of any private interpretation.**
> **21 For the prophecy came not in old time by the will of man: but holy men of God spake as they were moved by the Holy Ghost.**

Even though he had this supernatural vision and experienced this revelation of Christ, he reminds us that we have *a more sure word from prophecies of the Scriptures*. We have the Word of God given through the prophets by the inspiration of the Holy Spirit. What a privileged people we are to have a copy of these prophetic utterances.

HOSEA'S PROPHECY

Hosea is one of the prophets to whom Peter referred, and he does give a more sure word concerning Israel and end-time events.

> Hosea 6:1 **Come, and let us return unto the Lord: for he hath torn, and he will heal us; he hath smitten, and he will bind us up.**
> **2 AFTER TWO DAYS will he revive us: in the THIRD DAY he will raise us up, and we shall live in his sight.**

Allow me to reiterate: There were two days (2000 years), from Adam to Abraham. There were two more days (2000 more years) from Abraham to Christ. This total of four days represents 4000 years of human history before Jesus was born. Then Hosea states: *After two days* (making a total of six days), *He will revive Israel. In the third day* (third Millennium from Christ's first coming) *He will raise Israel up, and they shall live in His sight.* Here again, God has given us prophetic insight into the time span of the Church Age, which began when Jesus was born on earth. Since we have scriptural precedent that two days represent 2000 years, it becomes clear that in the third day (Millennial Reign of Christ) Israel will be raised up and live in His sight.

INCIDENT SUPPORTING HOSEA'S PROPHECY

There is another interesting incident recorded in Luke 2:41-46 that I believe gives support to Hosea's prophecy concerning the two days. When Jesus was twelve years old, He went with His parents to the Feast of the Passover in Jerusalem. When Mary and Joseph left Jerusalem, they assumed that Jesus was in their company. They had gone a day's journey out of the city when they discovered He was not with them. They returned to Jerusalem, which was obviously another day's journey. Now we know that they were Jewish, so we could say the Jews were without Jesus for two days. Then, on the third day, they found Him in the temple.

According to Zechariah, that is exactly where Jesus will be found on the third day (during the Millennial Reign), ruling from the temple which He will build in Jerusalem. (Zechariah 6:12-13.) There is a prophetic implication in this incident when viewed in the light of these and other prophecies.

Is it a coincidence that these events of the past seem to so vividly reveal future events? I hardly think so. Some of these scriptural pictorials are so exact that it is obvious God has used events, even from the beginning, to give us insight concerning the end of the Church Age and His Millennial kingdom.

Let me reiterate that I am not setting dates. I am only pointing out the general time frame revealed in God's Word.

Get another cup of coffee.

There is much more to come concerning Moses and Elijah.

Moses and Elijah:
God's Composite of the Rapture

There has been a great deal of speculation over the years about why Moses and Elijah were present at the Transfiguration of Jesus. Some people believe Moses and Elijah were there because they will be the Two Witnesses referred to in Revelation 11:3. However, I don't believe that to be the case.

Here are some of the reasons why I don't believe Moses will be one of the witnesses destined to die in Jerusalem just prior to Christ's Second Advent (Revelation 11:7). First, Moses had been dead for 1500 years at the time of the Transfiguration. Moses has already died, and after his resurrection, he cannot die again. And there is evidence in a skip sequence in the original Hebrew indicating that Moses has already been resurrected. I'll give more details later in this chapter.

So it would seem that Moses could not possibly be one of the Two Witnesses who will be killed in the streets of Jerusalem near the end of the Tribulation Period

Some have asked the question, "But if Lazarus died after he was raised from death, why couldn't Moses also die again?" The reason lies in the fact that Lazarus was restored to mortal life. We know at the time of the Rapture, all who are resurrected become immortal.

Now let's consider Elijah. It's true that Elijah would qualify as one of the Two Witnesses, and this seems to be confirmed in

Malachi 4:5-6. But I don't believe that is the *reason* Elijah appeared in the vision of the Transfiguration. I will explain later.

Judging from scriptural accounts, Enoch seems to be the only prophet from that time period, other than Elijah, who would qualify to be one of the Two Witnesses. First, we know that he didn't die but was caught up into Heaven and is still living there today in a natural body. (Hebrews 11:5-6.)

But the question still remains: *Why* was Moses involved in the event referred to as the Transfiguration?

We will gain some insight into this matter by calling to remembrance the fact that Moses was born with a death warrant on him. (Exodus 1:22.) Pharaoh had declared that every male child born of the Hebrew women in Egypt were to be cast into the river. But Moses' parents hid him for three months. Then he was placed in the river, inside an ark of bulrushes, where he was discovered by Pharaoh's daughter.

Moses' life was miraculously spared for many prophetic reasons. The most obvious reason was that he was to lead the children of Israel out of the land of Egypt. However, there was a more significant reason which concerns prophetic events that would transpire over 6000 years of human history. I believe Moses appeared at the Transfiguration because he *represents the righteous dead of the 6000-year period foreshadowed in the Genesis account.* That 6000-year period represents the time span of the earth lease which God gave to mankind.

MAN'S DAYS ARE LIMITED

We also find a confirmation of this in Genesis 6:3: **"And the Lord said, My spirit shall not always strive with man, for that he also is flesh: yet his days shall be an hundred and twenty years."**

The fact that the Lord said his *days* shall be 120 years reveals that a "day" in this verse represents a year. This gives us our first clue that this statement is connected to an end-time event.

In the ninth chapter of the book of Daniel, the seventy weeks are "weeks of years." Therefore, a day represents a year, just as stated also in Genesis 6:3. This is a significant clue, as we shall see as we continue.

Dr. Lester Sumrall, in his book entitled *I Predict 2000 A.D.*, states:

"Man experiences three main limitations while living on planet Earth. He is limited by time. It cuts man short of his ambitions. Secondly, man is limited by space. He can only be in one place at a time. The third is energy. All energy of man is calibrated and limited. The fateful year of 2000 A.D. is approaching. Leaders have a foreboding that important changes are about to happen. *The Kipling Letter*, written and mailed in the mid-eighties, already warned man to prepare for 2000 A.D...."

Earth's golden Jubilee will occur after six thousand years of human history.

"The year 2000 A.D. will be the golden Jubilee of planet Earth.... A Jubilee is fifty years. In Israel's history, the year of Jubilee was celebrated by forgiving all debts and releasing every slave. Earth's golden Jubilee will occur after six thousand years of human history."[1]

MAN'S DOMINION IS LIMITED

This seems to be the only reasonable conclusion concerning the statement in Genesis 6:3. In other words, the Scriptures indicate that man, or mankind's days of dominion on planet Earth, will be 120 Jubilee years. It is quite interesting that in the *Strong's Concordance* the number assigned to the Hebrew word "man" is (0120). Could it have been the inspiration of God that caused them to use that number as a concordant number for man?

We know that Noah lived 350 years after the flood and that his total life was 950 years. So it is evident that God didn't establish man's lifespan to be 120 years. But if you consider the 120 years in Genesis 6:3 to be 120 "Jubilee years," this would seem to establish the time span of the earth lease in which man has dominion over the earth.

When Israel came out of Egyptian bondage, God commanded them to let the land rest every seventh year for "seven sabbaths of years," which would be forty-nine years. The fiftieth year they were to blow the trumpet and proclaim the year of Jubilee.

> Leviticus 25:8 **And thou shalt number seven sabbaths of years unto thee, seven times seven years; and the space of the seven sabbaths of years shall be unto thee forty and nine years.**
> **9 Then shalt thou cause the trumpet of the jubilee to sound on the tenth day of the seventh month, in the day of atonement shall ye make the trumpet sound throughout all your land.**

Every fiftieth year was declared a year of Jubilee—a year in which all debts were canceled. Everything they had lost or sold was restored to them. This seems to be a scriptural pictorial of what God had planned to do for mankind after 6000 years of human history. This would correspond perfectly with what we found in the Genesis account and other prophetic Scriptures.

REASON FOR MOSES' PRESENCE REVEALED

If Moses and Elijah were exact composites of both the righteous dead and living who will be caught up to Heaven at the time of the Rapture, they had to both be caught up together. This seems to be the real reason that Moses was present with Elijah at the Transfiguration event.

We know Moses lived exactly 120 years. This indicates that Moses was symbolic of the *righteous dead* of all the 120 Jubilee years (6000 years) whose bodies will not be found in the earth.

> Deuteronomy 31:1 **And Moses went and spake these words unto all Israel.**

2 And he said unto them, I am an hundred and twenty years old this day; I can no more go out and come in: also the Lord hath said unto me, Thou shalt not go over this Jordan.

The reason that Moses could no more go out or come in was that time had run out for him. He was going to die the very day that he wrote these verses. Moses was allowed to see the Promised Land, but he wasn't allowed to enter it.

> Deuteronomy 34:5 **So Moses the servant of the Lord died there in the land of Moab, according to the word of the Lord.**
> **6 And he buried him in the valley in the land of Moab, over against Bethpeor: but no man knoweth of his sepulchre unto this day.**
> **7 And Moses was an hundred and twenty years old when he died: his eye was not dim, nor his natural force abated.**

It is quite evident from verse 7 that time ran out for Moses. There was no natural reason for him to die; he seemed to be in good health.

Moses fulfilled the 120 natural years which seem to represent 120 Jubilee years of man's dominion on earth. God buried him in the land of Moab, and no one ever found his body. It was necessary that it happen in that manner and time frame for him to represent all the righteous dead of 120 Jubilee years.

REASON FOR ELIJAH'S PRESENCE REVEALED

In 2 Kings 2, when Elijah was about to be caught up to Heaven, God sent him from Gilgal to Bethel. When they arrived in Bethel, the sons of the prophets said to Elisha, **"...Knowest thou that the Lord will take away thy master from thy head to day? And he said, Yea, I know it; hold ye your peace"** (v. 3).

The Lord sent Elijah to Jericho where the sons of the prophets said the same thing to Elisha. They also knew that Elijah was going to be caught up that very day. Then the Lord sent Elijah across the Jordan River—*to the place where Moses was buried.*

I find it very significant that Elijah was sent to the place where Moses was buried to be caught up into Heaven in an angelic chariot of fire.

> 2 Kings 2:11 **And it came to pass, as they still went on, and talked, that, behold, there appeared a chariot of fire, and horses of fire, and parted them both asunder; and Elijah went up by a whirlwind into heaven.**

The word translated "whirlwind" also means "storm cloud." It seems that God sent one of His chariots to take Elijah to Heaven. Psalm 68:17 gives us insight concerning God's chariots: **"The chariots of God are twenty thousand, even thousands of angels: the Lord is among them, as in Sinai, in the holy place."** The only visible appearance of angels on Mt. Sinai was a thick cloud of fire and smoke. (Exodus 19:16-18.) It seems from 2 Kings 2:11 that the chariot of fire and horses of fire were actually angels manifest as a chariot—providing Elijah's transportation from earth to Heaven.

Then Jeremiah describes chariots as a *whirlwind.*

> Jeremiah 4:13 **Behold, he shall come up as clouds, and his chariots shall be as a whirlwind: his horses are swifter than eagles....**

In light of all these Scriptures, it is significant that 2 Kings also states that Elijah went up by a whirlwind into Heaven. All these descriptions seem to be clouds of angels (chariots of God) that are in charge of catching away the righteous from the earth to Heaven. In Habakkuk 3:8, angels seem to be referred to as chariots of salvation or deliverance. Then Hebrews 2:3 states, **"How** shall we escape, if we neglect so great salvation...." And it is clear from the context that the reference is to angelic deliverance.

Second Kings 2:11 gives a vivid description of how Elijah was raptured from earth to Heaven while he was alive. We know from 1 Thessalonians 4:16-17 that Elijah had to be caught up to Heaven without dying to represent the Church (Body of Christ) being caught up alive.

MICHAEL'S DISPUTE WITH THE DEVIL

The Book of Jude also gives a rare bit of information which carries a strong prophetic implication concerning this event. For years we've wondered what it meant, but now the meaning seems to be quite obvious.

> Jude 9 **Yet Michael the archangel, when contending with the devil** HE DISPUTED ABOUT THE BODY OF MOSES, **durst not bring against him a railing accusation, but said, The Lord rebuke thee.**

When teaching concerning these end-time events, for several months, every time I referred to Moses and Elijah, this verse in Jude came to mind. Finally, I did some investigation of the Scriptures and found that Michael the archangel seems to be in charge of the Rapture of the Church. In 1 Thessalonians 4:16, Paul states, **"For the Lord himself shall descend from heaven with a shout, with the voice of the archangel, and with the trump of God: and the dead in Christ shall rise first."**

Michael's assignment includes the resurrection of the righteous dead, as well as catching up the righteous who are alive at the time of the Rapture. This gives insight into why both Moses and Elijah appeared in the vision of the Transfiguration. They are God's composites foreshadowing the Rapture of the Church.

When Moses died God buried him in the land of Moab. And that's where God sent Elijah to be caught up into Heaven. Allow me to do some scriptural speculation concerning this matter.

MICHAEL IN CHARGE OF RAPTURE

I believe that Moses and Elijah were God's exact scriptural pictorial composites of the Rapture.

I believe that Michael the archangel, who is in charge of the Rapture, was also in charge of that spirit chariot (composed of angels) which came to pick up Elijah. It was at that time that he contended with the devil about the body of Moses, just as Jude 9 reveals. It would seem that the dispute was over the fact that it was not yet time for the righteous dead to be taken out of the earth. But if Moses was God's composite of the righteous dead whose bodies cannot be left in the earth at the time of the Rapture, then Moses' body had to be caught up in the same chariot with Elijah. This seems to be the reason God sent Elijah across the Jordan River to the place where Moses was buried.

I believe Michael was the driver of that chariot. After his dispute with the devil, he took Moses up into the chariot before catching Elijah up in the same chariot. There is evidence that they were *both* caught up together at the same time.

Moses and Elijah were God's scriptural pictorials revealing the results of the Rapture.

Every detail fits prophetically. This would solve the mystery of why Moses and Elijah were with Jesus at the Transfiguration. Allow me to go over the details once more for clarity.

Moses represents all the righteous dead of the 120 Jubilee years whose bodies will not be left in the grave. The 120 Jubilee years are represented by his life span of exactly 120 years. To give an exact scriptural profile of the Rapture, Moses had to rise first, and then Elijah had to be taken up along with Moses in the same time frame.

Since we don't have an exact statement in the Bible concerning Moses' being caught up in that chariot, I realize this will be considered speculation. But I have found some confirmation concerning Michael's dispute about the body of Moses which I consider to be profoundly important.

CONFIRMATION HIDDEN FOR THIS GENERATION

Allow me to digress a little to inject this information which will shed light on this matter.

When this book first went to print in July of 1997, I was convinced that Michael had taken the body of Moses in the chariot before he caught up Elijah and they both went to Heaven together. It seemed to be the only explanation of why Elijah was sent to where Moses was buried to be caught up to Heaven.

While this book was at the publisher for the first printing, the book *The Bible Code* by Michael Drosnin was released. It revealed information concerning a hidden code and ELS sequencing in the Hebrew text of the Bible.

Eli Ripps, a Jewish mathematician and scientist from Israel, and many others had worked for years trying to unlock the code which they believed to be in the Hebrew text. Some Rabbis centuries ago had counted the letters by hand and found that there were hidden messages in the Hebrew text. This was done by counting the exact distance between letters. They found that there were certain messages hidden in a skip sequence in the Hebrew text which named names, dates, and events. However, this code could not be confirmed until the age of the computer.

Einstein tried to break the code and couldn't. Many others worked for years on it but were unable to unlock the time code hidden in the Scriptures for this generation. Daniel's prophecy gives us a clue into this when it says, **"...shut up the words, and seal the book, even to the time of the end: many shall run to and fro, and knowledge shall be increased."** (Daniel 12:4). Proof that a code existed under the surface of the Scriptures was not possible until the computer age, when knowledge had increased.

Michael Drosnin heard of "the code" and was very skeptical and set out to prove that it was not true. However, in his quest to disprove "the code" he became convinced that the Bible was truly coded with messages underneath the surface of the Scriptures. They show up in a hidden code of skip sequences in the original Hebrew text. The major event that caused him to believe in the Bible code was the fact that there was in the Scriptures a hidden message that seemed to say that Prime Minister Rabin would be assassinated by gunfire in Tel Aviv. He sent a warning to him, but he said, "Oh, if it is in the Bible, who can change it?" and he was assassinated in Tel Aviv. After the man was arrested, Drosnin searched again the Hebrew text and found, in the same area where he'd found "evil fire against Rabin," the name of Rabin's assassin.

We know every nation has codes they use to keep certain information from the wrong people. It seems that this is what God has done concerning certain revelations and confirmations of His Holy Word. He has infused revelation that confirms the written Word in a skip sequence in the original Hebrew for this generation which has not been released to any other generation.

I believe these messages which have been hidden in the Scriptures serve as proof to this "end-time generation" that the Bible is truly the inspired Word of God. It is possible that this information is being revealed to this generation because we will experience the total fulfillment of all end-time prophecy. No other generation needed this information, because they would not live to see the total fulfillment of these prophecies.

The revelation of this code and letter sequencing in our lifetime seems to magnify God's message to this generation. It is a message of profound importance revealing events of past history in great detail. It also seems to confirm in some instances future events prophesied in Scriptures which will soon take place on planet Earth.

When this book went to print in 1997 I was convinced that Moses was caught up to Heaven with Elijah. He had to be, if in fact Matthew 16 and the first part of chapter 17 was an exact profile of the Rapture of the Church. Since verse 9 of the Book of Jude gives support to that view. I put it in the book, knowing that I was on thin ice, so to speak, if I did not have more confirmation of Moses' resurrection.

CONFIRMATION FOUND

A few months after *The Bible Code* was released a friend of mine called and said, "I have a man staying with me for a few days who has worked with the Bible Code computer program for nine years. He wanted to know if there was anything you would like for him to search out in the Hebrew text. I was ecstatic. I said, "Oh yes!" I asked him to search 2 Kings chapter 2 for the "Jude connection." I told him what I had put in my book concerning Moses' body being caught up with Elijah into Heaven. In very short order, I received a fax stating, "I've found in a skip sequence in the text, Head Chief Angel Michael—more information will be forthcoming." The next fax I received stated: "Head Chief Angel Michael, he contended, Moses, he resurrected." This was all found from 2 Kings 2:1-13. Not only was it found once; it was doubled in the text.

He found in 2 Kings 2 the word "Moses" in the first verse of the Hebrew text. It appears in the plain text without any skips within the phrase "into Heaven." The word "Moses" appears again in the phrase "into Heaven" in verse 11. The other words were found in short skip sequences, the longest being every fourth letter, which would seem to be more significant. This is called an ELS sequence, which stands for "Equidistance Letter Sequencing." Although this may not be considered to be a scientific code, it does give us credible evidence that Jude verse 9 fits in 2 Kings 2:1-13, and seems to be revealing that Moses was resurrected and went to Heaven with Elijah, for they both appeared together in the vision on the mount and talked with Jesus.

A REVELATION TO THIS GENERATION

It is obvious that God has hidden information in the Hebrew text to be revealed to this generation. This was all the confirmation that I needed to be fully persuaded that Moses was resurrected, and taken to Heaven with Elijah. This would correspond perfectly with the apostle Paul's writings in 1 Thessalonians 4:16-17: "...**the dead in Christ** (represented by Moses) **shall rise first: Then we which are alive and remain** (represented by Elijah) **shall be caught up together with them in the clouds, to meet the Lord in the air....**" This seems to be a prophetic revelation of the Rapture to this generation that will experience this glorious event.

Sometime later, I received another fax from the man searching the text of 2 Kings 2 stating that he had found an unusual thing in verse 13. He found the word *Yeshua*, the Hebrew word for "Jesus," but it was not doubled in the text; it was only there one time. All the others had been doubled in the text. He said it looks as though Jesus encoded this message in 2 Kings 2 and signed his name to it. That may very well be what happened. The name Moses is found in the phrase "into heaven." In verses 1 and 11 in the Hebrew text.

> 2 Kings 2:1 And it came to pass, when the Lord would take up Elijah INTO HEAVEN by a whirlwind, that Elijah went with Elisha from Gilgal
>
> 3 And the sons of the prophets that were at Bethel came forth to Elisha, and said unto him, Knowest thou that the Lord will take away thy master from thy head to day? And he said, Yea, I know it; hold ye your peace.
>
> 5 And the sons of the prophets that were at Jericho came to Elisha, and said unto him, Knowest thou that the Lord will take away thy master from thy head to day? And he answered, Yea. I know it; hold ye your peace.

The very fact that Elijah, Elisha, and the sons of the prophets knew the exact day of Elijah's rapture could indicate that God may reveal the time of the Rapture to the Church before it happens.

> 9 And it came to pass, when they were gone over, that Elijah said unto Elisha, Ask what I shall do for thee, before I be taken away from thee. And Elisha said, I pray thee, let a double portion of thy spirit be upon me.
>
> 10 And he said, Thou has asked a hard thing: nevertheless, if thou see me when I am taken from thee, it shall be so unto thee; but if not, it shall not be so.
>
> 11 And it came to pass, as they still went on, and talked, that, behold, there appeared a chariot of fire, and horses of fire, and parted them both asunder; and Elijah went up by a whirlwind INTO HEAVEN (Moses).
>
> 12 And Elisha saw it, and he cried, My father, my father, the chariot of Israel, and the horsemen thereof. And he saw him no more: and he took hold of his own clothes, and rent them in two pieces.
>
> 13 He took up the mantle of Elijah that fell from Him....

The following is the Hebrew text showing the ELS skip sequence:

2 CHAP. II KINGS BOOK

◄———— Hebrew goes from right to left.

ספר מלכים ב פרק ב

א1 ויהי בהעלות יהוה את־אליהו בסערה

הַשָּׁמַיִם וילך אליהו ואלישע מן־הגלגל ————Moses

ג3 ויצאו בני־הנביאים אשר־בית־אל

אל־אלישע ויאמרו אליו הידעת כי ————He resurrected

הַיּוֹם יְהֹ־ה לקח את־אדניך

מֵעַל רֹאשֶׁךָ וַיֹּאמֶר גַּם־אני ידעתי החשׁו ————Head Chief angel

He contended ———— ————Michael

ה5 ויגשו בני־הנביאים אשר־בִּירִיחוֹ

אל־אלישע ויאמרו אליו הידעת כי ————He resurrected

הַיּוֹם יְהֹ־ה לקח את־אדניך

מעל ראשך ויאמר גם־אני ידעתי החשׁוּ

יא11 ויהי המה הלכים הלוך ודבר והנה רכב־אשׁ

וסוסי אשׁ ויפרדו בין שניהם ויעל

אליהו בסערה הַשָּׁמָיִם ————Moses

יג13 וירם את־אדרת אליהו אשר נפלה

מֵעָלָיו וַיֵּשָׁב וַיַּעֲמֹד עַל־שְׂפַת הירדן ————Yeshua (Jesus)

The fact that Elisha stayed on earth and received a double anointing would seem to indicate that Elisha profiles the 144,000 of Revelation chapter 7.

This message would seem to confirm that on the Mount of Transfiguration Moses represented the righteous dead that will be resurrected at the time of the Rapture and Elijah represented the Church caught up alive.

If there was any doubt whether or not the last two verses of Matthew 16 and first few verses of Matthew 17 were an exact scriptural profile of the Rapture of the Church after six days* (6000 years) of human history, this should be proof enough. I believe the

---

*This phrase "after six days" is not meant to imply that the Rapture will happen exactly at the end of 6000 years. It is intended to convey the fact that this event cannot happen before the end of the 6000-year earth lease. There are other indications that there will be a short period of time after the earth lease expires in which the glorious Church will reap the end-time harvests before being caught up to Heaven. (See chapter 16.)

events recorded in Matthew 17:1-5 and 2 Kings 2:1-13 are profound revelations from God to this end-time generation.

MOSES' LIFE—A TALE THAT WAS TOLD

What marvelous insight God has hidden in His Word—insight which has only been revealed to this last generation, confirming the Rapture of the Church. The prophetic implications of the 120 Jubilee years are also magnified as we read the ninetieth Psalm, which is a prayer of Moses. In the light of what we have just learned, his prayer is very revealing.

Psalm 90:9 **For all our days are passed away in thy wrath: WE SPEND OUR YEARS AS A TALE THAT IS TOLD. 10 The days of our years are threescore years and ten; and if by reason of strength they be fourscore years, yet is their strength labour and sorrow; for it is soon cut off, and we fly away. 12 So TEACH US TO NUMBER OUR DAYS, that we may APPLY OUR HEARTS UNTO WISDOM. 13 RETURN, O LORD, HOW LONG? and let it repent thee concerning thy servants.**

It seems that Moses realized the number of years of his life would actually be a tale that was told in human history. It seems that God used scriptural pictorials and biblical numerics to reveal the length of the earth lease which God gave mankind. If we number the days of Moses and apply our hearts unto wisdom, it would seem to answer the question that Moses asks in verse 13, even before he asks it. **"Return, O Lord, how long?"**

GOD USED SIMILITUDES

It is possible that the number of years that Moses lived being 120 reveals that there will be a time span of 120 Jubilee years before the Lord returns. This may be one of the similitudes referred to in Hosea 12:10, when God said, **"I have also spoken** by the prophets, and I have multiplied visions, and used similitudes, by the ministry of the prophets." There is no doubt that this Scripture was at least partially fulfilled in the vision of the Transfiguration.

Notice the words of Moses' prayer: **"Make us glad according to the days wherein thou hast afflicted us, and the years wherein we have seen evil."** (Psalm 90:15.) Even this verse seems to have some prophetic implications concerning Israel's seventy years of Babylonian captivity.

The seventy years of captivity in Babylon seem to represent seventy Jubilee years in which Israel will be under Gentile bondage. If we count from the time that Israel came out of Egypt until the year A.D. 2001, it seems to be seventy Jubilees. Is this a coincidence, or is it God's way of revealing end-time insight through biblical numerics?

The House of the Lord–A Prophetic Time Line

Solomon asked for wisdom instead of riches, and God gave him his request and much more. He revealed to him in a subtle way a valuable key in understanding God's revelation concerning the end of the age.

> 1 Kings 3:12 **Behold, I have done according to thy words: lo, I have given thee a wise and an understanding heart; so that there was none like thee before thee, neither after thee shall any arise like unto thee.**

THE SOLOMON CONCEPT

People came from all over to hear the wisdom of Solomon. Even though he had allowed other things to draw him away from God at the time he wrote the Book of Ecclesiastes, Solomon reveals a God-given concept which I call the Solomon Concept. Actually it is *God's Concept* that He revealed to Solomon.

> Ecclesiastes 1:4 **One generation passeth away, and another generation cometh: but the earth abideth for ever.**
> **5 The sun also ariseth, and the sun goeth down, and hasteth to his place where he arose.**
> **6 The wind goeth toward the south, and turneth about unto the north; it whirleth about continually, and the wind returneth again according to his circuits.**

7 All the rivers run into the sea; yet the sea is not full; unto the place from whence the rivers come, thither they return again.

A careful study of these verses gives us a wealth of understanding. Everything God created seems to revolve in cycles; each event that happens reveals another event to follow. The rivers run into the sea, form a cloud and rain, return only to run into the sea again and again in a different time frame. The things that have been are the things that shall be repeated in another time frame.

Verse 9 gives us a major key to understanding how events profile other events to follow.

Ecclesiastes 1:9 The thing that hath been, it is that which shall be; and that which is done is that which shall be done: and there is no new thing under the sun. 10 Is there any thing whereof it may be said, See, this is new? it hath been already of old time, which was before us.

SHADOW OF THINGS TO COME

This seems to be God's way of revealing future events thousands of years before their time of complete fulfillment. This concept is much the same as in Isaiah 46:10, which reveals that God declares the end from the beginning and from ancient times things that are not yet done. Paul states in Colossians 2:16-17 that the holy day, the new moon, and the sabbath are *only a shadow of things to come.* Many other Scriptures confirm that God has put His DNA, so to speak, in His Word in a consistent pattern throughout the Bible, revealing future events by events that have already happened.

So let's apply this concept, **"Things which have been, is that which shall be...THAT WHICH IS DONE IS THAT WHICH SHALL BE DONE,"** and watch the revelation unfold concerning the house of the Lord which Solomon built.

MEASURING THE TIME LINE

2 Chronicles 3:1 **Then Solomon began to build the house of the Lord at Jerusalem in mount Moriah, where the Lord appeared unto David his father, in the place that David had prepared in the threshing floor of Ornan the Jebusite.**
3 Now these are the things wherein Solomon was instructed for the building of the house of God. The length by cubits after the first measure was threescore cubits, and the breadth twenty cubits.
4 And the porch that was in the front of the house, the length of it was according to the breadth of the house, twenty cubits, and the height was an hundred and twenty: and he overlaid it within with pure gold.

It is interesting that the main building was 60 cubits by 20 cubits, which when added together would be 80* cubits, and the porch was 20 cubits by 20 cubits. When added together all these dimensions total 120 cubits without the measurements of the most holy place, which was inside the 120-cubit structure. The porch was also 120 cubits high. Now, remember in Genesis 6:3 the Lord said, "**...My spirit shall not always strive with man...yet his days shall be an hundred and twenty years.**"

We have already discovered that the 120 years is in reference to 120 Jubilee years, which seems to be the length of the earth lease. Could it be that the 120 cubits being the height of the porch, which is how you approach the Lord's house, would also be a clue subtly revealing the approaching 120th Jubilee as the general time frame when the Father's house will be prepared and ready for us? It is certainly a possibility, and as we continue the evidence becomes more

---

*Numerals instead of spelled out numbers will be used in this chapter to show their significance in certain prophetic events.

convincing. Verse 8 reveals that the most holy place was 20 cubits by 20 cubits, which when added together is 40 cubits.

Now let's consider the fact that the house itself was 80 cubits by the first measure without the most holy place. It seems that the 80 cubits possibly represent 80 Jubilee years (4000 years) of human history, which brings us to the birth of Christ. The 40 cubits.of the most holy house where God's Word was kept reveals the Church Age as being 40 Jubilees, which is 2000 years. This would fit prophetically with all of the other biblical numerics we have found in the Scriptures pointing to the same time frame.

> *He said it so many ways throughout the Scriptures that it is obvious that these numbers reveal a prophetic time line.*

It is also important to notice that God keeps things in numerical order throughout the Scriptures. Verse 9 states the weight of the nails for the house of the Lord was 50 shekels of gold (the number of years that make up one Jubilee). So the measurements were 120 (the number of Jubilee years given man in Genesis 6:3), and the weight of nails that held it all together was 50 shekels (the equivalent of one Jubilee). Is that a coincidence? Not at all, but it is a good example of the Solomon Concept revealing things to come.

First God revealed it in measurements; then He revealed it in the weight of gold. He said it so many ways throughout the Scriptures that it is obvious that these numbers reveal a prophetic time line.

The 120 cubits of Solomon's building were held together with 50 shekels of gold nails. A 50th anniversary is a golden anniversary. A Jubilee is 50 years, and 50 multiplied by 120 = 6000. The 120 cubits height of the porch was overlaid with gold which covered

---

*Numerals instead of spelled-out numbers will be used in this chapter to show their significance in certain prophetic events.

the approach to the house of the Lord—which would seem to indicate that after 120 golden Jubilees, the house of the Lord will be perfected. But God is not through yet. If you multiply 60 cubits by 20 cubits, you get 1200 cubits. The dimensions of the Most Holy house were 20 x 20 = 400; then the dimensions of the porch 20 x 20 = 400. Then add the total square cubits—1200 + 400 + 400 = 2000. Is it a coincidence that this number is the same as the length of the Church Age and could be indicative of the year A.D. 2000? This consistent thread of revelation begins in Genesis and weaves its way through the Scriptures into the Book of Revelation. This seems to be a time line for end-time events.

THE HOUSE OF THE LORD FINISHED

> 2 Chronicles 5:1 **Thus all the work that Solomon made for the house of the Lord was finished: and Solomon brought in all the things that David his father had dedicated; and the silver, and the gold, and all the instruments, put he among the treasures of the house of God.**

In this chapter, we find another scriptural pictorial in the celebration of the house of the Lord being finished, which also has prophetic implication concerning the fulfillment of the prophecy of Jesus in John 14. Let's refresh our memory.

> John 14:1 **Let not your heart be troubled: ye believe in God, believe also in me.**
> 2 **In my Father's house are many mansions: if it were not so, I would have told you. I go to prepare a place for you.**
> 3 **And if I go and prepare a place for you, I will come again, and receive you unto myself; that where I am, there ye may be also.**

It is obvious from these verses that the Lord is bringing prophetic insight concerning the Rapture of the Church. Jesus declared that He was going away to prepare a place for us in His

Father's house so that we could be there with Him. It goes without saying, if we are to be there with Him, we must be caught up to Heaven where He is.

Then in John, chapter 17, in his prayer to the Father, Jesus confirms again that we are to be brought to the Father's house to be with Him.

> John 17:24 **Father, I will that they also, whom thou hast given me, be with me where I am; that they may behold my glory, which thou hast given me: for thou lovedst me before the foundation of the world.**

Now, with these Scriptures fresh in mind, let's take a look at God's method of revealing from ancient times things that were not yet done. He gives us a scriptural profile of an event that foreshadows another future event which will fulfill the prophecies of Jesus and also reveal the general time frame for that fulfillment. Remember, Solomon said in Ecclesiastes 1:9, **"The thing that hath been, it is that which shall be; and that which is done is that which shall be done...."**

MOSES BROUGHT LAW BUT JESUS BROUGHT TRUTH

In 2 Chronicles 5, the Scriptures reveal that when Solomon finished building the house of the Lord, the priest brought in the ark of the covenant and placed it in the most holy place.

> **10 There was nothing in the ark save the two tables which Moses put therein at Horeb, when the Lord made a covenant with the children of Israel, when they came out of Egypt.**

It is important to remember the fact that when God gave the Law to Moses, a cloud covered the mountain *six days* before God gave him the tables of stone which were put in the ark. I believe it is significant that this verse mentions there was nothing in the ark at that time except the two tables of stone which Moses put in at Horeb.

120 PRIESTS SOUND TRUMPETS

In 2 Chronicles 5, God has woven into the celebration of the house of the Lord being finished, a revelation which corresponds perfectly with the prophetic promise of Jesus to receive us unto Himself, after *our* place in the Father's house is finished.

> **11 And it came to pass, when the priests were come out of the holy place: (for all the priests that were present were sanctified, and did not then wait by course: 12 Also the Levites which were the singers, all of them of ASAPH, of HEMAN, of JEDUTHUN, with their sons and their brethren, BEING ARRAYED IN WHITE LINEN, HAVING CYMBALS and psalteries and harps, stood at the east end of the altar, and with them AN HUNDRED AND TWENTY PRIESTS SOUNDING WITH TRUMPETS).**

In considering these verses, let me remind you that in 1 Chronicles, Asaph, Heman, and Jeduthun, were chosen because of their names. They were to prophesy with trumpets. So, let's analyze verses 11 and 12 in the light of this information.

First of all, the names in verse 12 are very revealing. Asaph means "gatherer"[1]; Heman means "faithful"[2]; Jeduthun means "praising."[3] Here is what their names and their actions seem to reveal: the high priest (Jesus), the gatherer of the faithful, praising God with sons and brethren, arrayed in white linen, having cymbals, psalteries, and harps, as the 120 priests prophesied with their trumpets of earth's coming 120th Jubilee.

This seems to be prophetic of Jesus, our High Priest, Who is the gatherer of the faithful, praising God with His sons and brethren arrayed in white linen. This has profound prophetic implications of what will happen in the New Jerusalem after the

Church is raptured. This account has amazing similarities with Revelation 19:7-9 concerning the Marriage Supper of the Lamb, in which the New Jerusalem was seen by John arrayed in fine linen, clean and white. John was told that fine linen was the righteousness of the saints.

This Marriage Supper will take place in the New Jerusalem during the time frame of the seven years of tribulation on the earth.

Verse 9 states, **"And he saith unto me, Write, Blessed are they which are called unto the marriage supper of the Lamb...."** This Marriage Supper will take place in the New Jerusalem during the time frame of the seven years of tribulation on the earth. It is also very interesting that Solomon held a **seven day feast** after the house of the Lord was finished. (2 Chronicles 7:8.)

The very context of these verses and their similarities with the celebration of the house of the Lord being finished would indicate that this is at least a parallel foreshadowing of that blessed event of the Marriage Supper of the Lamb, after our place in the Father's house has been finished.

EARTH'S GOLDEN JUBILEE

The ultimate confirmation of this matter would be the fact that there were 120 priests who blew 120 trumpets. This certainly seems to be a scriptural profile of the earth's *120th Jubilee*. Remember that God commanded Israel to blow the trumpet every 50th year and declare a year of Jubilee. (Leviticus 25:8-10.) So the 120 priests sounding 120 trumpets is indicative of earth's 120th "Total Time Jubilee." This would seem to signal two things of major importance—the 6000-year earth lease has expired and the time to favor the glorious Church—that set time—has come, as revealed in Psalm 102:13: **"Thou shalt arise, and have mercy upon Zion:**

for the time to favor her, yea, the set time, is come." Zion, at least by double reference, is a type of the Church. Verses 15 and 16 say, "So the heathen shall fear the name of the Lord, all the kings of the earth Thy glory; When the Lord shall build up Zion, He shall appear in His glory."

> 18 This shall be written for THE GENERATION TO COME: and the people which shall be created shall praise the Lord.
> 19 For he hath looked down from the height of his sanctuary; from heaven did the Lord behold the earth;
> 20 To hear the groaning of the prisoner; to loose those that are appointed to death;
> 21 To declare the name of the Lord in Zion, and his praise in Jerusalem;
> 22 When the people are gathered together, and the kingdoms, to serve the Lord.

I believe the phrase "the generation to come" in verse 18 refers to *the end-time generation* that will be alive at the time of the Rapture. Verse 20 speaks of loosing "those who are appointed to death." Could this be referring to the last righteous generation of the sixth millenium who will not die but be caught up alive?

The apostle Paul said: **"Behold I show you a mystery; we shall not all sleep, but we shall all be changed, in a moment, in the twinkling of an eye, at the last trump: for the trumpet shall sound, and the dead shall be raised incorruptible, and we shall be changed."** (1 Corinthians 15:51-52).

The prophetic words of Psalm 102 would seem to reveal that there is a time coming when the Church will be favored, not only by God but also by many in the world system. The indication in the Scriptures seems to reveal that after the earth lease expires there may be a short space of time of six months to a little less than a year, for the end-time harvest just before the Rapture takes place.

I realize this will be called speculation by some, but it all fits with the prophetic implications of the six days of the Genesis account and the prophetic time statement in Genesis 6:3.

The following verse also seems to indicate the glory of the Lord coming upon the Church for the end-time harvest.

2 Chronicles 5:13 **It came even to pass, as the trumpeters and singers were as one, to make one sound to be heard in praising and thanking the Lord; and when they lifted up their voice with the trumpets and cymbals and instruments of musick, and praised the Lord, saying, For he is good; for his mercy endureth for ever:** THAT THEN THE HOUSE WAS FILLED WITH A CLOUD, **even the house of the Lord.**

Is it a coincidence that the statement is made that "the trumpeters and singers were as one"? And Paul said the Body of Christ has many members but **one Body.**

The fact that the house of the Lord was filled with a cloud at the sound of 120 trumpets seems to be indicative of earth's 120th Golden Jubilee. This takes on a stronger prophetic implication when compared to other Scriptures which reveal that the glory of God as well as angels are sometimes manifest as clouds. I believe there is a double reference here possibly revealing that angels are going to play a greater part in revealing the glory of God that's coming on the Church just before the Rapture.

THE CHARIOTS OF GOD

Psalm 104:3-4 reveals that God **"...maketh the clouds his chariot: who walketh upon the wings of the wind: who maketh his angels spirits...."** Is it possible that the cloud that filled the house of the Lord represents not only the anointing of God but also a cloud of angels that will eventually transport the

Body of Christ to the house of the Lord when the great end-time harvest is finished?

We have a biblical precedent of angelic activity which took the spiritually body of the begger to paradise. Luke 16:22: **"...the beggar died, and was carried by the angels into Abraham's bosom...."** It seems that Michael the archangel is also in charge of the Rapture of the Church. (1 Thessalonians 4:16.) And Psalm 68:17 reveals that, **"The chariots of God are twenty thousand, even thousands of angels...."** It also states that **"...the Lord is among them, as in Sinai, in the holy place."**

In studying this account, the only visible presence that could be attributed to angels at Sinai was the cloud that covered the mountain and the fire. Then, the very next verse in Psalm 68 seems to connect these angelic chariots of God with the ascension of Christ.

> *...There seems to be a pattern of increased angelic activity at the death of saints and also when people are raptured.*

18 Thou hast ascended on high, thou hast led captivity captive: thou hast received gifts for men....

The fact that the chariots of God are thousands of angels would indicate that it was the "chariot of God" that appeared as a chariot of fire and took Elijah from the earth to Heaven.

We also know when Jesus ascended to Heaven, a cloud received Him out of their sight. So there seems to be a pattern of increased angelic activity at the death of saints and also when people are raptured.

THE GLORY OF THE LORD FILLS THE HOUSE

We need to take note of the fact that after the 120 trumpets sounded, **"...the house was filled with a cloud, even the house of the Lord; So that the priests could not stand to minister** by reason of the cloud: for the glory of the Lord had filled the house of God" (2 Chronicles 5:13-14).

The prophetic implications of these verses are also magnified in the light of Colossians 3:4: **"When Christ, who is our life, shall appear, then shall ye also appear with him in glory."**

Then in Romans 8:17-18, the apostle Paul states that we are joint-heirs with Christ and that if we suffer with him, **"...we may be also glorified together...the sufferings of this present time are not worthy to be compared with the glory which shall be revealed in us."** In Colossians 1:27 Paul reveals that **"Christ in you** [is] **the hope of glory."** The glory of God is coming on the Church (house of God) to make a quick work of righteousness on the earth.

TOTAL-TIME JUBILEE

It seems in the light of all these related Scriptures, that this account of celebrating the house of the Lord being finished is a profile of the earth's 120th TOTAL-TIME JUBILEE in which God will pour out His glory on the Body of Christ as never before so we can finish the work of righteousness on earth just before being caught up to meet Him in the air. I believe it is possible that when the earth lease expires, the righteous of the earth will have restored to them the power that was lost in the fall of man for the purpose of accelerating the end-time harvest.

The scriptural case is quite strong that the total time of man's dominion on planet Earth is to be 6000 years, or 120 Jubilees.

QUEEN OF SHEBA REVEALS JACOB'S TROUBLE

After the house of the Lord was finished, the Queen of Sheba came to visit Solomon. This may seem on the surface to have been a social visit; however, as we investigate the Scriptures, we continue to see end-time events revealed in numerical order.

2 Chronicles 8:16 **Now all the work of Solomon was prepared unto the day of the foundation of the house of the Lord, and until it was finished. So the house of the Lord was perfected.**

Could it be that this last sentence of verse 8, is by double reference, revealing the time frame when the Church (house of the Lord) will come to full maturity as Paul said in Ephesians 4:12-13?

2 Chronicles 9:1 **And when the queen of Sheba heard of the fame of Solomon, she came to prove Solomon....**

We have observed the Scriptures closely enough to know that almost immediately after the Church is caught up to be with the Lord in the Father's house, there is coming a seven year period of tribulation upon the earth.

SHEBA MEANS SEVEN

The queen of Sheba was the first to show up after the house was finished. Sheba was a Benjamite tribe which is part of Ethiopia today. It is listed in Ezekiel 38:5 as one of the countries that will come with Russia against Israel in a battle which seems to take place during the first part of the Tribulation Period. The name "Sheba" means "seven." Is it a coincidence that the first person to come on the scene after the house of the Lord was perfected had a title which means "seven"? I don't believe so; this seems to be God's way of revealing the time frame of the seven years of tribulation, called Jacob's Trouble.

It was customary in those days when they came to a king, to bring him gifts. One of the gifts the queen of Sheba brought Solomon was 120 talents of gold. The amount of gold is interesting, for it is a prophetic number, the same as the measurements of the house of the Lord. It is also the same as the number of trumpets. But it becomes even more intriguing in verse 13, which reveals in that same year, Solomon received 666 talents of gold.

"Now the weight of gold that came to Solomon in one year was six hundred and threescore and six talents of gold."

God had already said it in several ways, and this seems to be another confirmation that within a year of the 120th Jubilee the Antichrist will come on the scene and that seven-year period of tribulation will begin.

The same year the house of the Lord was perfected the queen of Sheba brought 120 talents of gold, and the number 666 shows up in the scripture, profiling the time line. We recognize this to be the number the Antichrist will use when he is revealed. (Revelation 13:18.) This is the first of three places in Scripture where the Antichrist's number appears as a profile of the timeline. A coincidence? Not at all. I believe this was God's way of confirming His prophetic Word through measurements, times, numbers, and events which have happened in the past.

Since the number 666 showed up the same year the house of the Lord was perfected, this seems to indicate that within a year of the 120th Jubilee the Antichrist will be revealed. My study of the Scriptures brings me to the conclusion that the seven years of tribulation cannot fit into the sixth millennium nor the seventh millennium. This is evident from the profile that we see in Matthew 17:1-3:

> 1 And after six days Jesus taketh Peter, James, and John his brother, and bringeth them up into an high mountain apart,
> 2 And was transfigured before them: and his face did shine as the sun, and his raiment was white as the light.
> 3 And, behold, there appeared unto them Moses and Elias talking with him.

These passages indicate that the Rapture will take place after 6000 years; therefore the seven years of tribulation cannot begin until sometime after the sixth millennium.

PROFILE OF THE TIME LINE

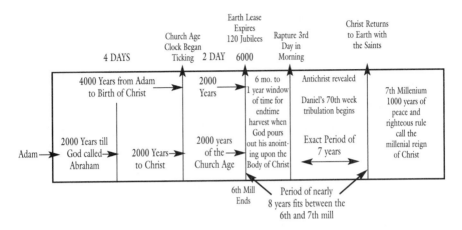

LAST SABBATICAL CYCLE

The Seventieth Week of Daniel is a sabbatical cycle. It is the last seven-year cycle of the 70 weeks of Daniel's prophecy. Therefore it must start at the beginning of a seven-year sabbatical cycle. The next seven-year cycle would seem to begin in the fall of the year 2000 or the early part of 2001 A.D.

We know from the Scriptures that Christ will return to earth after tribulation and establish an earthly kingdom for 1000 years of peace. So the seven years of tribulation can't fit into that millennium, because it will be a full 1000 years of peace and righteous rule and that period cannot begin until the end of the seven years of tribulation. (Revelation chapters 19-20; Matthew 24:29-30) The time period between the sixth and seventh millennia seems to be a parenthetical period of time what does not fit into either the sixth or the seventh millennium. It appears that the seven-year period is God's time bridge between the sixth and seventh millennia.

We have seen that Solomon received 666 talents of gold the same year the house of the Lord was perfected. This indicates that there is a space of time of less than a year between the time that the earth lease expires and the Church is raptured. He reveals that the seven years of tribulation begin after the Rapture. (2 Thessalonians 2:7-8) This gap of time shows up also in other passages.

If this is as accurate as it seems to be, this period of time between the sixth and seventh millenia will be a time in which the glorious Church will come into full maturity and reap an awesome end-time harvest of souls. In Romans 9:28 Paul reveals that **"He (God) will finish the work, and cut it short in righteousness: because a short work will the Lord make upon the earth."**

THE RIGHTEOUS SHALL BE RECOMPENSED IN THE EARTH

Major changes are coming to planet Earth before we enter the Seventh Millennium.

I believe the message God gave the prophet Isaiah applies to this generation:

Isaiah 3:10 **Say ye to the righteous, that it shall be well with him: for they shall eat the fruit of their doings. 11 Woe unto the wicked! it shall be ill with him: for the reward of his hands shall be given him.**

Proverbs 11:31 says it in a different way, but it confirms the words of Isaiah:

31 Behold, the righteous shall be recompensed in the earth: much more the wicked and the sinner.

I believe all this will happen before the Body of Christ (Church) leaves this earth.

In 2 Chronicles we have another confirmation of the same **time line** in a different way.

2 Chronicles 9:17 **Moreover the king made a great throne of ivory, and overlaid it with pure gold. 18 And there were six steps to the throne, with a footstool of gold, which were fastened to the throne....**

GOLDEN FOOTSTOOL

This passage is speaking of Solomon's earthly throne. However, it also seems to be a profile of the earthly throne from which Jesus will rule during the Millennial Reign of Christ. Take note of the fact that there were six steps which led to the throne with a footstool of gold fastened to the throne. These six steps would seem to be indicative of 6 days (6000 years) of human history before Jesus puts His enemies underfoot and rules for 1000 years here on earth.

Matthew 5:35 reveals that the earth is His footstool.

Psalm 110:1-2 states, **"The Lord said unto my Lord, Sit thou at my right hand, until I make thine enemies thy footstool. The Lord shall send the rod of thy strength out of Zion: rule thou in the midst of thine enemies."**

These verses reveal the prophetic importance of the golden footstool attached to the throne. The prophet Isaiah gives another view connected with a question about the house of the Lord and His place of rest. **"Thus saith the Lord, the heaven is my throne, and the earth is my footstool: where is the house that ye build unto me? and where is the place of my rest?"** (Isaiah 66:1).

All of these Scriptures together seem to confirm that within a year of the 120th Jubilee, a seven-year period will begin when the Antichrist shows up associated in some way with the number 666. The six steps leading up to the throne seem to confirm that six days (6000 years) must transpire before Jesus will rule from His throne in Jerusalem with His feet resting upon the golden footstool. Paul states that He must rule until He has put all enemies under His feet. (1 Corinthians 15:25-26.) This prophetic revelation stretches from Genesis to Revelation, confirming the sequence and timing of these end-time events in numerical order. It is done subtly through the Solomon Concept. (The things that have been are the things that shall be, and the things that are done are the things that shall be done.)

This same **time line** is found in the Book of Isaiah, confirming again in a different way these prophetic events connected with the end of the age.

In the next chapter we will find that this insight begins with Israel's release from Babylonian captivity.

Israel's Release:
A Composite of Their 70th Jubilee

The prophet Isaiah gave us another prophetic composite when he prophesied that Israel would be released from Babylonian captivity by a man named Cyrus.

In Isaiah 44:28, God said of Cyrus, "**...He is my shepherd, and shall perform all my pleasure: even saying to Jerusalem, Thou shalt be built; and to the temple, Thy foundation shall be laid.**" This verse seems to have a double reference revealing that Christ, God's shepherd, will also build the millennial temple after His return to earth after the Tribulation Period. The prophecy continues into chapter 45.

> **1 Thus saith the Lord to his anointed, to Cyrus, whose right hand I have holden, to subdue nations before him; and I will loose the loins of kings, TO OPEN BEFORE HIM THE TWO LEVIED GATES; and THE GATES SHALL NOT BE SHUT;**
> **2 I will go before thee, and make the crooked places straight: I will break in pieces the gates of brass, and cut in sunder the bars of iron:**
> **3 And I will give thee the treasures of darkness, and hidden riches of secret places, that thou mayest know that I, the Lord, which call thee by thy name, am the God of Israel.**

4 For Jacob my servant's sake, and Israel mine elect, I have even called thee by thy name: I have surnamed thee, though thou hast not known me.

This amazing prophecy concerning Cyrus was spoken 150 years before he was born. In these Scriptures Cyrus seems to be a type of Jesus Christ. He is even called God's shepherd. When Cyrus overthrew Babylon they had left the levied gates open from the city to the river. Cyrus diverted the river and came through those two gates that had been left open, thereby fulfilling Isaiah's prophecy exactly.

Verse 13 says, **"I have raised him up in righteousness, and I will direct all his ways: he shall build my city, and he shall let go my captives, not for price nor reward, saith the Lord of hosts."**

Cyrus seems to be a type of Christ, Who set the captives free when he arose from the dead. (Ephesians 4:8; Matthew 27:50-53.) He will again set Israel free when He returns at His Second Advent and will also build the millennial temple. (Zechariah 12:6.) Then Israel will be free from Gentile bondage for the first time in several thousand years.

SABBATH: A PERPETUAL COVENANT

We find in Exodus 31 that God had spoken to Israel concerning the sabbath Israel was to observe.

15 Six days may work be done; but in the seventh is the sabbath of rest, holy to the Lord: whosoever doeth any work in the sabbath day, he shall surely be put to death.
16 Wherefore the children of Israel shall keep the sabbath, to observe the sabbath throughout their generations, for a perpetual covenant.

17 It is a sign between me and the children of Israel for ever: for in six days the Lord made heaven and earth, and on the seventh day he rested, and was refreshed.

Keeping the sabbath was a perpetual covenant and a sign between the children of Israel and God throughout all generations. This was actually to be a rehearsal of appointed times to be kept over thousands of years. The prophetic reality of these events will be fulfilled after the Tribulation in a Seventh Millennium. It will be a time of peace and rest in which Israel will be set totally free from Gentile bondage.

> *It will be a time of peace and rest in which Israel will be set totally free from Gentile bondage.*

In Leviticus 25 God spoke to Israel saying:

**2 ...When ye come into the land which I give you, then shall the land keep a sabbath unto the Lord.
3 Six years thou shalt sow thy field, and six years thou shalt prune thy vineyard, and gather in the fruit thereof;
4 But in the seventh year shall be a sabbath of rest unto the land, a sabbath for the Lord: thou shall neither sow thy field, nor prune thy vineyard.**

God not only commanded them to keep the sabbath themselves, which was a rehearsal of events to transpire throughout their generations; He also commanded a sabbath year of rest for the land. In verses 8 through 13, God instructed them to number the "sabbaths of years" (seven times seven years), which would be a space of seven sabbaths, or forty-nine years.

They were to cause the trumpet of Jubilee to sound at the beginning of the 50th* year. They were to hallow the 50th year by proclaiming liberty throughout all the land. It was to be a year

---

*Numerals instead of spelled-out numbers will be used in some places in this chapter to show their significance in certain prophetic events.

of Jubilee in which *every man was returned his own possessions, and every man returned to his family.*

Concerning the sabbath year, verse 21 states, **"Then I will command my blessing upon you in the sixth year, and it shall bring forth fruit for three years."**

God promised to reward them abundantly if they obeyed, but Israel did not keep the covenant. Therefore, they went into Babylonian captivity for 70 years, as prophesied by the prophet Jeremiah. (Jeremiah 25:11-12.)

THE LAND ENJOYED HER SABBATHS

Second Chronicles 36 reveals that Judah was carried away into Babylon, where they were servants until the reign of the Kingdom of Persia: **"To fulfil the word of the Lord by the mouth of Jeremiah, until the land had enjoyed her sabbaths: for as long as she lay desolate she kept sabbath, to fulfil threescore and ten years"** (2 Chronicles 36:21).

Again, this verse could fit prophetically with Moses' prayer in Psalm 90:10, where he stated, **"The days of our years are threescore years and ten...."** This would seem to be a possible double reference, referring also to the 70 years in Babylonian captivity which were fulfilled at that time.

However, it also seems to have a prophetic implication of the 70 Jubilees during which time Israel would be in Gentile bondage. The year 2001 A.D. will be earth's 120th Jubilee and Israel's 70th Jubilee.

After threescore and ten years were fulfilled, the land had kept her sabbaths. The 70 years Israel was in captivity is exactly the number of "sabbaths of years" in the 490 years known as the Seventy Weeks of Daniel. (Daniel 9:24.) Is it a coincidence that all these numbers relate to prophetic events? I hardly think so. I believe they are clearly what Moses prophesied in his prayer when he said:

Psalm 90:9 **For all our days are passed away in thy wrath: we spend our years as a tale that is told. The days of our years are threescore years and ten [70]....**

It seems possible that these prophetic words of Moses also reveal that Israel will suffer 70 Jubilees of Gentile bondage.

ISRAEL PUNISHED SEVEN TIMES MORE

There also seems to be a correlation between the 70 years in Babylonian captivity and the prophecy in Leviticus 26:18, where God states, **"And if ye will not yet for all this hearken unto me, then I will punish you seven times more for your sins."**

This statement is made three times in the context of seven verses.

The 70 years in Babylonian captivity were Israel's punishment for not keeping the perpetual covenant of sabbaths. If God punished them seven times more, that would be 70 x 7, which is 490 years.

This fits perfectly with Daniel's prophecy in Daniel 9 commonly called the Seventy Weeks of Daniel. The angel revealed to Daniel that God would deal with Israel for 70 weeks of years (490). This time span was determined by God to deal with Israel and make an end of sins, to make reconciliation for iniquity, to bring in everlasting righteousness, to seal up the vision and prophecy, and to anoint the most holy (Daniel 9:24).

But after 69 weeks of years (483 years) had passed, they crucified the Messiah; then it seems that God turned off His time clock, postponing His final week of dealing with Israel until after the Church Age. He turned His attention to the Gentiles for two days (2000 years). This left one week (7 years), which is commonly referred to as the Seventieth Week of Daniel, in which God will finish dealing with Israel.

The Seventieth Week is that seven-year period referred to by many Bible scholars as the Tribulation Period. It is an exact period of 7 years and begins immediately after the Church has been raptured. (Revelation 6:2.)

In those seven years, God will fulfill the prophetic Word He gave to Daniel.

Daniel 9:24 **Seventy weeks are determined upon thy people and upon thy holy city, to finish the transgression, and to make an end of sins, and to make reconciliation for iniquity, and to bring in everlasting righteousness, and to seal up the vision and prophecy, and to anoint the most Holy.**

It is clear that by the end of Daniel's Seventieth Week God will have fulfilled this prophecy completely. There will be no more iniquity, and there will be everlasting righteousness in Jerusalem.

TOTAL-TIME JUBILEE

Scriptural evidence seems to reveal that earth's 120th Jubilee and Israel's 70th Jubilee will both be somewhere around the year 2001.* The prophetic implications seem to reveal that we experience the earth's 120th Jubilee about the time we enter the great end-time harvest. And that would seem to be a few months before the Body of Christ is caught up with the Lord to the Father's house.

I believe the Church will truly experience Total-Time Jubilee, with everything being restored that was lost in the fall of man. Then after the harvest is completed there will be a reunion in Heaven for seven years before we come back to rule and reign with Christ.

However, for those left on the earth, *their* Jubilee celebration will be delayed seven more years while God fulfills His prophetic Word concerning Israel and the wicked of the earth.

---

*This is not to be confused with Israel's first Jubilee as a nation after being restored in 1948. They celebrated that Jubilee in 1998. Their normal Juilee will be in the fall of the year 2000.

Since neither Israel nor the wicked of the earth have lived out that seven years prophesied by Daniel, God has the prerogative to insert this parenthetical time period of seven years back into his calender of events, for it must be fulfilled before the nation of Israel is totally restored. (Isaiah 32:15-18.)

The Seventieth Week of Daniel will complete the prophesied 490 years of God's dealings with Israel. During that time frame He will finish transgressions to bring an end to sin, make reconciliation for iniquity, and usher in everlasting righteousness in Jerusalem. God's thread of prophetic truth continues into 2 Chronicles 36 and the Book of Ezra, confirming again the *time frame* in which the Antichrist and his number, 666, appear on the scene.

> *Earth's 120th Jubilee and Israel's 70th Jubilee will both be somewhere around the year 2001.*

CYRUS FULFILLS JEREMIAH'S PROPHECY

In the closing chapter of 2 Chronicles, Zedekiah reigned over Jerusalem doing that which was evil in the sight of the Lord. The Lord in His mercy sent messengers many times because He had compassion on His people. But they mocked the messengers of God, despised His words, and misused His prophets until the wrath of the Lord arose against them. (2 Chronicles 36:16.)

Then Nebuchadnezzar's army burned the house of the Lord and broke down the walls of Jerusalem, and Israel went into Babylonian captivity for seventy years:

> 2 Chronicles 36:21 **To fulfil the word of the Lord by the mouth of Jeremiah, until the land had enjoyed her sabbaths: for as long as she lay desolate she kept sabbath, to fulfil threescore and ten years.**
> **22 Now in the first year of Cyrus king of Persia, that the word of the Lord spoken by the mouth of Jeremiah might be accomplished, the Lord stirred up the**

spirit of Cyrus king of Persia, that he made a procla-
mation throughout all his kingdom, and put it also in
writing, saying,

23 Thus saith Cyrus king of Persia, All the kingdoms
of the earth hath the Lord God of heaven given me;
and he hath charged me to build him an house in
Jerusalem, which is in Judah. Who is there among you
of all his people? The Lord his God be with him, and
let him go up.

Cyrus seems to be a type of Christ, Who sets his people free
and builds the millennial temple when He sets up His kingdom.
(Zechariah 6:12.) It is significant that Cyrus released Israel after
70 years of captivity, which had been prophesied by Jeremiah. We
have seen previously that the 70 years of Babylonian captivity evidently represent 70 Jubilee years (3500 years) in which Israel will
be in Gentile bondage after their exodus from Egypt. The time
frame of this event corresponds perfectly with the prophetic
Scriptures, for the earth's 120th Jubilee will mark Israel's 70th
Jubilee from the first pentecost of Exodus 19.

ADONIKAM BRINGS BACK 666

Then, as we look into the Book of Ezra, the number 666
shows up in the exact prophetic time frame that was revealed in 2
Chronicles, chapter 9. When Cyrus released the Jews from captivity, those who chose to leave Babylon to rebuild the house of the
Lord in Jerusalem were listed. Ezra 2:13 states, **"The children of
Adonikam, six hundred sixty and six."** This statement is
prophetic, not only because it contains the number 666, but also
because the name Adonikam means "the Lord has risen."[1] This
has profound prophetic implications when considered in the time
frame of their return to Jerusalem. This is the second time that the
number 666 shows up in the Scriptures as a time line profile. It is
in the exact prophetic time frame as the number 666 we found in
2 Chronicles 9:13. This is revealed in the fact that when the house

of the Lord was finished, the number 120 appeared numerous times. It was in measurements and also in the amount of gold the queen of Sheba brought to Solomon. It was also revealed in the height of the porch and the 120 priests sounding trumpets.

Israel's 70 years of Babylonian captivity would seem to represent 70 Jubilee years (3500 years) before Israel will be totally free. When Adonikam came back to Jerusalem, his descendants numbered 666. A coincidence? Not at all. It is God's pattern of prophetic truth woven through the Scriptures from Genesis to Revelation, revealing the same time line of these end-time events.

It seems that God has decided to give us this revelation in so many different ways that it would be almost impossible not to recognize this as being scriptural pictorials profiling His time line to this generation.

ADONIKAM PROFILES RAPTURE

The name "Adonikam" also magnifies the prophetic implications concerning the time frame of the earth's TOTAL-TIME Jubilee. His name means *The Lord has risen,* or *the Lord arose.* This is very significant in light of the fact that Paul states that Jesus is the Head of the Body, the Church. (Colossians 1:18.) The Church is now the Body of Christ, and remember when the bright light blinded Paul on the road to Damascus, Jesus said, **"Why persecutest thou me?"** (Acts 9:4). Paul was persecuting the Church, but Jesus took it personally, because He considered the Church to be Him (His Body).

So, it is clear that Jesus considered the Church to be Him. For we are members of His Body—His flesh, and His bone. We are many members but one Body in Christ. (Romans 12:5; 1 Corinthians 10:17.)

1 Corinthians 12:12 **For as the body is one, and hath many members, and all the members of that one body, being many, are one body: so also is Christ.**

It is possible that this is the message God has placed in the pattern of this event so that the name of Adonikam subtly reveals that the Church, being His Body, will be caught up with Him just before the Antichrist, with the number 666, comes on the scene after Israel's 70th Jubilee. It is the second confirmation of three Scriptures in which the number 666 is revealed in the exact prophetic time frame.

So, it appears to be a subtle revelation of God's time frame of end-time events. This revelation continues with Christ's ascension, confirming the same time line for events that will end this age.

Christ's Ascension and His Return

John 14:1 **Let not your heart be troubled: ye believe in God, believe also in me.**
2 In my Father's house are many mansions: if it WERE NOT SO, I would have told you. I go to prepare a place for you.
3 And if I go and prepare a place for you, I will come again, and receive you unto myself; that where I am, THERE ye may be also.
4 And whither I go ye know, and the way ye know.

These words of Jesus in verses 1-3 are prophetic. In this generation, those who are without the knowledge of God's Word are truly troubled because of the chaotic condition of world affairs. Yet at the time of His betrayal, Jesus gave a prophetic message of comfort by saying He was going to prepare a place for us in the Father's house. Then He would come again to receive us to Himself so we could be with Him in the Father's house.

Notice Jesus' statement in verse 4: **"...whither I go ye know, and the way ye know."** (They knew that after His death.) Jesus was seen of them *forty days;* then He was raptured (caught up to the Father's house) before their very own eyes. This has prophetic implications that the Church (Body of Christ) will depart the same way they saw Jesus go after 40 Jubilees of the Church Age. How long after 40 Jubilees? We don't know exactly, but the indication is that it will be a short time after that 2000-year period.

Those who believe God should also believe these prophetic statements and consider their implications carefully.

> **The stabilizing force for the righteous of the earth is God's Word which abides in them.**

The stabilizing force for the righteous of the earth is God's Word which abides in them. The stabilizing forces of the Church are found in the prophetic Scriptures. In John, chapter 17, just before Jesus was betrayed, He prayed, **"Father, I will that they also, whom thou hast given me, be with me where I am; that they may behold my glory..."** (v. 24). This too is another confirmation of His plan that the righteous shall be with Him where He is now.

When Jesus had finished His work on the earth and was about to depart to be with His Father, His disciples thought that He would at that time set up His kingdom on the earth.

THEIR QUESTION

Acts 1:6 **When they therefore were come together, they asked of him, saying, Lord, wilt thou at this time restore again the kingdom to Israel?**

Jesus had given them inside information which they didn't understand because of their own preconceived ideas about the time of His kingdom.

He told them He was going to suffer, die, and be raised from the dead. But at the time of His approaching death, they were still arguing about who would sit on His right and on His left when He set up His kingdom. (Mark 10:35-45.)

In Acts, chapter 1, after His resurrection, they were *still* questioning Him concerning things to come. He had appeared to them off and on for forty days, and they thought surely He would at that time set up His kingdom on the earth.

HIS ANSWER

Acts 1:7 **And he said unto them, It is not for you to know the times or the seasons, which the Father hath put in his own power.**

Jesus made similar statements on several occasions. (Mark 13:32; Matthew 24:36.)

The Scriptures reveal that it would be foolish for anyone to try to set the exact date of the Rapture at this time. However, the fact that Elijah and Jesus knew the exact day they were to be raptured would seem to indicate that God may reveal that information before the Rapture takes place. Both Elijah and Jesus are profiles of the Church.

But I want to reiterate that it is not my purpose to try to set an exact date for the Rapture, but rather to point you to the prophetic revelation which does establish a general time frame for all end-time events. We are children of the day and should not be in the dark concerning the events that are about to be fulfilled in this generation.

Jesus continued His answer by shifting His emphasis to receiving the Holy Spirit.

Acts 1:8 **But ye shall receive power, after that the Holy Ghost is come upon you: and ye shall be witnesses unto me both in Jerusalem, and in all Judaea, and in Samaria, and unto the uttermost part of the earth.**

Jesus seemed to emphasize that there was something more important that had to transpire on earth before God's prophetic time table would permit Him to set up His kingdom on earth. First, the Holy Spirit (Spirit of Truth) must come, and He would teach us and guide us into all truth and show us "things to come."

(John 16:13-15.) Could this be a clue that the Holy Spirit may reveal the time of the Rapture to those who will experience that blessed event? We don't know for sure. We will have to wait and see.

> Acts 1:9 **And when he had spoken these things, while they beheld, he was taken up; and a cloud received him out of their sight.**
> **10 And while they looked stedfastly toward heaven as he went up, behold, two men stood by them in white apparel;**
> **11 Which also said, Ye men of Galilee, why stand ye gazing up into heaven? this same Jesus, which is taken up from you into heaven, shall so come in like manner as ye have seen him go into heaven.**
> **12 Then returned they unto Jerusalem from the mount called Olivet, which is from Jerusalem a sabbath day's journey.**

Remember the words of Jesus in John 14:4, **"And whither I go ye know, and the way ye know."** The disciples watched Jesus ascend into the heavens as a cloud received Him out of their sight. This is how they knew where He had gone and the way He had gone; it is obvious that He was raptured while they watched.

Let's consider some interesting observations. When Jesus was born, the physical *body of Christ* came to earth. That was His personal body. Then in John 12:24, Jesus said, **"...Except a corn of wheat fall into the ground and die, it abideth alone: but if it die, it bringeth forth much fruit."** When His physical body died, it was placed in a tomb, and when He arose from death, His physical body had gone through a transformation and was a spiritual body (see 1 Corinthians 15:35-50). Then, after he was seen of them 40 days*, He was caught up into Heaven and the believers (the Church) became the only *body of Christ* on earth. And Paul

---

*We will again use numerals instead of spelled-out numbers in this chapter to show their significance in certain prophetic events.

said, **"Now ye are the body of Christ, and members in particular"** (1 Corinthians 12:27).

Acts 1:3 reveals that He showed Himself alive after His passion by many infallible proofs, being seen of them 40 days, and speaking of things pertaining to the kingdom of God. Then after 40 days, He (the body of Christ) was raptured. This would seem to have profound prophetic implications when we consider that God told His people they would spend a year in the wilderness for each of the 40 days they searched the land in unbelief. (Numbers 14:34.)

The implications are that the Church will depart the same way the original body of Christ (Jesus) departed the earth.

He fed them supernaturally with manna for 40 years. They were commanded to gather just enough manna on each of the five days for one day; but on the sixth day, which seems to bear witness of the 6000th year of human history, they gathered twice as much.

Then, consider the scriptural precedent in Daniel 9:24 which reveals an end-time event in which a day represents a year. We have already seen that the 120 years spoken of in Genesis 6:3 seem to represent Jubilee years.

Since all of these are connected with end-time events, the prophetic implications seem to indicate that the 40 days in which Jesus was seen on earth after He arose was a scriptural pictorial revealing that the Church (Body of Christ) will be on the earth for at least 40 Jubilees (2000 years) before being caught up to Heaven. The implications are that the Church will depart the same way the *original* body of Christ (Jesus) departed the earth by being caught up after the 40 Jubilees of the Church Age.

CHRIST'S TEMPTATION—COMPOSITE OF THE CHURCH

Let's consider another time period of 40 days, which could also be of prophetic importance.

Luke 4:1 **And Jesus being full of the Holy Ghost returned from Jordan, and was led by the Spirit into the wilderness,**
2 Being forty days tempted of the devil.

Here again the Scripture reveals that Jesus, the physical body of Christ, was in the wilderness 40 days being tempted of the devil. It seems that Jesus Himself was a true living pictorial of the Church. Since we have precedent for a day in the wilderness representing a year, this would fit as a parallel of the the Body of Christ (Church) being tempted on earth for 40 Jubilees (2000 years) of the Church Age before being raptured.

To say the least, the prophetic implications are astoundingly accurate. In any event, we shall soon know the truth of this matter.

HIS ASCENT

Jesus ascended to Heaven from the Mount of Olives. This will be the exact place where He will return with the saints on the evening of the last day of the Tribulation Period. (Zechariah 14:1-5, Revelation 11:3-20.)

It's interesting that Acts 1:12 mentions that it is a "sabbath day's journey" from the Mount of Olives into Jerusalem, which is less than a mile. The Scriptures reveal that Jesus will descend on the Mount at the beginning of the Seventh Millennium. This seems to be what the sabbath day represented to Israel under the Old Covenant—a day of peace and rest.

The six days God labored plus the seventh day of rest represent a time period of 7000 years in which He will deal with mankind to weed out the wicked of the earth and gather the righteous into an eternal state.

God hallowed the seventh day and told Israel to honor it. It represented the last Millennium before eternity, in which Israel will be raised up and live in His sight. (Hosea 6:2.)

PROFILE OF THE RAPTURE–THIRD DAY

We find in Exodus 19 an event which gives us marvelous insight concerning both the Rapture and Christ's Second Advent.

Exodus 19:10 **And the Lord said unto Moses, Go unto the people, and sanctify them to day and to morrow, and let them wash their clothes,**
11 And be ready against THE THIRD DAY: for the third day the Lord will come down in the sight of all the people upon mount Sinai.

The Lord instructed Moses to sanctify the people two days. The prophetic implication of this phrase seems to confirm the Church Age to be two days, which would be two 1000-year days. The people were to be sanctified and prepared for the third day, for on the third day the Lord was coming down on the mountain in the sight of all of His people.

These verses give us both a profile of the Rapture of the Church and also a parallel to the Second Advent. The significance of the third day is that when you begin counting from the birth of Jesus to measure the 2000 years of the Church Age, then the third day would indicate at least the time frame of His appearance to catch away the Church.

The two paragraphs below are from YACOV RAMBSEL'S Book *His Name Is Jesus.*

In Exodus 19:13, starting with the first letter of the sixteenth word, counting every third word, and reading only the first letter spells *Jehovah* יהוה. In Exodus 19:15, starting with the seventh word, and reading the first letter of every third word spells *Jehovah* יהוה. In Exodus 19:16, starting with the first letter and reading only the first letter spells *Oshiah* הושע, which means "He will save." Note that in Exodus 19:23 when we combine in sequence the second, third, and fourth words, it spells "Moses and Elijah"

Moshe Eliyah משה אליהו. Moses and Elijah were together on the Mount of Transfiguration with Jesus many years later.

In Exodus 19:13, starting with the ninth word and counting the first letter of every sixteenth word from left to right spells [Jehovah] יוהי. In Exodus 19:15, starting with the seventh word, the first letter of every fourth word from left to right uncovers [Jehovah] יוהי. In Exodus 19:11, starting with the first letter of the fourth to last word, counting every third word, and reading only the first letter spells "the jubilee ." היבל

> **It's obvious that only those who are ready for the Rapture will see Jesus when He appears to catch away the Church.**

I find this to be a very significant revelation in the fact that the names of Moses and Elijah appear together in verse 23, which reveals that all the people could not come up to meet with God. Then the words *"the jubilee"* appear in verse 11. The acceptable year of the Lord would be considered the final Jubilee that Jesus referred to in Luke 4:19.

Hebrews 9:28 states, **"Christ was offered to bear the sins of many; and unto them that look for him shall he appear the second time without sin unto salvation** (deliverance)." It's obvious that only those who are ready for the Rapture will see Jesus when He appears to catch away the Church. Exodus 19:16-17 seem to accurately profile the Rapture. Any time after the 2000 years (two days) of the Church Age would be considered the "third day," and that seems to indicate the time frame when Jesus will come down in the sight of all His people to receive them unto Himself.

When Jesus appears to catch away the Church, He does not come physically to the earth. He appears about mountain-top high, and we are caught up to meet Him in the air. This could also serve as a parallel to the Second Advent. It will still be considered the "third millennial day" after the Tribulation when

Jesus descends on the Mount of Olives to destroy the armies of the Antichrist and set up His righteous rule for 1000 years.

Keep in mind the Solomon concept—**"The thing that hath been, it is that which shall be; and that which is done is that which shall be done"** (Ecclesiastes 1:9). It is through this concept that Exodus 19:16 gives us unusual insight which seems to confirm a time frame for the Rapture of the Church in a most interesting way.

Exodus 19:16 **And it came to pass on the third day IN THE MORNING, that there were thunders and lightnings, and a thick cloud upon the mount, and the voice of the trumpet exceeding loud; so that all the people that was in the camp trembled.**

This verse reveals that it was the morning of the third day when they heard the voice of a trumpet exceedingly loud. It's interesting that it says "the voice of a trumpet" instead of "the sound of a trumpet." Why the voice of a trumpet? The apostle Paul said, **"The Lord himself shall descend from heaven with a shout, WITH THE VOICE OF THE ARCHANGEL, and with the trump of God: and the dead in Christ shall rise first: Then we which are alive and remain shall be caught up together with them in the clouds, to meet the Lord in the air..."** (1 Thessalonians 4:16-17). Notice that Paul mentions the voice of the archangel, which would be Michael. It is his voice blended with the trump of God.

MOSES BROUGHT THE PEOPLE TO MEET GOD

It's obvious there was a voice blended with this trumpet and it was exceedingly loud. Verse 17 reveals that Moses **"brought forth the people out of the camp to meet with God."** This seems to be a scriptural profile revealing the Rapture of the Church to be a short time after the two days of the Church Age have expired. It is said to be the third day in the morning. This is where it becomes very interesting because the Hebrew day does not begin in the morning. It begins in the evening at sundown. We pick up on this in the Genesis account where it describes the days as "the evening and the morning". It was on the third day of creation that God's creation produced fruit after his kind. If it is the third day in the morning when the Rapture takes place, then it would not be immediately after the second day. There would be a time gap between the end of the second day and the morning of the third day when the Lord came down in the sight of His people.

The third day seems to be an all inclusive term which begins at the end of the two days of the Church Age and includes the transition into the new millennium. This transition period would include the endtime harvest, the rapture of the Church, the seven years of Tribulation as well as the millennial reign of Christ (See Hosea 6:2).

Let's look again at some facts to refresh our memory. Jesus was born after four days (4000 years) of human history; then adding the two days (1000-year days of the Church Age) makes the 6000 years. It seems that between the sixth and the seventh millennia there is a time gap of at least seven years and possibly eight years. And that period of time is not considered the Seventh Millennium as far as God is concerned. The time period of the Tribulation and the few months for the end-time harvest between the sixth and the seventh millennia is a parenthetical period of time (in other words, it fits in parentheses between the two millennia). During that period of time, a day represents a year.

So if this profiles the time frame of the Rapture being the third day in the morning, it is obvious that the two days of the Church Age will have expired. It also indicates there will be a time gap between the end of the second day and the morning of the third day of at least twelve hours and possibly as many as twenty-four hours, which would represent a period of at least six months to a year.*

TORAH REVEALS RAPTURE

Here is what Yacov Rambsel has found in the original Hebrew Torah. Starting with the fourth letter in verse 16, reading every other Hebrew letter from left to right spells the Hebrew word *B'Shilhuv*.[2]

The Hebrew phrase *B'Shilhuv* בשלהוב means "In the rapture"

Exodus 19:16

ויהיביומהשלישיבהית

B'shilhuv is found* backwards using an interval of 2.

It is found embedded in the phrase "and it came to pass on the morning of the third day." This gives us an obvious clue that this verse profiles the Rapture of the Church, and it would seem to indicate a time frame of somewhere between six months and a year after the earth lease expires.

Exodus 19:20 **"And the Lord came down upon mount Sinai, on the top of the mount: and the Lord called Moses up to the top of the mount; and Moses went up."** Now remember Moses, who to us represents the righteous dead of 120 Jubilees, was called up to the mountain of God. The fact that Moses was called up to the mountain the morning of the third day seems to indicate a time frame of the resurrection and the Rapture.

I had a Hebrew scholar check chapter 19 for the word "Elijah" to see if it was embedded in the original Hebrew in an ELS skip sequence. Elijah's name is found six times in this chapter imbedded

---

*Hebrew day is divided in only two segments evening and morning so the morning of the third day could be any time from 12 hours to 24 hours from the end of the second day.

˙ Hebrew is read from right to left, so the fact that this message is found reading from right to left could be because the church is made up of mostly Gentiles and this message would not be backwards to us.

in the phrase "unto the Lord." I would say that is significant revelation because of the fact that Moses represents the righteous dead of 120 Jubilees, and Elijah represents the Church that will be caught up alive. They are both named in this chapter—Moses being called up to the top of the mountain, Elijah's name being in the Hebrew text. This would seem to be an astounding revelation that has been hidden in the Hebrew text to be revealed to this generation.

> *God has kept these end-time events in perfect numerical order throughout the Scriptures.*

While searching this chapter for more confirmation of the Rapture in an ELS sequence, we found another significant message embedded in the Hebrew: "Michael, he took, Church into Heaven." Could it be that through the Solomon concept God has revealed the fulfillment of end-time prophecy in detail? **"The thing that hath been, it is that which shall be; and that which is done is that which shall be done"** (Ecclesiastes 1:9). One thing is sure—we won't have to wait long to know if these messages are accurate revelations of the Rapture.

CLOUD COVERED MOUNTAIN SIX DAYS

There is another incident concerning Moses and this same mountain which also parallels the resurrection of the righteous dead at the time of the Rapture. It is found in Exodus 24.

> **16 And the glory of the Lord abode upon mount Sinai, and the cloud covered it SIX DAYS: and the seventh day he called unto Moses out of the midst of the cloud.**
> **18 And Moses WENT INTO THE MIDST OF THE CLOUD....**

The fact that Moses went up into the cloud after six days corresponds perfectly with Matthew 17:1-3. When applying the 1000-years-as-a-day concept, this again confirms the time frame of the Rapture to be *after* 6000 years.

Since Moses was God's profile of the righteous dead of 120 Jubilee years (6000 years), the details of this event certainly have prophetic implications. The 6 days of the Genesis account, representing 6000 years, would correspond with the 6 days in which the cloud covered the mountain before Moses was called up into the cloud. So it is apparent that the 6-day emphasis in Genesis continues through the Bible into the Book of Revelation, revealing a consistent time frame of prophetic events. All of these Scriptures point to the same time line—6 days, or 6000 years, plus about a year for the awesome end-time harvest. The 7 years of Jacob's Trouble must be fulfilled before the seventh 1000-year day of peace, at which time Satan will be bound in the bottomless pit.

God has kept these end-time events in perfect numerical order throughout the Scriptures. Exodus 21 reveals that a Hebrew servant was to serve *six years* and be released the *seventh year.* Then there were the six days that Joshua marched around Jericho with seven priests blowing seven trumpets. Then the six days that Jesus waited before taking Peter, James, and John up to a high mountain apart to be transfigured before them. These are all connected by the same *time line.*

It also seems obvious that God chose Moses to represent all the righteous dead of the 120 Jubilee years, who will be caught up in the clouds to meet the Lord in the air *after six days.* Those six days indicate the total time in which God will deal with mankind under the earth lease of Genesis 1:26-31. These events seem to be God's way of revealing, through the Solomon Concept, what the twenty-first century holds for both the Church and planet Earth.

EARTH LEASE PROFILE

In Mark 12 Jesus gives us a profile of the earth lease in a parable.

1 "And He began to speak unto them by parables. A certain man planted a vineyard, and set an hedge about it, and digged a place for the winevat, and built

a tower, and let it out to husbandmen, and went into a far country.

2 And at the season he sent to the husbandmen a servant, that he might receive from the husbandmen of the fruit of the vineyard.

3 And they caught him, and beat him, and sent him away empty.

4 And again he sent unto them another servant; and at him they cast stones, and wounded him in the head, and sent him away shamefully handled.

5 And again he sent another; and him they killed, and many others; beating some, and killing some.

6 Having yet therefore one son, his well-beloved, he sent him also last unto them, saying, They will reverence my son.

7 But those husbandmen said among themselves, This is the heir; come let us kill him, and the inheritance shall be ours.

8 And they took him, and killed him, and cast him out of the vineyard.

9 What shall therefore the lord of the vineyard do? He will come and destroy the husbandmen, and will give the vineyard unto others."

Notice Jesus asked the question; then He gave the answer, which I believe to be prophetic. He reveals that the vineyard will be given to those who are willing to deliver the fruit of the vineyard to its rightful owner.

POSSIBLE SCENARIO OF FUTURE EVENTS

Let me give you a scenario of what I believe could possibly happen during that period of time after the earth lease expires just before the Rapture. It seems that the authority of the earth will be delivered to the righteous who are here on the earth at the time the earth lease expires.

I see indications that God will restore to the righteous the authority and dominion that was lost in the fall of mankind by pouring out His anointing on the Body of Christ. This seems to be a window of time of possibly six months to a year in which God turns up His power to expedite the great end-time harvest.

Remember the Ananias and Sapphira incident in the early days of the Church? The anointing of God was so strong that when they lied they died. You may see it again when God pours out His anointing for the end-time harvest. The prophet Isaiah spoke of a time in the future when **"moreover the light of the moon shall be as the light of the sun, and ...the light of the sun shall be sevenfold, as the light of seven days, in the day that the Lord bindeth up the breach of His people, and healeth the stroke of their wound** (Isaiah 30:26). The fourth day of the Genesis account profiles Christians as the moon, which reflects the light of the sun of righteousness to a sin-darkened world. When the light of the moon becomes as the light of the sun, the prophetic implications are that we will minister as Christ ministered. This seems to be what Paul referred to in the fourth chapter of Ephesians.

> *...the Body of Christ will reap an awesome end-time harvest of souls into the kingdom of God.*

THE MATURED CHURCH—A PERFECT MAN

Ephesians 4:7 **But unto every one of us is given grace according to the measure of the gift of Christ.**
11 And he gave some apostles, and some prophets, and some evangelists, and some pastors and teachers;
12 For the perfecting of the saints, for the work of the ministry, for the edifying of the body of Christ;
13 Till we all come in the unity of the faith, and of the knowledge of the Son of God, unto a perfect man, unto the measure of the stature of the fulness of Christ...."

How will all this come about? It seems that when the wicked of the earth lose their authority, demons also lose their power over humanity for a short time in which the Body of Christ will reap an awesome end-time harvest of souls into the kingdom of God.

SUPPOSE DEMONS WERE EVICTED

Even though God gave mankind authority and dominion over this earth for 6000 years, the devil and demons have been able to influence wicked men and use their authority to kill, steal and destroy. The apostle Paul said **"...the god of this world hath blinded the minds of them which believe not, lest the light of the glorious Gospel of Christ... should shine unto them"** (2 Corinthians 4:4). But suppose demons were evicted from humanity for a window of time for the end-time harvest. If that were the case you couldn't build churches big enough nor fast enough to hold all the converts. I see some indication in the Scriptures that this may very well happen. We get some clues from the fifth chapter of Mark.

> **2 And when He was come out of the ship, immediately there met Him out of the tombs a man with an unclean spirit,**
> **3 Who had his dwelling among the tombs; and no man could bind him, no not with chains.**

LEGION—A POSSIBLE PROFILE OF 6000 YEAR OF LEASE

When Jesus asked him his name he said: "My name is Legion for we are many." (A Roman legion in Jesus' day was generally considered to be 6000 foot soldiers).

2000 POSSIBLY PROFILES END OF CHURCH AGE

Mark 5:12 And all the devils besought Him saying, send us into the swine that we may enter them. And

**forthwith Jesus gave them leave and the unclean spir-
its went out and entered into the swine; and the heard
ran violently down a steep place into the sea (they were
about *two thousand)* and were choked in the sea.**

Notice in these verses that the number 6000 and the number
2000 are associated with demons being evicted from a man who
was then clothed and in his right mind. Could this be a profile of
demons being evicted from humanity for a short period of the
glorious end-time harvest? These numbers correspond perfectly
with the time lines we have followed through the Scriptures.

Demons and evil spirits have to usurp the authority of mankind
to do anything on the earth. We know they have perverted the
minds of men and kept them from the Gospel. Could it be that
when they lose access to mans authority, they also lose their ability to confuse the minds of men?

This could be one of the reasons that Jesus said we would do the
greater works. (John 14:12) I believe there is a time coming in this
end-time harvest when wicked men dare not come against the work
of God lest their obituaries appear in the morning paper as a Sover-
eign Act of God's Judgment. There is no doubt that God is fed up
with the wicked ruling the earth, and it's not God's style for the
Church Age to end in defeat. We've looked at the Church for years
with the thought, *When is this Glorious Church which Paul referred to
in Ephesians 4 going to show up?* I think we've found the clue. When
God's commitment to the earth lease is fulfilled He can do anything
He well pleases here on earth. It seems His first move will be to turn
the power and light up for the endtime harvest.

The story continues with Mark 5:15: **"And they come to
Jesus, and see him that was possessed with the devil, and had
the legion, sitting, and clothed, and in his right mind; and
they were afraid."** This could be a profile of the fear which will
come upon the wicked when they see the Body of Christ ministering with that stronger anointing.

Now as you follow Jesus the next event of prophetic significance seems to be the healing of the woman who had an issue of blood twelve years. She slipped up behind Him and touched His clothes, and the anointing that was upon Jesus brought her instant healing.

When satan came to earth he brought sin, sickness and disease. When the earth lease expires I believe, as far as the Body of Christ is concerned, sickness and disease will melt like a snowball in the August sun.

The next event with prophetic implications was the fact that Jesus went to Jairus' house and resurrected his daughter who had died. Isn't it interesting that his daughter was born the same year this woman came down with the issue of blood? She had that disease twelve years, and Jairus' daughter was twelve years old.

Lets review the sequence of events: Demons were evicted from a man called Legion (6000). The demons entered into 2000 swine, and they were choked in the sea. The sick were healed and the dead was raised to life. Is it possible that these events profile the expiration of the earth lease, revealing that demons will be evicted from humanity for a short period of time and that the sick will be healed? If so, then the raising of Jairus' daughter would seem to profile the resurrection that will accompany the Rapture. You can be the judge of this matter; but to say the least, it looks very suspicious.

The scriptures indicate that after that window of time for the glorious end-time harvest the Church will be raptured. Then it seems that demons will come back seven times worse during the seven years of tribulation (Luke 11:24-26) because that seven-year period is a delayed Sabbatical cycle from earth lease time which has never been fulfilled. Will this scenario really happen? One thing is sure: We shall soon know if we are reading the scriptural time line and profiles accurately.

When you consider this scenario in the light of the words of Solomon and Isaiah you realize the possibilities are very real, but only time itself will fully reveal the truth of this matter (Ecl. 1:9-10).

Isaiah 3:10 **Say ye to the righteous, that it shall be well with him: for they shall eat the fruit of their doings. 11 Woe unto the wicked! it shall be ill with him: for the reward of his hands shall be given him.**

COMPASSED ABOUT WITH A CLOUD OF WITNESSES

It seems at this point in our scriptural journey we can surely say that we are compassed about by a cloud of prophetic witnesses concerning these end-time events. Let's do a quick review to bring these events into focus again before the conclusion of this book.

REVIEW OF PROPHETIC WITNESSES

We began our journey in Genesis, where we found that the six days of the Genesis account represent 6000 years of human history before the Seventh Millennium of rest, in which Christ will rule the earth.

Then we found in Genesis 6:3 that the 120 Jubilee years are in reference to the same 6000 years. This serves as the second witness of the same time line found in Genesis 1.

As we have gone through the Scriptures, we have found that God fed Israel for forty years with manna in the wilderness. (Exodus 16.) And it is very likely that forty years is symbolic of forty Jubilee years (2000 years) in which the Church is fed with manna (Bread) from Heaven. (John 6:32-35.)

They gathered just enough manna on each of the five days for one day; but on the sixth day, which seems to be symbolic of the six thousandth year of human history, they gathered twice as much. This indicates that this last generation will receive twice as much revelation as any other generation.

We were witnesses of the fact that Joshua (who was a type of Jesus) marched around Jericho once a day for six days. Seven priests blowing seven trumpets witness to the fact that God would warn the wicked world for 6000 years; then at the end of the Seventh Millennium He would make an end of all wickedness on planet Earth. (Joshua 6:3-4.)

We have found that the Hebrew servant served for six years and the seventh year was to go free, indicating that in the Seventh Millennium Israel will be totally free from Gentile bondage. (Exodus 21:2.)

Moses was born with a death sentence hanging over him, but God preserved his life, and the years of his life were as a tale that was told. He lived 120 years, representing 120 Jubilee years which would encompass all the righteous dead of the 6000 years of human history. (Exodus 1:22-2:10.)

We witnessed the fact that in Matthew 16:28 Jesus said there were some standing there that would not taste death until they saw the Son of Man coming in his kingdom.

Then after six days, Jesus took Peter, James and John up to a high mountain and was transfigured before them, and He talked with Moses and Elijah. Moses was a profile of the righteous dead and Elijah the Body of Christ's (Church's) being caught up alive after six 1000-year days.

We have witnessed the biblical numerics in the Book of 2 Chronicles, which seem to confirm that the house of the Lord will be finished and ready for the Body of Christ at the time of the earth's 120th Jubilee.

God gave us a subtle witness by the height of the porch's being 120 cubits and also in the dimensions of the house of the Lord. We found that 50 shekels of gold nails held the 120-cubit dimensions of the house together—a significant number indeed in view of the fact that today the 50th year is considered a golden anniversary and in Bible days was a Jubilee.

The scriptural witness continues in 2 Chronicles 5, as they celebrated the house of the Lord being finished. There were 120 priests sounding trumpets, which profiles earth's 120th Golden Jubilee. Then the house of the Lord was filled with a cloud, which by double reference could be symbolic of the glory of God that will come on the Church when the earth lease expires.

We have witnessed the fact that after the house of the Lord was finished, there was a *seven day* feast held by Solomon, which could be a subtle indication of the Marriage Supper of the Lamb.

Second Chronicles 9 revealed that the queen of Sheba was the first to visit Solomon after the house of the Lord was finished. Sheba means "seven," and the fact that she brought 120 talents of gold seems to confirm the time to be the 120th Jubilee. The same year that the queen of Sheba (seven) came, Solomon received 666 talents of gold, which indicates the time frame when the Antichrist will be revealed.

The same chapter reveals that there were *six steps to Solomon's throne* with a golden footstool attached to the throne. This same time line began in Genesis with the six days representing 6000 years. The six steps are symbolic of the same six days of human history. The golden footstool represents Christ having all enemies under His feet during the Millennial Reign as He rules from an earthly throne in Jerusalem. (Isaiah 66:1-2; Jeremiah 3:17.)

The Scriptures reveal that Israel was in Babylonian captivity 70 years. This foreshadows 70 Jubilee years in which Israel will not be totally free from Gentile bondage. It was at the end of that 70 years of captivity that Adonakim brought 666 of his descendants back to help rebuild Jerusalem.

We also found that the name Adonakim means "the Lord has risen" or "the Lord arose." Since the Church is the Body of Christ, when the Church is taken up it can be said that the Lord has risen because we are one with Him.

The critics may call all this coincidental. Some modern-day theologians may call it spiritualizing the Bible, yet the Bible is indeed a *spiritual book* and is spiritually discerned. In this journey through the Holy Scriptures, we can't help but witness the incredible accuracy of these time lines in relation to the prophetic Scriptures.

God Himself is the only One Who could give such revelation and insight through events that happened thousands of years ago. These prophetic threads have been woven into the fabric of God's Word from Genesis to Revelation with amazing consistency.

Then they are all brought into prophetic focus in Revelation, chapter 13. The context of this chapter reveals that the people who are left on the earth during the Tribulation Period will be faced with many terrible dilemmas.

ROMAN EMPIRE REVIVED

John reveals that one of the heads of the beast was wounded to death and his deadly wound was healed. All of the world wondered after the beast. We know the devil does not have resurrection power. Some believe that the Antichrist will be assassinated and resurrected from the dead, but I believe this is in reference to the fact that the Antichrist will come from the territory of the old Roman Empire. We know that empire died but has been revived or resurrected under the name of the European Economic Community (EEC). Revelation 13 reveals that in the last forty-two months of the Tribulation Period the Antichrist will be at his worst.

7 And it was given unto him to make war with the saints, and to overcome them: and power was given him over all kindreds, and tongues, and nations.
8 And all that dwell upon the earth shall worship him, whose names are not written in the book of life of the Lamb slain from the foundation of the world.

The Antichrist will wage war against the Tribulation saints. Here is a note of caution: Please don't confuse these with the Church. These are Tribulation saints who will be born again after the Rapture of the Church. The Rapture takes place in the time frame of Revelation 4:1, before the Antichrist is revealed.

> Revelation 13:16 **And he causeth all, both small and great, rich and poor, free and bond, to receive a mark in their right hand, or in their foreheads:**
> **17 And that no man might buy or sell, save he that had the mark, or the name of the beast, or the number of his name.**
> **18 Here is wisdom. Let him that hath understanding count the number of the beast: for it is the number of a man; and his number is Six hundred threescore and six (666).**

SECULAR HUMANISM WANTS TO RULE THE WORLD

Jesus, Who is the Head of the Church, revealed to John in one verse of Scripture the same revelation that we have followed from Genesis to Revelation. This verse and related Scriptures subtly reveal the sequence and timing of three major end-time events. John said, "The Antichrist's number is the number of a man." Man's number is six. Man was created in the image of God on the sixth day. The number 666 represents an unholy trinity of the Antichrist, the False Prophet and the beast system powered by Satan himself. It is man's effort, inspired by Satan, to try to rule the world by an unholy trinity of secular humanism.

Remember there were six steps to Solomon's throne. The first six Roman numerals add up to exactly the number the Antichrist will use—666. The seventh Roman numeral is the letter "M," which in Latin is *mille*, which means one thousand.

So you can see that the prophetic time line has stretched from Genesis to Revelation and every time frame matches perfectly with the prophetic Scriptures.

What a marvelous revelation Jesus gave John in one verse of Scripture. Man's days of dominion on planet Earth are numbered, and that number seems to be six 1000-year days. The first six Roman numerals represent six days of human history that will bring us very near to that seven-year period when the Antichrist and his number, 666, will be revealed to the world. After the Tribulation there will be 1000 years of peace on earth which is referred to by most bible scholars as the Millennial Reign of Jesus Christ. The graph on page 261 illustrates how the six 1000-year days relate to the Roman numerals.

WATCH & PRAY

It is clear from the parable in Luke chapter 21:29-36 that Jesus has revealed that by watching the things that will transpire on earth people would be able to discern the season of His appearing. In this chapter Jesus is generally referring to what will happen during the tribulation period, after the church has been raptured.

The Lord of the harvest is about to gather the first harvest from the earth.

Luke 21:34: **"and take heed to yourself lest at anytime your hearts be overcharged with surfeiting and drunkenness and the cares of this life so that day should come upon you unawares. v. 35—For as a snare shall it come upon all them that dwell on the face of the whole earth"**.

It is evident from verse 35 that He is referring to people who will be on the earth during the tribulation period. Then in verse 36 Jesus reveals how we can escape all of these things that are coming on the earth and stand before the Son of Man.

V 36—*"Watch ye therefore and pray always that you may be accounted worthy to escape all these things that shall come to pass and stand before the Son of Man"*. In this verse Jesus alludes to the

ROMAN NUMERALS as they relate to NUMERICAL VALUES revealing the TIME OF THE ANTICHRIST

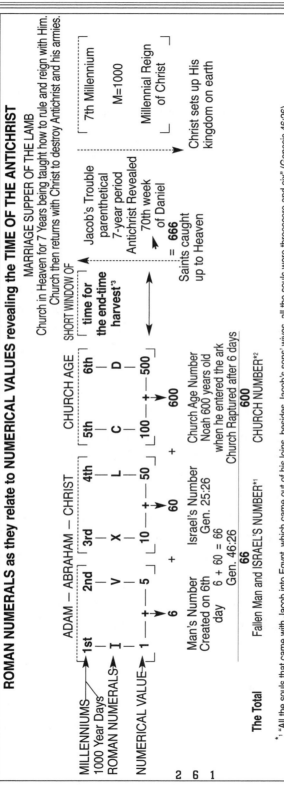

MARRIAGE SUPPER OF THE LAMB

Church in Heaven for 7 Years being taught how to rule and reign with Him. Church then returns with Christ to destroy Antichrist and his armies.

		ADAM — ABRAHAM — CHRIST		CHURCH AGE					
MILLENNIUMS 1000 Year Days	1st	2nd	3rd	4th	5th	6th			7th Millennium
ROMAN NUMERALS	I	V	X	L	C	D			M=1000
NUMERICAL VALUE	1 + 6	5	10 + 60	50	100 + 600	500			Millennial Reign of Christ

Man's Number Created on 6th day
6 + 60 = 66
Gen. 46:26

Israel's Number Gen. 25:26

Church Age Number Noah 600 years old when he entered the ark
Church Raptured after 6 days

SHORT WINDOW OF **time for the end-time harvest***[3]

Jacob's Trouble parenthetical 7-year period Antichrist Revealed 70th week of Daniel
= **666**

Saints caught up to Heaven

Christ sets up His kingdom on earth

The Total   Fallen Man and ISRAEL'S NUMBER*[1]   CHURCH NUMBER*[2]

66   600

*[1] "All the souls that came with Jacob into Egypt, which came out of his loins, besides Jacob's sons' wives, all the souls were threescore and six" (Genesis 46:26). It seems that both fallen man and Israel's number is 66. Adam's number was 6 and Isaac was 60 years old when Jacob was 60 years old when his name God changed to ISRAEL (Genesis 35:10).

*[2] "And he made the most holy house, the length whereof was according to the breadth of the house, twenty cubits; and the breadth thereof twenty cubits: and he overlaid it with fine gold, amounting to six hundred talents" (2 Chronicles 3:8). The most holy house seems to represent the Church, for it was where the Word of God was kept. The measurement 20 cubits by 20 cubits seem to represent 40 Jubilees or 2,000 years of the Church Age. This prophetic implication is further magnified by the fact that the most holy house was overlaid with 600 talents of fine gold, and as we can see from the chart, the 5th and 6th Roman numerals indicative of the 5th and 6th millenniums add up to the very same number, 600. Then considering the fact that Noah was 600 years old when he entered into the ark, it seems quite obvious that the number 600 represents the Church Age being fulfilled just before the Antichrist comes on the scene with the number 666.

*[3] There seems to be a window of time at the end of the 6th millennium before the Rapture. During that time I believe we will see the Glorious Church stand to the true height of God's anointing for the awesome end-time harvest of souls into the kingdom just before the Rapture. (Exodus 19:10-18)

Rapture, as the way to escape all of these things that are coming on the earth during the tribulation period.

Even though there is no one scripture in the Bible that would give us a date for the Rapture of the Church, Jesus indicated in this chapter if we would watch and pray there would be significant information concerning the times and the seasons available to us before He appears.

I believe what the Apostle Paul taught in I Thessalonians 4 and II Thessalonians 2 is part of what vital information that we need today.

In II Thessalonians 2:6 Paul states, *"and now ye know what withholdeth that he might be revealed in his time"* (The phrase "his time" is referring to the time of the antichrist). v 7—*"For the mystery of iniquity doth already work, only he who now letteth will let until he be taken out of the way"*. v 8—*"and then shall the wicked be revealed, whom the Lord shall consume with the spirit of His mouth and destroy with the brightness of His coming"*. The word "let" or "letteth" means to "withhold or restrain".

These verses leave no doubt that Paul is referring to the Church being taken out of the earth before the anti-christ is revealed. The very fact that Paul states "that he (antichrist) might be revealed in his time" let us know that there is a determined time which the anti-christ will be revealed on earth. That time is an exact period of seven years, no more and no less. It is called the 70th week of Daniel, it is called Jacob's Trouble, and also referred as the Tribulation Period.

The 70th week of Daniel is a seven year Sabbatical cycle. In fact it is the only Sabbatical cycle of that seventy Sabbatical cycles mentioned in Daniel chapter nine that has not been fulfilled and must be fulfilled before the millennial reign of Christ. I believe this may be one of the reasons why we are instructed by Jesus to watch. If there was no information to be gained by watching, then there would obviously be no reason to watch. The tribulation period is the only Sabbatical cycle of that seventy weeks of Daniel that have not been fulfilled.

Therefore, to fulfill that seven year Jewish cycle the tribulation must of a necessity begin at the beginning of a Sabbatical cycle. When God brought the children of Israel out of Egypt, He told them to let the land lay out every seventh year. The Jews were to observe the Sabbath day and let the land lay out every seventh year. Since they did not let the land enjoy her Sabbaths, God sent them into Babylonian captivity for seventy years so that the land would enjoy its Sabbath.

Those seventy years in Babylonian captivity represent seventy Sabbatical cycles of Daniel chapter nine, which is determined time.

Daniel 9:24—**"seventy weeks are determined upon thy people and upon the holy city to finish the transgression, to make an end of sins, to make reconciliation for iniquity, to bring in everlasting righteousness, to seal up the vision and prophecy and to anoint the most Holy"**.

This determined time must of necessity be fulfilled before the millennial reign of Christ.

There are different opinions but some who have researched this matter say that the next Jewish Sabbatical cycle will begin in the late fall of the year 2001. Could this be some of the information which Jesus said we should watch for and pray about? To say the least, the time between now and the next Sabbatical cycle is a time in which we should make time to watch and pray during this great endtime harvest. If the rapture does not occur before the next Sabbatical cycle, that would seem to indicate that we have at least seven more years. One thing for sure, we are definitely in the season of His appearing and the words of Jesus recorded in Mark 13:37 are more meaningful than ever before, **"what I say unto you I say unto all, watch"**.

It seems that God has truly spoken the end from the beginning by using events of the past to reveal what the future holds for both the righteous and the wicked. Mankind will be without excuse if he is not prepared for the events which will end this age and begin to usher in the last Millennium before eternity. There are multitudes who are not prepared for the change that is coming to planet Earth in the twenty-first century.

"DETERMINED TIME"

In this book we have followed scriptural profiles revealing God's time-line. We have seen scripture after scripture confirming that time-line to be accurate. However, I want to give a word of caution. Since we don't know for sure whether our calendar is anywhere near accurate, we should never place our faith in man's calendar concerning dates for these endtime events. Our faith should be firmly established in the fact that God has always fulfilled His every promise within His own time frame.

The scripture in Daniel 9:24 revealed that God would deal with Israel in a time frame which was referred to as "determined time" of seventy weeks of years (490 years). That time was determined by God Himself. A study of Daniel 9:25-27 reveals that after sixty-nine of those weeks Christ was crucified and that seventieth week (7 year period) of determined time has been delayed until after 2000 years of the Church Age. We must take into consideration the fact that from time to time God has delayed prophetic fulfillment of the scriptures at His will. Then in His own timing turns the prophetic time clock on again for the total fulfillment.

To understand "determined time" we have only but to consider a football game. It is divided into four-fifteen minute quarters. The total determined time being one hour, but there has never been a football game played in one hour of real time. There are time-outs, there are delays of the game in which the time clock in stopped for an indefinite period of time. Then the time clock is turned on again and the determined time begins to be counted.

We must realize that it is at least a possibility that our calculations of the calendar of time does not exactly fit God's "determined time". Only time itself will reveal the whole truth concerning this matter. But yet we must not take lightly the prophetic profiles in the Word of God which give us a definite determined time-line for God's dealing with mankind.

In Job chapter fourteen, Job was speaking prophetically.

Job 14:1—"Man that is born of a woman is a few days and full of trouble. He cometh forth like a flower, and is cut down, he fleeth also as a shadow, and continueth not"

v 5, "Seeing his days are determined, the number of his moths are with the, thou hast appointed his bounds that he cannot pass".

These verses allude to the fact that God has determined man's days of dominion on this planet and he cannot pass those bounds determined by God Himself.

Have there been other delays in that determined time that we have not noticed in which God did not measure the time? We cannot be absolutely sure at this point but we do have precedent that He has delayed the prophetic fulfillment of Daniels 70th week until the end of the Church Age.

There are two questions that Job asked which seems to confirm that mans days of dominion are limited.

Job 7:1; "Is there not an appointed time to man upon earth? Are not his days also like the days of a hireling"?

I believe man's appointed time of dominion upon the earth was revealed in Genesis chapter one. When the six days of creation were finished man was in the image and the likeness of God.

The six days of the creation account by prophetic profile is strong evidence that mans "determined time of dominion" is six thousand years.

There is much confusion about calendars, for they have been tampered with and changed over the centuries but you can rest assured that God is the master time keeper and He is keeping "determined time". History records the fact that many people have set dates for the Rapture. There has been one thing in common with date setters, they have all been 100% wrong. This is why I sound a word of caution about date setting. There were some who had set dates and then committed suicide when it didn't happen on that date. It is obvious that there faith was not in the promise of God but in a date which man had set with faulty information. When the date had come and gone their faith vanished with it therefore they had no hope.

The apostle Paul in I Thess. 4:13 admonished us saying: "that we should sorrow not as others which have no hope". The blessed hope of the Rapture is based not on man made calendar dates, but rather on God's "determined time". The apostle Paul states in Ephesians 1:10 **"that in the dispensation of the fullness of times He might gather together in one all things in Christ, both which are in heaven, and which are on the earth; even in Him".** The key phrase here is "the dispensation of the fullness of times". In other words, when God's determined time is fulfilled.

In verses 11-14 Paul reveals that we were sealed with the Holy Spirit of Promise and states that it was the earnest of our inheritance until the redemption of the purchased possession. The redemption of the purchased possession refers to the redemption of the body and Paul connects it with the dispensation of the fullness of times, which no doubt, refers to the fullness of God's "determined time".

WARNING FOR ALL MANKIND

These prophetic composites and profiles should be viewed as a warning for all mankind: Get prepared for the third day, for it will bring the most traumatic change on Earth in 6000 years of human history.

There is no doubt about it—we are in the end-time harvest. It is the season of His appearing. The tares are coming together in bundles. The Lord of the harvest is about to gather the first harvest of the righteous from the earth.

THE KING IS COMING—ARE YOU PREPARED TO MEET HIM?

MESSAGE TO READER –BEFORE THE RAPTURE

If you are reading this book before the Rapture of the Church and you are not prepared to meet the Lord when He appears, pray this prayer. It may sound too simple to you but that's why it is called the simple plan of salvation. Do it now. Don't put it off any longer.

Lord Jesus, I believe You are the Son of God. I believe You died for my sins and You were raised the third day for my justification. I repent of my sins and receive Your forgiveness. I ask You to cleanse me from all unrighteousness. I confess that Jesus Christ is my Lord and true Messiah. I receive my forgiveness by faith on the authority of Your Word. Now I thank You, Father, that I am Your child and You are my Father and Jesus is my Lord. My sins are gone. Thank You, Heavenly Father; I am born again. I have become a new creature in Christ Jesus, and according to Romans 10:9-10 and 1 Thessalonians 5:9, I am now saved from the wrath to come, Amen.

I encourage you to get a Bible and begin reading the Book of Romans.

MESSAGE TO READER–AFTER THE RAPTURE

If you are reading this book after the Rapture of the Church has taken place, obviously you missed His appearing. But God's grace still extends to you at this point in time. But you must act quickly, because there are traumatic changes taking place on earth which will make it much harder to make a decision in the near future.

Pray this prayer: Oh, God in Heaven, I ask You in the name of Your Son Jesus, to have mercy on me now. I repent of my sins, and I resign every evil work. Forgive my sins and cleanse me from all unrighteousness. I believe that Jesus Christ is the true Messiah Who died for my sins to redeem me. Have mercy upon me now and receive me into Your kingdom; give me divine direction and guidance of the Holy Spirit during these troublesome times. I confess that Jesus Christ is my Lord and Messiah. Thank You, Lord, that because of Your divine mercy and grace I am born again; I am now a child of God. I have become a new creature in Christ, and I depend on Your wisdom, mercy, and grace to divinely guide me so that I may lead others to the saving knowledge of the Christ, the true Messiah.

Thank You, Father, for Your divine forgiveness, which makes it possible for me to be with You in eternity.

Find a bible and read the book of Revelation. It will reveal what is happening on earth and warn you against taking the mark of the beast.

Endnotes

CHAPTER FIVE

[1] *Dakes Annotated Bible* Note J 4th Column, p. 71 in the N.T.

[2] Strong, James. "Greek Dictionary of the New Testament," *Strong's Exhaustive Concordance of the Bible*, (Nashville: Abingdon, 1890), p. 22, #1220.

CHAPTER SEVEN

[1] *The Amplified Bible,* New Testament copyright © 1958, 1987 by the Lockman Foundation, La Habra, California, p. 1403.

[2] Strong, James. "Greek Dictionary of the New Testament," *Strong's Exhaustive Concordance of the Bible*, (Nashville: Abingdon, 1890), p. 41, #2722.

CHAPTER EIGHT

[1] Strong, James. "Greek Dictionary of the New Testament," *Strong's Exhaustive Concordance of the Bible*, (Nashville: Abingdon, 1890), p. 47, #3346.

[2] *The Amplified Bible, New Testament,* copyright © 1958, 1987 by the Lockman Foundation, La Habra, California, p. 1403.

[3] Strong, James. Op. Cit., p. 15, #646.

CHAPTER NINE

[1] Strong, James. "Greek Dictionary of the New Testament," *Strong's Exhaustive Concordance of the Bible,* Nashville: Abingdon, 1890, p. 73, #5207.

[2] Ibid., p. 50, #3565.

[3] Ibid., p. 55, #3933.

[4] Ibid., p. 12, #435.

[5] Ibid., p. 12, #444.

CHAPTER TEN

[1] Brown, Francis, Driver, R., Briggs, A. "The New Brown—Driver—Briggs—Gesenius Hebrew and English Lexicon," (Massachusetts: Hendrickson Publishers), p. 988, #7620.

CHAPTER TWELVE

[1] Strong, James. "Greek Dictionary of the New Testament," *Strong's Exhaustive Concordance of the Bible,* (Nashville: Abingdon, 1890), p. 37, #2398.

CHAPTER THIRTEEN

[1] Lester Sumrall, *I Predict 2000 A.D.* (South Bend: LeSEA Publishing Co., 1987), p. 69.

CHAPTER FOURTEEN

[1] Strong, James. "Hebrew and Chaldee Dictionary of the Old Testament," *Strong's Exhaustive Concordance of the Bible,* Nashville: Abingdon, 1890, p. 15, #623.

[2] Ibid., p. 33, #1968.

[3] Ibid., p. 47, #3038.

CHAPTER FIFTEEN

[1] Strong, James. "Hebrew and Chaldee Dictionary of the Old Testament," *Strong's Exhaustive Concordance of the Bible,* Nashville: Abingdon, 1890, p. 8, #140.

CHAPTER SIXTEEN

[1] Rambsel, Yacov A. *His Name is Jesus.* Toronto: Frontier Research, p. 136.

[2] Ibid.

READER'S INDEX OF WORDS AND PHRASES

Since I will use many phrases and words that may be unfamiliar to many of our readers, I felt that it would be good to put an index dictionary of words that could be referred to from time-to-time to make sure that they understand the words and phrases and how they are used in this book.

"RAPTURE," "BLESSED HOPE," and "CATCHING AWAY OF THE CHURCH" are all used in this book as synonymous terms to Rapture, which is simply a catching away of the Body of Christ from earth to heaven just before the seven years of tribulation begins.

The phrase "CHURCH" and "BODY OF CHRIST" are synonymous terms referring to those that are born again and have a current relationship with the Lord Jesus Christ.

The phrase "THE LAST DAYS" generally refers to the two days which represent two thousand years of the Church Age.

The phrase "CHRIST'S FIRST COMING," or, "FIRST ADVENT," refers to when Christ was born on earth. "SECOND ADVENT" is a future coming of Christ and refers to the second time that He comes to earth, which will be at the end of the seven years of tribulation, to set up His earthly kingdom here on the earth.

"COMING OF THE LORD" — This phrase most generally refers to the Second Advent.

The phrase "OUR GATHERING TOGETHER UNTO HIM" refers to the Rapture of the Church.

"THE DAY OF CHRIST" refers to and is a synonymous term with the Day of the Lord, which is the Seventh Millennium that begins when Christ returns from heaven to earth with the saints to set up His kingdom here on earth. It is a time-span of one thousand years.

The word "MILLENNIUM" is used of that one thousand-year period, which on some occasions will also be referred to as the millennial reign of Christ, or the last Millennium.

"THE TRIBULATION PERIOD" — "DANIEL'S SEVEN-TIETH WEEK" — "TIME OF THE ANTICHRIST" — "TIME OF JACOB'S TROUBLE" — are all synonymous terms and refer to one event, which is the seven-year period of tribulation that begins immediately when the Church is raptured and continues until the Church comes back with Christ from heaven to set up His kingdom on earth.

The phrase, "WHEN HE SHALL APPEAR — WHEN HE SHALL APPEAR IN THE AIR — AND — AT HIS APPEAR-ING" are all used in reference to the Rapture, unless otherwise specified by referring to the Second Advent when He appears to the whole world.

The phrase "LAW OF DOUBLE REFERENCE," or "BY DOUBLE REFERENCE," refers to the fact that many prophetic Scriptures have a literal fulfillment that may have taken place many years ago, but also foreshadow a future fulfillment.

About the Author

Charles Capps is a retired farmer, land developer, and ordained minister who travels throughout the United States sharing the truth of God's Word. He has taught Bible seminars for twenty-four years, sharing how Christians can apply the Word to the circumstances of life and live victoriously.

In the mid-'90s the Lord gave Charles an assignment to teach end-time events and a revelation of the coming of the Lord.

Besides authoring several books, including the bestselling *The Tongue, a Creative Force,* and the mini-book *God's Creative Power,* which has sold 3 million copies, Charles Capps Ministries has a national daily syndicated radio broadcast called "Concepts of Faith."

For a complete list of tapes and books
by Charles Capps, or to receive his
publication, *Concepts of Faith*, write:

Charles Capps Ministries
P. O. Box 69
England, AR 72046

*Feel free to include your prayer requests
and comments when you write.*

OTHER BOOKS BY CHARLES CAPPS

Available from your local bookstore.
Harrison House • P. O. Box 35035 • Tulsa, OK 74153

The Harrison House Vision

Proclaiming the truth and the power
Of the Gospel of Jesus Christ
With excellence;

Challenging Christians to
Live victoriously,
Grow spiritually,
Know God intimately.